HUMANNESS IN
ORGANISATIONS

HUMANNESS IN ORGANISATIONS

A Psychodynamic Contribution

edited by

Leopold Vansina

Routledge
Taylor & Francis Group

LONDON AND NEW YORK

First published 2013 by Karnac Books Ltd.

Published 2018 by Routledge
2 Park Square, Milton Park, Abingdon, Oxon OX14 4RN
711 Third Avenue, New York, NY 10017, USA

Routledge is an imprint of the Taylor & Francis Group, an informa business

British Library Cataloguing in Publication Data

A C.I.P. for this book is available from the British Library

ISBN 9781780491936 (pbk)

Edited, designed and produced by The Studio Publishing Services Ltd
www.publishingservicesuk.co.uk
e-mail: studio@publishingservicesuk.co.uk

CONTENTS

ACKNOWLEDGEMENTS

I wish to thank the publishers mentioned below for their permission to reproduce the articles from our colleagues:

Gilles Amado, 2009. Psychic imprisonment and its release within organizations and working relationships. *Organisational & Social Dynamics*, 9(1): 1–20.

Much of the material in this chapter was originally published as the Keynote paper presented at the OPUS Conference, London, 21–22 November 2008 and is reprinted here with the kind permission of Karnac Books.

Dominique Lhuilier, 2009. Travail, management et santé psychique. *Connexion*, 91: 85–101, reprinted with permission.

The article is translated into English as "Work, management, and psychic health", by Lianne J. M. Van de Ven, Turn A Phrase Translations, Williamsburg VA 23185, USA.

My special thanks go to my long-time colleagues for their gentle encouragement and valuable suggestions. I am grateful to all those who contributed their thinking to the book and their patience with me.

I wish to express my gratitude to Marina Vansina, who, inspired by the manuscript, drew a human face for the cover of the book, and to her daughter, Melina Vanhelmont, who assisted me in editing the various chapters.

Gilles Amado, Psy Dr, is Professor Emeritus of Organisational Socio-psychology, HEC School of Management, Paris, a consultant, and an action researcher. He is a founding member of the International Society for the Psychoanalytic Study of Organizations (ISPSO) and the International Centre for the Socio-psychological Research, Training and Intervention (CIRFIP). He is co-editor-in-chief of the *Nouvelle Revue de Psychosociologie* and the author of numerous books and articles in the areas of group dynamics, leadership, and organisational psychodynamics.

Kenneth Eisold, PhD in Clinical Psychology, is a psychoanalyst with a private practice in organisational consultation and psychotherapy. He has been a consultant in Group Relations Conferences in various countries, for example, Australia, Israel, UK, USA. He supervises organisational consultations at the William Alanson Institute, New York. Kenneth has published widely in several psychoanalytic journals and books. His latest book: *What You Don't Know You Know: Our Hidden Motivations in Life, Business, and Everything Else* (2010) has reached readers from different disciples and practices.

Thomas N. Gilmore is Vice President of CFAR, a consulting firm that spun out of the Wharton School. He is a Senior Fellow in the Health Care Systems Department, where he taught for many years as an adjunct associate professor. He is a Senior Fellow in the Leonard Davis Institute of Health Economics. He is the author of *Making a Leadership Change: How Organizations and Leaders Can Handle Leadership Transitions*. Tom has been involved in many executive development programmes for corporate, governmental, and non-profit executives, including HEC, Oxford Said, Wharton, and with many associations. He has published extensively on leadership dynamics, especially among top teams, boards, and in the context of transitions.

Nora I. Grasselli studied management, with focus on organisations. She completed her PhD on group dynamics at HEC School of Management, Paris. She was visiting fellow at the Wharton School of the University of Pennsylvania and at RMIT (Melbourne). She joined The Boston Consulting Group as a strategy and organisation consultant, lectured at various business schools such as HEC, Oxford, and Reims prior to becoming a Programme Director at ESMT (European School of Management and Technology, Berlin) where she pursuits her academic interest in group dynamics, leadership, and organisational psychodynamics.

James Krantz is an organisational consultant and researcher from New York City. He is Managing Director of Worklab, which concentrates on strategy implementation, senior team development, and work process design. Dr Krantz has a PhD in Systems Sciences from the Wharton School and a BA in Philosophy and Economics from Wesleyan University. He is a past president of the International Society for the Psychoanalytic Study of Organizations (ISPSO), a Fellow of the A. K. Rice Institute, member of OPUS, and currently Director of the Socio-Analytic Program in Organizational Development and Consultation at the Institute for Psychoanalytic Training and Research (IPTAR). His writing has focused on the unconscious background of work life and on the socio-psychological challenges posed by emerging forms of organisation.

Dominique Lhuilier, Psy Dr, is Professor Emeritus of Work Psychology at the Conservatoire National des Arts et Métiers (CNAM), Paris.

She is a member of the scientific board of the Work and Development Research Centre (CRTD) and of the International Centre for Socio-psychological Research, Training and Intervention (CIRFIP). She is the author of a dozen books and numerous scientific articles in the areas of work psychology and social exclusion processes. She is an action researcher and a consultant in these two main areas.

Edgar H. Schein is the Sloan Fellows Professor of Management Emeritus at the MIT Sloan School of Management. He received his PhD in Social Psychology from Harvard in 1952, worked at the Walter Reed Institute of Research for four years, and then joined MIT, where he taught until 2005. His publications in the fields of organisational psychology, culture and leadership, and process consultation are all well known. He studied Singapore's economic miracle (*Strategic Pragmatism*, 1996), and Digital Equipment Corp's rise and fall (*DEC is Dead; Long Live DEC*, 2003). He continues to consult, and recently has published a book on the general theory and practice of giving and receiving help (*Helping*, 2009). He is the 2009 recipient of the Distinguished Scholar–Practitioner Award of the Academy of Management and the 2012 recipient of the Life Time Achievement Award from the International Leadership Association.

Sandra G. L. Schruijer, PhD, is Professor of Organisation Sciences at the Utrecht University School of Governance and Professor of Organisational Psychology at TiasNimbas Business School, Tilburg University, both in the Netherlands. Her research involves the psychological dynamics of conflict and collaboration within groups and between organisations. Sandra heads Professional Development International, an institute that organises the International Professional Development Programme and consults to organisations and managers with respect to collaboration and large-scale change. Sandra is a member of ISPSO.

Leopold Vansina, PhD in Psychology, is Professor Emeritus of Organisational Behaviour at the University of Leuven and l'Université de Louvain-la-Neuve (Belgium). He founded the International Institute for Organization and Social Development (IOD, Leuven) a multi-disciplinary consulting, training, and research institute that he directed for twenty-five years. After retirement, he continued his professional activities in the Professional Development Institute (Pro-Dev. Ltd) until he became freelance in 2009. He regularly wrote about his consulting and action research work in journals and books, for example, *Psychodynamics for Consultants and Managers* (2008), co-authored with his wife, M. J Cobbaert, PhD. Leopold is a member of the Academy of Management, and ISPSO.

FOREWORD

Although we have had our fights and our differences, Leopold, with his background in psychology, and I, with my background in engineering, share a passion for humanness in human work. I am very grateful to him that he asked me to write the Foreword for this book with a theme that is more than relevant today.

In spite of all kinds of theories about human nature, there is one specific aspect to us, as a species. We shall never stop enquiring about what it means to become a human being. All ideologies that claim to know what human nature *is* are bound to fail. The converse of this is that we only learn our way further into the meaning of humanness by being confronted with what we, at a certain point in history, have discovered to be inhuman. For example, the notion of slavery as a normal human way of organising became labelled as inhuman. But, nowadays, we seem not to recognise the similarity between the selling of the slaves of a Roman villa, together with the villa, or of a feudal domain with its serfs, and the selling of companies with their anonymous workforce, defined as human resources and calculated as FTE, full time equivalents!

The first part of this book in fact clarifies the inhumanity emerging from the application of mainstream management and organisational hypes nowadays. What strikes me in reading it is an underlying mechanism that has been labelled as the virtualisation of management. To me, the basic trigger of that mechanism comes from the tendency to split the staff of organisations into thinkers and doers, and the higher status which is attributed to those who only "think" and are not troubled either by their own bodies, or by the confrontation with the material aspects of all meaningful human work: strategic forums peopled by staff specialists and consultants, whose main discourse is not about themselves, but why, and how the "others" should change to increase performance, engagement. I refer also to all forms of what I call "Management by Excel", unable to discern the difference between facts and figures. Most of what is called management education is focused on figures, and certainly not interested in embodiments! Human beings are embodied beings: denying it is inhuman and leads to inhuman behaviour.

For this reason, I have read the second part, which is developing experiences to counteract the virtualisation of work, as focusing at least on the embodiment of the relevant forums. People who meet each other and work through their own experience, their own fears and hopes, have a greater opportunity to be confronted by the rich strata of their humanness, which go beyond the cognitive and the logical–rational. Tapping into these strata enables them to develop their own humanness, and, hence, to recognise the humanness of those they influence by their decisions.

I hope that the reader will sense in this book, beyond the concepts and methods illustrated in the various chapters, the deep engagement of all the authors in discovering more and more what humanness means in our working life.

Luc Hoebeke

General introduction

Leopold Vansina

Aren't social scientists more often leaders in following the market, than leading parts in creating well-being?

It is not easy for me to spell out what drove me to edit this book. I do know I am touched by the confrontation with three dominant trends in our society: the increasing presence of virtual worlds, the deification of performance and its ideology of excellence, and the progressive individualisation in society. These developments seem to silently penetrate our thinking and practices. They turn human beings into handy instruments for production processes in commercial, public, and private organisations, and educational and even health-care institutions. I often doubt whether many leading persons in universities and consulting firms are aware of the negative impact of these developments on respect for the human being and the resulting integrity of the social fabric. If they are, do they care enough to counter them?

The more I explore the underlying dynamics, the more I come to reflect on myself: what am I, as a social scientist, manager, or consultant, contributing to these processes? Can we look beneath these often gratifying modern developments to study and explore their undesirable consequences, which often become visible in other domains, such as mental disturbance, the abuse of drugs, criminality, and increasing discrepancy between the rich and the poor, etc.? These disturbing consequences are most often not reflected in statistical averages of satisfaction scores of societies, because these trends affect predominantly its most vulnerable inhabitants. The problems simply disappear in the averages.

Is it still possible to curb or to redirect these developments by creating alternative methods of organising or managing workplaces and educational systems? What can be my part in mobilising networks of like-minded people and institutions to create a fairer world, in which it is good to live for all people, now and in the future? It is this inner turmoil of observations, experiences, reflections, and questions that encouraged me to invite colleagues to contribute their thinking to the issues of humanness in organisations.

Let me first elaborate somewhat further on these three dominant trends in society.

The increasing presence of virtual worlds. Some twenty years ago, when I was teaching at the International Management School in St Petersburg, a Russian reporter wrote in the local English newspaper, *The Press*: "We know that our leaders are lying and they know that we know. But they go on deceiving us!" Many Russians resented these dishonest relations and cherished hope that "Glasnost" would open a free-minded search for truth. However, becoming honest in facing daily realities proves to be a slow and painful process. Is the Western world doing any better? We know that many of our leaders are deceiving us, too. When their deceptions become public and they can get away with it, we applaud!

These leading political figures, managers, and even social scientists are not necessarily lying. They might deceive by deflecting or partly distorting the facts, hiding them to manipulate the truth to their own advantages or to make them fit into their locked-in views of the world. Others take a lead with one-liners, often with a deceptive intent or as a sign of a mental incapacity to grasp the complexities of the world. Still others respond with a well-intended, paternalistic perspective attempt to teach the ignorant. The reasons might vary, but the consequences are the same: they do create virtual "make-believe" worlds. I call them virtual worlds, composed of a rich mixture of inspiring statements, incomplete, massaged facts, company philosophies, spiritual campaigns, and well-sounding extrapolations of partial or even tentative research findings.

Regrettably, many of our social scientists are yielding to university pressures to "publish or perish". Consequently, they concentrate on easy to study human interactions in artificial, experimental situations, completely divorced from the real, organisational complexities. Unfortunately, they come to live in that self-created artificial world, believing that it is the real world of organisational life. Furthermore, the attention and interest of their students in gaining a deeper under-standing of the specific socio-economical and structural context of an issue becomes neglected, even rejected. One can obtain a doctoral degree in organisational psychology simply by doing a meta-analysis of already published studies, without having spent even a week in an organisation. Yet, the more we become fixed on the modal organisa-tion, the modal person, the more we forego the particularities of the interactions with the specificities of the organisational context or environment.

Consultants too become so specialised that they unknowingly exclude the fields of tension in the organisational context, or become blind to the lack of knowledge competences required to solve even recurrent problems. Do intervention techniques become popular by turning real issues that should be dealt with by processing factual and non-factual data into opinions or internal psychic constructions? Some say, "It's all a matter of perception!" However, this frequently heard one-liner is deceptive, too. It is misleading in the sense that not all upsetting or pleasurable experiences are entirely due to inter-nal, deranged psychic processes; paradoxically, there is an outside world, too.

Do psychological inventories and group interventions hit the market by providing personality or psychoanalytic labels to individu-als or psychodynamic processes, thereby neglecting the real work of learning to work with differences and group dynamic processes?

Those involved in interpersonal skills—including leadership—training, stress management, positive thinking, and resilience, or other "experience providing" techniques, might, in fact, lead people into an illusory world in which everything is possible, and everything is fine once your mind is properly fixed. In this way, they might well collude with management's wishes to keep tight control over the structural design of work systems and management practices, based on the so-called imperatives of costs and global competition. Training in such settings often serves to make employees believe they are in control, or make them feel good, while leaving the disturbing daily realities of the system untouched.

These virtual worlds, only remotely connected to the realities of organisational life, are on the increase. Some virtual worlds are designed for entertainment, such as amusement parks, computer games, and films. They provide pleasure and a temporary relief from daily preoccupations. The ones we mean to discuss are those that create a "virtuality" that is hard to distinguish from reality, or, worse, those in which one is forced to live and work. The latter was recently illustrated by Greg Smith, a successful manager at Goldman Sachs, from which he resigned due to the conflict between the stated policy of the bank to serve the interests of the client and the rewarded practices to exploit their innocence to the benefit of Goldman Sachs (Smith, 2012).

Not only technologies and globalisation, but also "psychologising" creates virtual worlds: for example, through meaning-providing practices that reduce human experiences to mental processes, states of mind, or simple neurological activities in which the actual realities of the situation and the history of experiences are ignored. Virtual worlds are, in essence, unhealthy. They erode the ability to distinguish what is "real" or "true" from what is "make-believe". Living in these man-made virtual worlds demands more energy to sort real from unreal, but also to sort through one's assumptions about what is really going on. Without such verifications, human beings are totally dependent on the sanity of their inner worlds. Furthermore, inadequacy in reality checking destroys trust in persons and institutions. At times, as mentioned earlier, the real and the make-believe become two different worlds that people have to live in, and they will have to cope with the inherent discrepancies. One might not be fully aware of the tensions thereby generated. Yet, they are there, under one's skin, so to speak, and likely to emerge as dis-identification with the organisation, cynicism, internal unrest, and even explosions of aggression. Regrettably, these are too often diagnosed and dealt with as personal problems. The real causal context in the external world is left undisturbed.

Another element in my turmoil is the *deification of performance*. Excellent performance, either bluntly stated in financial terms or under the guise of record-breaking achievements, tends to become the ultimate goal at the expense of the overall purpose of organisations, which is to contribute to the well-being of society.

Even children are being pushed around: from school to their music classes, ballet courses, or sports activities. "If you don't start practising at a very young age, you'll never make it on any international platform!" Parents are encouraged through gentle social pressures to go with the trends. How moving, is it not, to see parents making personal sacrifices for the "good" of their children or being proud to see them selected to perform on a stage or win a medal? However, the exclusive emphasis on excelling performance deprives human beings of the intrinsic satisfaction and enjoyment of the act of performing.

In the business world, we find management courses and training programmes that can be seen as retreats in this cult. They emphasise the importance of stretching oneself for high performance in a highly competitive world, often with that repeating idea of how gratifying and self-enhancing it feels to be the best, to win. It is as if employees at work are athletes, continuously engaged in a competitive sport. Funnily though, although excelling in performance is presented as so self-gratifying and self-enhancing, business courses continue to teach the newest techniques to motivate people, reward them, and, of course, to control the performance of these very same enthusiastic, dedicated employees!

The god of performance—like most gods—demands sacrifices. For some, it means giving up pleasure, or care for colleagues, in order "to make it", to "pursue one's talents", or simply to serve the performance god. The pressures to make "sacrifices" take various forms: some subtle, some more blunt. The performance god likes you to replace honest negative emotions with positive feelings and thoughts, so you will turn potential clients into actual buyers, all to the detriment of being authentic. Straying away from authenticity, however, is not so far removed from giving up integrity.

The undue appeal to duty and compassion in the healthcare professions often seeks to extract extra efforts from professionals while increasing time pressure to "serve" a fixed number of patients (or beds!). Demands for working overtime and being reachable twenty-four hours a day (even during holidays) are considered legitimate, along with an implicit threat of losing one's job. Unfortunately, all of these sacrifices cut deep into people's psychic health and social life.

One might lose honesty, invent short-cuts, and manipulate data. One might become deprived of "mental free time" to care for the education of one's children and balance work and family life. Not surprisingly, more and more people want to retire early, either to get away from work or because they feel unable to continue to work in their workplaces at an "old" age. Others disidentify with their organisation and the make-believe to protect their real selves, or they start looking for other meaningful activities beyond what we used to call "being employed". Still others "dislocate" themselves, behaving in one way in the workplace, either as a manager or a ordinary employee, and behaving quite differently in other social settings, as if they are two different persons.

I think some have forgotten the relevance of the field studies conducted by Eric Trist and Ken Bamforth (1951) in the early years of the Tavistock Institute. These action researchers discovered that coal-miners had the ability to optimise technological demands as well as their own social requirements to realise economical objectives. They took the technical and economical realities into account and optimised their requirements with their social needs. In this way, they maintained their wholeness as human beings. These findings became the basis for socio-technical systems thinking and work systems design in Europe, the USA, and even India. Since the early 1960s, more supportive evidence has come up showing that there is no natural incompatibility between humanness and performance. Even more, under certain conditions and to a certain extent, performance and humanness do actually enhance one another. The challenge for all of us is to create those conditions and secure that balance. Maximising performance at the expense of well-being, or vice versa, eventually leads to social disintegration.

Another set of observations has twisted into a troubling concern, which I label *individualisation*, the processes of turning human beings into individuals as if they can exist in a void of social relations. The phenomena are not new. They have been studied before. However, they have not had the desired impact to counter the trend. Some of these individualisation processes start early and later gain increasing strength in working life.

The opening up of the labour market for married women created opportunities for emancipation, for social and personal growth, and for making an extra income, needed or not, to raise children and enjoy a healthy income. But there is also a price to be paid. When both parents are working, the care of their children, most frequently, is out-sourced to nurseries, day- and child-care centres. I wonder what the impact of moving babies around between working parents, nurseries, day-care centres, and/or grandparents is on attachment and belong-ing? Various studies show that these infants become independent at a much earlier age than those raised in families. Yet, without being nos-talgic, one has come to question this early independence. Is this but a manifest layer covering their tendencies to adjust quickly and get the best out of changing relations? Is it a more self-centred attitude? The opening up of the family at a very young age might well weaken the dependency on parental authority, but are these children, once young-sters, better equipped to deal with the peer pressures to "be in and be with" the trends of talking, thinking, dressing, and valuing?

Although work is essentially social in nature, many organisations are endorsing individualisation. In fact, it has become a standard prac-tice to conceive the individual as a "dissectible resource". The frequent changes in response to turbulent environments, such as strategic re-structuring and changes in management, redesigns of work systems, the introduction of new technologies, relocations, mergers, and acqui-sitions, raise the demands on human flexibility. It is almost inevitable that these changes entail breaking up work relations and establishing new ones. The latter becomes more difficult, the more frequently and painfully relations have to be given up. From experience, managers have learnt that recognising the person in a social context, that is, as a product of relationships of the past, the present and the future, and as operating in a socio-economical and technological setting, becomes an annoying obstacle to getting the work (re)organised or fast organisa-tional changes implemented. To further increase flexibility, work sys-tems are dissolved and cut up into chunks of work, which are easy to assign to (replaceable) individuals whose performance can be securely controlled and individually rewarded. Or, when needed, the chunks can readily be contracted out or cancelled as a company activity.

Some people thrive on job-hopping, trying to make a career by "following their talents". The hiring companies thereby show their employees that work relations and tacit knowledge of the business are less relevant than their belief that new and "uncompromising talents" enhance financial results. On the other hand, people low in employ-ability become more dependent and submissive in tolerating harsh and unfair working conditions under threats of losing their job, especially in a depressed labour market. When worse comes to worst, the individual employee is left alone to hold on to his/her job or find a new one.

Many organisations have pushed the individualisation processes even further, eroding work from a social activity to a job that is individually rewarded, or to the conception of an individual as an impersonal set of competences, even as a computer to be loaded and downloaded. This conception of the human being as a computer is mutually constitutive (e.g., the information technology and the human being using it). It can be found in new software programmes made for downloading the ideas of people without the need to discuss them in a (boring) meeting (Milian, 2012).

Some forms of individualisation seem to be a response to complexity. People reduce their interest and engagement in the world to those things they can readily influence. This withdrawal into one's own restricted world of direct influence can be seen as *dissociation*. The individual concerned may enjoy a less complex environment and a more peaceful life, but the dissociation creates free space for those in power positions to impose their views on the powerless and the self-made helpless.

The individualisation processes seem to be hard to stop, or even to attenuate, despite the overwhelming evidence that social relations at work have a marked positive effect on turnover, happiness, absenteeism, and productivity. Something as simple as having a friend at work to whom one can talk in confidence is a distinguishing feature of high performing organisations. "High levels of social support predict longevity as reliably as regular exercise does, and low social support is as damaging as high blood pressure" (Achor, 2012). Providing social support is even more beneficial than receiving it. It is common sense that all this requires a level of stability, some desirable organisational purposes, and work designs that cater to identity and a sense of belonging.

Disturbing phenomena like high employee turnover, burnout, absenteeism, difficult to handle persons, and various forms of aggression, such as bullying, "scapegoating", and discrimination, tend to be conceived as "individual" problems. As such, they can easily be handled by either removing/firing the aggressor/perpetrator, or by sending the "victim" or sufferer to an external coach. This conception and "treatment" of "personal problems", abstracted from its real context, allows organisations and even society to consider itself "problem free". Nothing in the organisation, its management, culture, procedures, and work designs is questioned.

Coaching is such a general concept that you and I do not know what to expect from those practices. With few exceptions, they have one common denominator: the individual is the focal point of attention. The organisational context is left out or, exceptionally, included as perceived through the eyes of the client/coachee. The client in this contextual vacuum too easily becomes a rich territory for "psychologising". While the individual may learn from coaching, the required improvements to the situation back home are left to the coachees themselves. The same must be said about training programmes for individuals to increase their resistance to stress, to become more resilient, mindful, or to engage in meditation. However beneficial these programmes might be to the individuals, at least temporarily, the attention and results are not system-wide. .

Why are these programmes and coaching sessions so popular? I assume that sending troubled or difficult persons for outside help has a somewhat hidden benefit for the managers/sponsors. They do not have to question their own practices and they are relieved not to have "difficult personal talks" with their employees. Difficult personal conversations can further be avoided by investing in technologies that substitute "unpleasant confrontations" with another human being with a computer printout. No time for uncomfortable explorations into why employees show up late, or even work late, and no personal confrontations about unprofessional behaviour or disrespecting company values. Even healthcare organisations do not shy away from the required financial investment to install such "depersonalising systems". If the organisation has designed out all difficult personal conversations with their employees, how do you expect them to have human conversations with their clients or patients? Are the most dedicated employees not pushed to live and work in two worlds: the impersonal one of the organisation and the personal one of care?

So far, it is my personal concerns that put me to work. But the book is not a rant on current practices in organisations and educational institutions. It would deny the laudable efforts of many managers, particularly those in family businesses, and social scientists in their teaching and/or consulting assignments. Neither does it intend to glorify the past.

Humanness in Organisations is a big title. It encompasses a variety of themes that can be studied from different perspectives. We have reduced the scope to a few issues or subjects that fit with the aim of the book. Its aim is twofold. First, we would like to sharpen the critical spirit of our readers, and, second, to provide some "actionable knowledge" that is useful in our work as managers, consultants, and academics. Both intents are insatiable; yet, they stand out as prerequisites for effective and responsible work in a turbulent world in transition.

A critical mind relies on the capacity and willingness to be in touch with oneself and to reflect on what is going on in society, in particular regarding the developments in society that are taken for granted, and our own involvement in them. However, one cannot develop that requisite self-awareness and critical look at what is going on all by oneself. Human beings need other trusted persons to open up self-confined reflections, and to enrich their perspectives to appreciate trends and practices. This is one of the benefits of belonging to a small group of honest and critical professionals.

"Consequence thinking" is an essential ingredient of critical thinking. Claes Planthaber, a Swedish colleague, once told me about his experience with the Iroquois, an Indian tribe, in which he was confronted with their concept of the "Seventh Generation". Their 800–900-year-old constitution has a reputation for its elegance in thinking of and managing the hardest possible situations. The Seventh Generation is a fundamental "Probierstein", or touchstone, for all choices and decisions that might be, or become, of a strategic nature, now or later. Each generation is responsible for the people to come in the seventh generation following their own. In this way, every generation is caring and being cared for regarding their living circumstances. Would it not be wise to add some reflective "consequence thinking" to our results-orientated behaviour also? Depending on the kind of actions and the context, our second thoughts or reflections might lead us to explore the likely consequences in quite other dimensions than just excelling in performance or individual freedom: for example, the likely socio-economical, ecological, societal, and/or political implications, now and for future generations. These reflective considerations become inevitably mixed with our values, implicit in our appreciations, judgements, actions, and non-action.

The second intent of the book is to share with you some selected written contributions that generate "actionable knowledge". Argyris (1996) coined this notion to mean knowledge that is understandable and can be used by most people without additional training. Perry (2012) talks about "useable knowledge", knowledge that ". . . meets users' priorities and needs and is research of high scientific quality" (p. 479). It has internal and external validity, and contextual realism (i.e., a broader audience can accept and apply it). Other voices in the social sciences are now pleading to engage in "actionable research". However, contributing to the body of actionable knowledge is not easy, especially in the field of psychodynamics. All too often, the psychodynamic approach is seen as predominantly focused on intrapsychic work, thereby neglecting the real conditions human beings are exposed to; conditions that might lie at the heart of the problems. Another trap in the psychodynamic literature is the number of studies explaining why things happened the way they did after the fact. Such "understanding" is informative, and interesting, but when it stops here, without any suggestion or proposal of how the disruptive or distressing behaviour could be prevented or brought back to acceptable proportions, it is far from being actionable knowledge.

Actionable knowledge is not simply a set of recipes to apply to research findings. Actionable knowledge most often requires a good touch of creative thinking to integrate it with the specifics of the situation. Consequently, by providing chapters describing some examples of how *conditions* can be created to improve systems, we hope to trigger your creative thinking to develop your own innovative interventions in real context.

With these risks in mind, we nevertheless chose to take a psychodynamic or "clinical" perspective in this book, because we do believe that such an approach can be rich in generating actionable knowledge and thinking. "Clinical", here, does not refer to psychopathology, but to its special meaning of understanding the uniqueness of a situation to be able to take action. Consequently, we are not very concerned with generating universal principles to control social systems or with advocating so-called "best practices". In addition, psychodynamic and clinical approaches bring a special human quality to our practices. It includes providing time and space to reconcile the inner world of needs, aspirations, experiences, and fear with the realities in the outer world. But, it does not end with that. On the contrary, it leads to the mobilisation of energy and knowledge to change unhealthy working conditions and degrading systems, not simply in order to solve, or even resolve, human and social problems, but to create conditions for developing well-being. To realise requisite whole system changes, psychodynamic approaches borrow from, and build on, other disciplines, such as systems thinking, organisational behaviour and development, and anthropology.

I am pleased to share the thinking of a selection of international authors. Each of them enjoys an established reputation in the broad field of consulting organisations with a psychodynamic or "clinical" perspective. Their studies are grouped in two parts. In Part I, "Taking a closer look", the chapters focus on the more subtle dynamics in work organisations, educational institutions, and society which create new fields of tensions that hamper well-being, development, and authenticity. By unveiling these dynamics, the authors draw our attention to specific trends and practices and open our minds for what can be done, either in terms of practices or further research, or what should be stopped, to counter the negative consequences for people, now and in the future.

In Part II, "Thoughts and ideas for the practice", the chapters deal with experiences, with approaches, and alternative designs that enable the development of the involved people and their organisation on the one hand, or bring humanness to life in the working relationships of one's managing, consulting or educational activities, on the other. All contributions have one solid element in common. They present ways of working and relating with the whole human being. They bring together what has been fragmented: the rational and the emotional, the body and mind, performance and psychic health in a healthy organisation. Working with the human employee as a whole person in his socio- economical setting and with a life of his own puts human resource and competence management in a quite different frame.

Humanness in organisations is a broad and complex domain. The presented thoughts and ideas do not provide solid solutions, they point to opportunities and choices: choices of actions within the area of our own competences and authority to make organisations more humane and effective in creating well-being. Maybe these ideas are small steps that we can hope will open boundaries in thinking and stimulate us to join efforts in creating a sustainable, socially desirable future.

References

Achor, S. (2012). Positive intelligence. *Harvard Business Review*, January–February: 100–102.

Argyris, C. (1996). Actionable knowledge: design causality in the service of consequential theory. *Journal of Applied Behavioral Science*, 32(4): 390–406.

Milian, M. (2012). It's not you, it's meetings. *Bloomberg Businessweek*, June 11–17: pp. 51–52.

Perry, J. (2012). How can we improve our science to generate more usable knowledge for public professionals? *Public Administration Review*, 72(4): 479–482.

Smith, G. (2012). Why I am leaving Goldman Sachs. *New York Times*, March 14, p. A27.

Trist, E., L., & Bamforth, K. W. (1951). Some social and psychological consequences of the longwall method of coal-getting. *Human Relations*, 4: 3–38.

PART I
TAKING A CLOSER LOOK

Introduction

Leopold Vansina

We do not often have the time or energy to take a deeper look at life in the organisations we manage, the workplaces we design, or the activities we are engaged in as consultants, academics, and researchers. The chapters in this part of the book guide us in thoughtful reflections by the sharing of experiences, observations, and studies of social scientists from France, the Netherlands, and the USA. Some studies might touch on indignation or disbelief. Others might point to gaps and neglect in research and consulting practices. At times, the unveiling of some underlying dynamics might affirm what we already suspected. Whatever it is, if we can sit with and hold on to these "strange" ideas and probably uncomfortable feelings about what should not be done, our creative thinking will be activated to invent alternative practices and come up with ideas about what to do to bring more humanness into organisational life. What conditions can be created that foster psychic and organisational health, which studies need to fill the gaps we see in consulting organisations and in the teaching of managers and social scientists?

Some chapters are aimed more directly at one category of readers: managers, consultants, academics, or researchers. However, all are of general interest and useful for sharpening our critical thinking.

In Chapter One, "Psychic imprisonment and its release within organisations and working relationships", Gilles Amado unveils the various attempts that organisations bring to bear on their employees to strengthen their hold on them. Participation as a form of social engineering, the destruction of professionalism, alibis to impose change, the fabrication of heroes and manipulation of emotions are all tricky practices. These techniques aim not only at engaging the skills and the knowledge of employees, but also their minds, values, and emotional lives. Here, we come close to what Goffman called "total institutions", that is, organisations that completely control the physical and emotional life of their employees. Yet, in such organisations, individual alienation is never absolute, as most of their members might preserve an authentic self by either de-identification with the organisation, taking a sort of ethnographic distance, irony, cynicism, and all sorts of secret and tactical ways, either individual or collective, to resist the capture of their intimate identity.

In Chapter Two, "Work, management, and psychic health", Dominique Lhuilier draws our attention to the most often neglected issue of work and its impact on psychic health. Psychic health is neither seen as the absence of illness, nor as a state of complete physical or mental well-being. Furthermore, it has less to do with the capacity to adapt to environments, but more with the power to create the environment a human being desires. First, a profound analysis is provided of contemporary forms of psychopathology of work in environments that are characterised by increased pressure to perform, along with a decrease in available means and resources to respond properly. Second, the study directs attention to managerial controls, the dominant discourse, and institutional systems put in place to "treat" suffering at work, all of which guide the categorisation of subjective experience and the demand for individual treatment. Engaging external coaches/therapists further contributes to the concealment of the links between the experienced problems and work. In addition, many debilitating effects of problematic psychic health and work still belong essentially to the field of public health and social work, which dilutes the fact that preventative work is an essential part of the responsibilities of consultants and managers. They are the ones in a position to create conditions for professionals and employees to rethink the workplace and allow for the co-creation of work. This is equally true for the enhancement of the beneficial effects of work (e.g., the reintegration) for ex-psychiatric patients, for the mentally and physically handicapped, and for marginalised people.

In Chapter Three, "Approaching twenty-first century, information-based organisations", James Krantz looks into some fundamental changes in the way organisations are managed and how work is organised: less hierarchy and more collaboration, shifting relationships, more global markets and re-sourcing, virtual teams in dispersed, decentralised enterprises, and computer-mediated work. Together, these factors begin to offer a descriptive framework for understanding the dilemmas of contemporary organisations. The purpose of this chapter is to study the emerging features of twenty-first century organisations and to raise questions of how research and consultation from a systems psychodynamic perspective must adapt to remain relevant. In doing so, it explores some of the dilemmas posed for consultation practices, including the dilution or diminishment of sentience, increasing difficulties to arrive at a reflective, balanced, integrated stance (depressive position), and the place of social defence systems in fostering integrated, productive, developmental work environments.

Krantz explores a new conceptual frame in system psychodynamics to enable humanity to develop in these emerging, "modern", information-based organisations.

In Chapter Four, "Are we losing the group in the study of group dynamics? Three illustrations", Sandra Schruijer investigates the decreasing interest in group dynamics; more precisely, in learning to work with dynamic processes, partly beneath the surface, that emerge when human beings are interdependent for achieving a given task. Has one forgotten the history of social sciences, or does one blindly follow the currents of societal trends? In either case, preference is given to inventories that "typify individuals", as if one thereby has gained proficiency in working in, and with, groups. Universities push research in social psychology towards experimental social psychology, into settings that are far removed from daily reality, and often with a focus on individual behaviour, away from the social. This is a general trend that is widely affecting education and research at university levels, thereby depriving future generations of becoming familiar with a rich body of knowledge.

Sandra Schruijer's study points to the need to research the impact of economical and societal forces on the social sciences, their research and their practices, and evaluates how this affects the forthcoming generations. Indeed, to what extent does the current, almost exclusive, emphasis on cognition lead us away from wisdom; wisdom in the Jewish sense of the word, meaning the emotional concern for, and the willingness to grapple with, the complexities of daily realities.

Chapter Five, "Notes towards a model of organisational therapy" is a transition between Part I, "Taking a good look", and Part II, "Thoughts and ideas for practice". In this chapter, Ed Schein titillates our thinking about "organisational health". Is the concept fundamentally different from individual or group health? Yes, it is! Nevertheless, the notion of health triggers, unwillingly, associations of pathology, treatment, and therapy. Yet, in the context of organisational health, these very notions have a special meaning, far removed from psychopathology. They relate only in an analogical way to individual healthcare.

Ed Schein brings his lifetime experiences and studies to bear on organisational health. He points to some basic "organisational pathologies" and describes some requisite skills and competences for consultants engaged in "organisational therapy", defined as "all interventions directed to enhance organisational health".

Although the advanced concept of organisational health provides a sufficient basis for differentiating the consulting work, when process consulting moves from dealing with individuals and groups to improving the health of large systems, it should not foreclose further study. On the contrary, such investigations might expose more clearly the dynamic balance between economical and ecological factors and well-being.

CHAPTER ONE

Psychic imprisonment and its release within organisations and working relationships*

Gilles Amado

I n order to develop my thinking on psychic imprisonment and its release within organisations and work relationships, I have chosen to start by referring to the intersubjective approach of Dorey, who stated thirty years ago,

> In the psychic imprisonment relationship, there is always an attack on a chosen individual because of his or her specific qualities. It is always the desire of the other that is targeted, given that it is essentially foreign and by its very nature escapes all understanding. Psychic imprisonment is thereby a fundamental tendency to neutralise the other's desire, that is to reduce all otherness, all difference, to abolish all specific characteristics, the aim being to reduce the other to the function and status of an object that can be completely assimilated. (1981, p. 118, translated for this edition)

The tendency to create psychic imprisonment is present in every one of us and can be observed in any interpersonal relationship,

---

*A French version of this paper has been published in the *Revue de Psychothérapie Psychanalytique de Groupe*, 2008, 2(51) under the title "Emprise et dégagement dans les organisations et les relations de travail", pp. 15–32. The author wishes to thank Marlene Spero for her help in the editing of this text.

although it is particularly common in perverse and obsessive prob-
lematics, perverse psychic imprisonment tending to be seductive in
nature and the obsessive being essentially destructive (Dorey, 1992).
Dorey speaks of the genesis of the psychic imprisonment as being
related to situations in which "control seems impossible or too costly
for the psychic economy of the subject" (1981, p. 139, translated for
this edition).

The difficulty in controlling and neutralising the desire of others,
the reduction of otherness, reification, perversion, and obsessiveness
are all traits and processes that define, to a certain extent, the universe
of modern or hypermodern organisations and work relationships
today. These are processes that we cannot reduce to the simple influence of perverse individuals, whether they are narcissistic, with or
without accomplices (Eiguer, 1989, 1995), or whether they are thanato-
phores (death bringers) (Diet, 2005), psychosocial (Sirota, 2003), or
more polymorphous, even though the clinical work on this subject is
highly valuable. As Racamier (1992) says, "The occasional circumstances, a complacent and favourable environment are all necessary to
the accomplishment of perversion" (p. 283, translated for this edition).
It is this environment, this fertilising ground, that I am now going to
look at in detail, by describing some of the ingredients that set the
scene for potential psychic imprisonment, and I then go on to explore
some of the possible means of release, often used by "resistant"
employees.

Let us go back at bit. At the beginning of the 1980s, when the
French population started to be reconciled with the world of business
enterprise, particularly after the triumphant left-wing government
had rung the changes, Pagès and his multi-disciplinary team made a
great splash by denouncing the psychic imprisonment set up by
multi-national companies which were a source of alienation and psychological disorders. In *L'emprise de l'organisation* (1979), they show
how the individual becomes trapped by the simultaneous presence of,
on the one hand, real compensations (high salary, career prospects,
and job security) and the communication of humanistic principles in
mission statements, and, on the other, the development of management techniques orientated towards autonomy, very heavy work-
loads, increasingly ambitious operational objectives, and the obligation to submit to the ideology of the company. A hypermodern
company such as IBM, they claim, obtained a hold over employees

worldwide by engendering regression to primary narcissism. These managers all internalised within their ideal self an organisation representing the archaic maternal imago, at once protective and threatening, an imago that was reinforced by the effacement of bosses and replaced by abstract policies defined by who knows whom. The employees were thus engaged in a system that mediated contradictions, a socio-mental structure that modelled their psychic structure.

The 1980s saw the development of the concept of company culture, that is, the creation of strong cultures by company management, a movement that I denounced at the time as potentially leading to a sectarian tendency (Amado, 1988). Indeed, there is but a small step between organisational cohesion and collective illusion and imprisonment, phenomena that have been analysed by some social psychologists who have revealed processes of influence (Moscovici, 1979), or who have denounced the dangers of groupthink (Janis, 1972), as well as by the group psychoanalysts following on from Freud (1912–1913, 1921c) and Le Bon (1916). I would, in particular, like to cite Anzieu (1984) and his explanation of group illusion, and also Kaës (1980, 1989, 2009) whose work on unconscious alliances, pacts of denial, and ideology is highly relevant here; not to forget the numerous other specialists of group psychoanalysis whose work provides useful insights into processes of psychic imprisonment (Abraham & Torok, 1978; Avron, 1997; Bion, 1961; Pinel, 1996; Rouchy, 1998).

The company culture movement is certainly not yet dead, given the persistence of many company directors' dreams of creating ever more compact, cohesive, and loyal units. Nevertheless, such dreams have had to face up to reality: the globalisation of the economy, the all-powerful nature of financial capitalism, of shareholders, and markets, and the merging of telecommunications and information systems, which give rise to the dictatorship of the just-in-time procedures and the immediacy of responses to the demands of the financial markets (De Gaulejac, 2005). All of these have led to innumerable employees being thrown out under the questionable pretext of restructurings, mergers, and cost reductions. The morbid side of the archaic maternal imago was at work (disillusionment and falling out of love were at stake), its impact increasing with the discovery of corruption by key figures of industry and the financial or ecological scandals of important firms such as Enron and Total. The increased importance of private life to the younger generations is no surprise, given this disillusionment. Their distrust of organisations leads them to be more prudent, or even instrumental, in their commitment to organisations, as long as they have the power and the means to do so. Does this mean that the hold of organisations and work relationships on people has diminished? Let us say that it has taken on new forms, which rely on the precariousness of the economic context, a certain resurgence of individualism, and what Diet (2005) calls "the destabilisation of the cultural containers" (that is, the traditional institutions) and the "default of symbolisation", elements on which sectarian movements feed.

I would like to point to some of the factors that seem to me to make up a form of system that takes a hold over people today.

The current psychic imprisonment system

The trap of participation

It is no longer possible to mobilise staff using centralising approaches. The average level of education has risen and people have become less dependent on authority, which itself has already been weakened by the fading of patriarchal society. As a result, it is necessary to get staff involved not only in implementing directives, but also in accepting the rules of the game, in defining regulations, and in evaluating results. However, very often the means to do this are insufficient. Thus, employees are trapped, in spite of themselves, in constructing procedures, which subject them to a normative power to which they have to adhere. By participating in defining concrete organisational policies, employees are moving in the direction of freely consented submission, thus realising the prediction of one of Orwell's characters in his famous novel *Nineteen Eighty-Four* (1949, p. 256): "We are not content with negative obedience, nor even with the most abject submission. When finally you surrender to us, it must be of your own free will". The trap arises with the psychological difficulty of declining an invitation to participate in a supposed collective construction and of refusing to put one's own personal mark on the principles and processes that are likely to influence one's own work.

As Ranjard (1972) explained in the 1970s when he denounced two ills, "groupitis" and "non-directivitis", based on Carl Rogers' ideas, these apparently tolerant approaches (which are, in fact, closer to the repressive tolerance so dear to Marcuse, 1963) are coloured by the maternal imago and, therefore, limit the expression of conflict.[1]

The destruction of professions and the advent of competences

"The deconstruction of the world of work" (Boltanski & Chiapello, 1999) is not due only to the increasing precariousness of employment and the intensified rhythm and volume of production. It is also linked to the disqualification of the points of reference to be found in professions that are now considered outdated (Lhuilier, 2006). Simply being an expert in one's field and taking part in the symbolic and historical precedents of a profession is equivalent to refusing the future. This is what misleadingly leads to the shift from the notion of qualification to that of competence. In addition to knowledge, the notion of competence generally implies a set of behavioural skills that are assessed by the hierarchy, and that involve the employee on a personal level in interpersonal relationships with colleagues, customers, or members of the public, without him or her having been trained to do so. In France, it is common to observe the dismay of many younger teachers at having to work in difficult areas, and of postal employees having to become sales representatives, or even sell financial services.

A competent person today is someone who manages to solve complex problems on his or her own, who takes initiatives, who markets him or herself, who imposes his or her own view while, of course, respecting the team spirit . . . It would be difficult to list here all of the paradoxical injunctions, or those that are experienced as such, that lead people to become tired of being themselves (Ehrenberg, 2000), or, rather, of being that "total" person, a sort of multi-faceted extrovert.

Total assessment and the quantophrenic delirium

Two more or less explicit reasons seem to justify, in the eyes of company management, the setting up of increasingly detailed and oppressive control and assessment systems: the all-powerful nature of economic factors which exert their pressure in a chain reaction, on the one hand, and the more guarded commitment of employees to the organisation's messages, on the other. This serves to illustrate Freud's "sphincter morality" in all aspects of professional life. People spend so much time accounting for and quantifying their work and results that they are prevented from deepening their professional knowledge and are even at risk of becoming under-qualified.

In addition to this, there is increasing use of a procedure known as 360°, which involves the assessment of employees' contributions by their colleagues, as well as the assessment done by the hierarchy. This kind of approach, despite its numerous positive qualities, has led to strange games of mutual surveillance. Indeed, in many ways, our society is becoming the controlling and normative society denounced by Foucault (1975): a socio-economic context which imposes an ethos of ever more volume in ever less time, without providing the necessary means to do so.

Stress, ill treatment, moral harassment, bullying (Hirigoyen, 1998), "placardisation" (putting on the shelf) (Lhuilier, 2002), and psychological breakdowns are currently common among employees, all in the name of profitability and quality. Whenever employees do not go along with the assessment system (after all, is it not logical to be accountable for one's work in exchange for one's pay?), conflicts are settled in court rather than through dialogue and regulation (for example, the exploitation of the concept of bullying by all those involved, in certain health institutions), which gives rise to paranoia and often leads to immobility.

As Dejours (2003) puts it, there is a growing gap between the subjective and the managerial descriptions of work. The clinical study of work has clearly shown that work cannot be directly observed. "Even if the work is well designed, if the work organisation is rigorous, if the rules and procedures are clear, it is impossible to achieve high quality by respecting the instructions to the letter" (Dejours, (2003, p. 13, translated for this edition), as incidents, breakdowns, anomalies, and incoherencies are inevitable. There is, therefore, always a difference between prescribed and real work, such that one could say, as does Dejours, that execution does not exist. For the clinical practitioner, he adds, work is defined as "what the person must add to the instructions in order to be able to satisfy the objectives he is given" (2003, p. 14, translated for this edition). It is the inevitable failure of instructions, the resistance of the "real" that informs and stimulates creativity. Thus, a good worker always violates orders, generally without the hierarchy knowing about it, except that the major swindle at the Société Générale, following that of the Barings

Bank (Stein, 2000), is a good example of a form of strategic *laisser faire*. However, it is a kind of tolerance of employees' tinkering, which inevitably goes against them when there is a problem. There is a sort of paradox: in order to do their jobs well, people must break the rules, but if there is a problem, they become the first targets.

It is important to remember that the reduction in productive activity and the related increase in service activity have led to a subjective mobilisation of employees in aspects that are invisible because they are relationship-based and intersubjective; the hold of this kind of work on people's private lives is one of the sources of technical efficiency. A relevant illustration is the psychic work of hospital staff (nurses and psychologists, for example) who continue to reflect on their patients after work. This kind of psychic work is, of course, not included in formal assessment. Real work is, therefore, subject to what Dejours calls "institutional denial". The fact that it is impossible to assess it today means that total quality is an absurd myth. This becomes transformed into normative prescriptions, with individual performance assessment contributing to the destruction of solidarity, of convivial work relationships, of loyalty, and sometimes of people going from shameful solitude to suicide. The French media, backed by research data (Conroy, 1989; Gournay, Laniece, & Kryvenac, 2004), specify that between 300 and 400 employees each year commit suicide, the cause of which is attributed to working conditions; these figures are probably far below the real ones.

Delusive alibis

Globalisation, economic warfare, total quality, submission to the all-powerful customer, and the requirement for permanent mobility and change (this being what defines the ideology of hypermodern times) are all presented to employees as natural choices, or self-evident and inevitable facts. Some managers have even modified their organisation charts in such a way as to position the customer at the top of the pyramid. The customer is a mythical, invisible, and all-powerful being, with whom all of us must be able to identify, a new totem before which even company executives must bow. There are no limits to the edicts—in particular, constraints—that are pronounced in the name of this new ghost-boss, which are often used as an alibi to cover up for the incompetence of people supposed to be in charge. On another level, and also linked to domination, Correale (2005) speaks of "hypertrophy of memory", which is a form of sedimentation of certain events in collective memory. We have observed a variation of this process during institutional interventions. An example of this is when more senior people refer to institutional history in order to force newcomers to conform and to stop them from changing traditional ways of functioning; this phenomenon I call the "castration of young shoots" in the name of respect for the elders and the *status quo*.

The "heroisation" of the individual

Given that all of us are encouraged to be heroes, we could become one of the principal actors of the great industrial or institutional adventure. Indeed, it is not certain whether or not we really have the choice. In any case, it is necessary to count only on one's own strengths, to fight against routine, to become a winner, and to constantly go beyond one's limits at the risk—which is always well hidden—of no longer recognising oneself! But what does it matter, is it not necessary to conquer in order to realise one's real self? The cult of performance is founded on the sports parable, according to which all of us are budding champions, and which gives rise to the quasi-evangelical use of sports coaches being invited to spread the good word on group work in order to achieve successful and faultless cohesion. Transference to the coach takes place on the basis of fascination and temporary collective illusion, which are phenomena that have contributed to the recent spectacular development of the coaching profession. The success of coaching is ambiguous and there are many critics. I myself have talked about the risk of "narcissistic inflation" (Amado, 2004), and of the psychologisation of the social arena at the expense of a more systemic analysis of the problems that have led to the demand for coaching in the first place. Gori and Le Coz (2006) have made a radical criticism of coaching, which they call "sports soup remixed with managerial sauce", and "the neoliberal recycling of humanistic psychology in the service of adaptation" through "a pretty pink approach to psychic life". Coaching can be seen as the symptom of a process of behavioural normalisation, which is anchored in an ideology of free will. Even if the problem is more complicated than Gori and Le Coz's view, it reminds me of the director of a large firm in the high-tech business who was generally calm and precise, but who, when he forcefully expressed his disagreement with an unethical approach to a business contract, was sent into coaching in order to learn how to control his emotions better . . .

The Carrefourised mind[2]

Alternatively, the director could be coached to develop his emotional intelligence (Chanlat, 2002), which is the same thing if one takes the original definition of this new intelligence (Salovey & Mayer, 1990), which came from the USA: "A form of social intelligence which implies being able to control one's emotions and those of others, to differentiate between them, and to use this information to guide both one's thinking and one's actions". The global success of Goleman's works (1995) has rapidly infiltrated the world of work. After all, how can one oppose the development of the four basic qualities of emotional intelligence: self-awareness, self-management, interpersonal intelligence, and relationship management? What is more, according to certain research (Feist & Baron, 1996), the emotional quotient is much more important than IQ, emotional skills being four times more significant in determining professional success and prestige than intellectual ones.

When endowed with such skills, it is possible, so they say without laughing, to become a "leader of resonance", capable of generating adhesion through one's own emotion and one's sensitivity to that of one's team, even to the point of crying together, as "the emotional leader acts like a 'limbique' magnet by exerting a tangible force on the emotional parts of brains" (Goleman, Boyatsis, & McKee, 2005) There is, however, a necessary condition to being able to manifest one's emotional authenticity, a condition that many North American psychologists have iterated for a long time: one must put one's negative emotions aside and expel them from one's brain, as things like resentment, chronic anxiety, and the feeling of uselessness draw people's attention away from the task to be accomplished (Dalgleish, Mathews, & Wood, 1999). Goleman implores us (1995, p. 21), "We must dissipate the fog created by toxic emotions", as this is a necessary condition to being able to play the role of a leader. "Once managers are established in the mode of systematic positive emotion, their management relationship skills enable them to interact in ways that catalyse resonance; they thereby drive the emotions in the right direction" (Goleman,

1995). Unfortunately, I doubt that any psychoanalyst would be able to deliver such a "driving" licence, given that they are not well established in the mode of positive emotion and might guide emotions in unpredictable directions, particularly in Europe. Here, our sensitivity to negative emotion can sometimes produce strange resonances. For example, when we hear "leader" we may think of Hitler or Stalin, and when we speak of the merits of organisations, images of Auschwitz or the gulag cross our emotional minds. Our minds not being properly "Carrefourised"[3] ("with Carrefour I am positive" is their slogan), some clinicians among us even think that negativity and creativity can go well together.

Thus, as some of us, and too many of those working in organisations and living in society, have badly orientated minds, it becomes necessary to try to persuade them that there are marvellous worlds around, using a new mystification technique: storytelling.

Storytelling: stories that make you daydream

Storytelling is a kind of machine for producing stories and formatting minds (Salmon, 2007). It was developed during the 1990s following the marketing and advertising crisis, and the denunciation of the means by which consumer goods were being manufactured. In order to hide the often terrible working conditions and the exploitation of children, large firms such as Nike hired professional storytellers to embellish their logo with beautiful stories. As Denning (2005, p. 105) says, "a brand is essentially a relationship". It was the beginning of a new era of narrative with alibi references to authors such as Roland Barthes, Tzvetan Todorov, Mikhail Bakhtine, and Guy Debord, and this movement was not restricted to the USA. Closer to home, in France, Henri Guaino, a talented storyteller and adviser to President Sarkozy, declared in July 2007, "It is not possible to transform a country without being able to write and tell a story". This means that the arrival of a new President today looks more like the start of a fiction rather than the taking up a new function. George Bush did not go wrong when he brought in Hollywood scriptwriters to tell the story of the Iraq war in his own way; the co-operation between Hollywood and the Pentagon is now official. This July, the search engine, Google, counted more than twenty million entries of the word "storytelling", and an increasing number of firms are using it. As the author of the best seller, *Shakespeare on Management*, Corrigan (1999) explains that rather than using dashboards, balance sheets, and end of year results, it is better to tell stories to employees.

This post-industrial company thinks of itself more as a story-producing machine, and I fear this movement could also reach the health and educational institutions. As Salmon states,

> Reality is now enveloped in a narrative net/mesh which filters perceptions and stimulates useful emotions. The great sagas that have marked history, from Homer to Tolstoy and from Sophocles to Shakespeare, spoke of universal myths and transmitted lessons from past generations. These were lessons of wisdom, the fruit of experience accumulated over time. Storytelling takes the opposite path: it relates reality in an artificial way, blocks exchanges, saturates the symbolic space with series and stories. It does not recount past experience, it accounts for behaviour and orients the flow of emotions . . . sets up narrative mechanisms by which people come to identify with models and conform to protocols. (2007, p. 16)

Examples can be seen in the marvellous collective fables about Disney, the World Bank, Coca Cola, the seven episodes of the legend of Chivas whisky designed to stall the decline of the brand, and Danone's story of the reconciliation between twins thanks to Danao. It is a question of getting us to "suspend incredulity temporarily", according to Coleridge, a specialist in the theory of narrative.

However, as Salmon (2007) states, the mechanism would not be complete if stories were only produced from outside. It is necessary to involve the employees, or, rather, to get them to tell the stories themselves. IBM has grasped this idea and encourages employees on the ground to propose stories, especially in times of mass redundancies, as is happening in Europe.

In February 2007, a study carried out by a consulting firm caused a great scandal. It was called "Silence leads to failure". The study was based on an enquiry into a group of 1000 directors of forty companies, to evaluate 2200 industrial projects in different sectors. The conclusion was that 85% of the failures of such programmes are due to organisational silence: things left unsaid, unresolved conflict, and the cult of Internet communication. The resulting recommendation was to get people talking, to create the voluble storytelling company and to insist on stories with an emotional content!

Intimacy is, thus, being spied upon, and the internal self solicited. The conversion of everything into stories becomes a means to ensure "a policing of behaviour and pedagogy for change".

And what if storytelling were simply a caricature of the modern world?

Let us sum up the different traps that create psychic imprisonment:

- a "collaborationist" form of participation which is virtually imposed, without people being able to question the objectives defined by the hierarchy and the almost perverse flattery of their sense of responsibility;
- the attack on professions, that is, on an important part of identity, and the increasingly continuous solicitation of behavioural skills that are always subject to sanction;
- the hypomania for individualised assessment, which increases self-inflicted pressure, solitude, or even a permanent fear of job loss;
- the ideological alibis that people end up internalising;
- the stimulation of the ego ideal, each person being a potential champion;
- the scrapping of conflict and the privilege associated with success and positive thinking;
- the capture of the imaginary through stories that make people dream, and the solicitation of the intimate self.

The attack on transitional thinking and the "psychologisation" of the social

Following this rather brief inventory of the elements that potentially contribute to creating psychic imprisonment, I would like to refer to the recent thinking of Honneth and the earlier work of Mendel.

Axel Honneth, currently the director of the Frankfurt School, where he took over from Jurgen Habermas, describes in his most recent book (2007) how the reforms of the neo-liberal economy have led to the development of a new kind of individual, whose relationship to himself is devoid of critical thinking, of the capacity for conflict, or for interior dialogue. Based on phenomena of self-reification, people have come to see themselves as having experiences and personal thoughts that can be produced. It is what Honneth calls a "self-objectivation" tendency, or is more in line with Lukacs' "self-reification" (Honneth, 2007).

Mendel, let us not forget, as early as the 1970s, describes how organisations, or, rather, their leaders, attempted to envisage and deal with complex problems related to the organisation of work in an essentially psychological way, thus leading to a "regression from politics to psyche" (or to the psycho-family personality, as he redefined it more recently (Mendel, 1998)). The following is an extract from an interview with a manager, which illustrates this phenomenon:

> "I have always said that the most important thing for me in a job is autonomy . . . I could not imagine working throughout my career with people who gave me orders or who told me what to do every morning. It would have been impossible for me. I have a real need to organise things as I like them, to work at my own pace, to decide how I want to go about things, to organise the work of others myself. Autonomy means freedom, adulthood, and responsibility. It means that people trust me and that I am capable of doing things in my own way. Of course, when you look carefully, I am still quite closely managed by someone who is autonomous. I have objectives to achieve, mandatory procedures, daily reporting, and the quality procedure; there is not really any room for manoeuvre and one cannot really improvise. In fact, no one says anything to me but I feel surrounded by such precise, constraining, unquestionable rules that I cannot see how I could go against them. What is more, I thought that autonomy meant some form of decision power . . . and 'margin of freedom'. Officially, of course, no one would contest that. My boss talks as I would expect him to . . . and yet in reality I feel terribly constrained. At the same time, as nothing is said officially, I cannot criticise anything either. Perhaps I am the one that is too demanding . . . but I am only taking up the notion of autonomy as it is used in the annual appraisal! In the end, I am wondering if I am the problem. Am I really autonomous? Have I really understood what it means in a company? Am I capable of being autonomous while respecting all of those constraints? That is it, and what if, after all that, I am the problem?" (Bellier & Laroche, 2005, p. 32, translated for this edition)

It is only a small step from there to getting into therapy or becoming mesmerised by a stress management course, thereby leaving the organisation of work and the management style intact and innocent.

It seems to me that this psycho-family regression (even if the intrapsy-chic resonance at work is also important (Amado, 1994)) and the reifi-cation process should be referred to by what I call "the attack against transitionality and depressivity". In other words, they are an attack on the psychic and environmental spaces that enable symbolisation processes (Amado, 2007), a "sane" relationship between fantasy and reality, play and creativity; they go against the capacity to think, and the tolerance of uncertainty, complexity, and ambivalence. Operative thinking and false-selves are not far away, and yet . . .

Sources of release

Let us come back, after those sombre observations, to Racamier's words and to the processes of release, but without inventing a happy ending for this story. What is intriguing in this process of psychic imprisonment is the need for "complacency", which Racamier refers to when talking about perversion. Now, it seems to me that this complacency is not systematic and, at least, not general, as people are capable of distancing themselves to a greater or lesser extent. There are not enough observations made of this distancing capability, because researchers and clinicians are generally confronted with what is problematic, what does not work, and words of complaint and suffering. This constitutes their basic material, some of which can overwhelm them if they have not sorted out their countertransference reactions. I would like to insist on one point to begin with: psychic imprisonment is never total within a system, and the enigmatic volun-tary servitude (Enriquez, 2007) is never completely guaranteed. The accounts of those who survived the concentration camps, gulags (Moscovici, 1979), and sects (Amado, 1990) are an illustration of that. Despite the "total" character of such institutions (Goffman, 1968), which are cut off from the world, the individual's internal being is not always destroyed. Even the collective suicide in Guyana (about 800 people) under the influence of Jim Jones was not carried out with total complacency. It was necessary to have recourse to threat and violent repression for total slaughter to be achieved.

Although today's institutions are tending to reduce barriers between the private and public spheres, there are ways of resisting. In their study of IBM, Pagès and his team (1979) might have somewhat underestimated the strategic or tactical dimension of the ways in which managers adapted to the organisation. Besides those who subscribed to the company religion (because they found in it what they needed, objectively or unconsciously), there were also those who used pretence, acted "as if", and silenced their real thoughts in order to put up with the constraints imposed on them. It is undeniable that there are advantages in this kind of submissiveness, even if it is only apparent. There is a good example to be found in some of the great French restaurants, where a creative, brilliant chef rules over an army of cooks who are subjected to a regime of conformity and apparent bad treatment. Nevertheless, this more or less freely accepted submissiveness does have another side to it: it provides an exceptional opportunity to learn a profession, which does not necessarily lead to repetition and mimicry. Once they are released from the chains of subordination, many cooks apply the tacit knowledge they have built in the shadow of their master. Free will can always be mobilised, even if it appears to be dormant.

In addition to the strategic conformism of agents, it is also possible to observe the strategic use of the prescribed tools:

Take the case of the National Police force. The assessment of each nightly patrol is based on the number of "sticks" collected, that is the number of times the intervention of an individual officer or patrol gives rise to a fine or an arrest. This leads to a nonsensical situation. A patrol works all night under cover in a difficult area to try to arrest a gang involved in drugs trafficking that is destroying the area. After six hours under cover, the patrol discovers that the gang has managed to get away because there have been leaks, or because the car that they are using has been noticed. It is very difficult, anyway, because the people on the other side are very clever. The patrol returns to the police station in the early hours of the morning. They have no "sticks". The hierarchy does not take into consideration the fact that this undercover work is necessary, that failure is an integral part of this work. Success is only possible after a number of disappointments. They want numbers, visible actions, which produce results that can be shown proudly to the mayor or police commissioner. This patrol is likely to be sanctioned, whether or not they have done their job well. The inevitable consequence of these absurd assessments is that on the following nights, the patrol will focus on checking on car drivers. At the end of one night they will come back having sanctioned a large number of offences, such as driving without papers, drunken driving, driving without a licence. When they return to the police station, they have fourteen "sticks". In the end, assessment leads to ineffective measures against public order offences. (Dejours, 2003, pp. 33–34, translated for this edition)

Coaching works in the same way; it cannot only be seen as imposed on people. In the case previously mentioned (the manager sent to coaching for expressing disagreement), the manager told me that he first chose his own coach from among the people he knew. He had drawn useful insights from the coach for his life in general and had adopted a more detached and cynical point of view in relation to his company, reducing his own risks and cleverly getting them to be taken on by his company. This is a good example of cynical resistance, which, by the way, is not without problematic implications in terms of the type of people and organisations it gives rise to.

In the same way, administrative assessment and control mechanisms can also be circumvented, exploited, or derided by employees, whenever they feel sufficiently safe to do so. For example, the secretary of a higher education institution, asked by the HR director to sum up her work using two figures, gave a first figure, 94,830, to describe the number of characters, including spaces, that she typed daily (emails, administrative forms, articles, etc.), and a second figure of twenty-eight to describe the number of useless daily interruptions to her work by her hierarchy!

Irony is becoming a prime element among the defence strategies used against psychic imprisonment, not only in practice, but also in research carried out on the subject in organisations. It is not surprising to learn that the Danish are ahead of us in that area (Johansson & Woodilla, 2005), since Kierkegaard (1861), following on from Socrates, had already developed a theory in his thesis about the unmasking function of irony (to do with power structures, hypocrisy, and prejudice), equivalent to a liberating function.

Derision is a closer cousin of irony and sometimes relies on the defence mechanism known as the "reversal into the opposite" of the affect. Nothomb, the novelist, illustrates this in her ferocious and playful denunciation of a Japanese firm. When, as an intern, she was demoted to the position of toilet cleaner, she gave the following account:

From the moment I was given this incredible assignment, I entered into a new dimension of existence: the world of pure and simple derision. I imagine this was a reflex action: in order to be able to bear the seven months I was to spend in that position, I needed a change of reference, I had to invert what had until now served as guidelines for me. And through a process that saved my immune capacity, that interior reversal was immediate. From then on, in my mind, everything dirty became clean, shame became glory, the torturer became the victim, and the sordid became comical. (1999, p. 127, translated for this edition)

A chapter on irony–cynicism would not be complete without mentioning the huge success of a particularly sinister booklet with therapeutic qualities written by Maier in 2004, *Bonjour paresse* (Good morning laziness), in which she gives "treacherous" advice to enable people to get away with doing the least possible amount of work in a company. Through a somewhat anarchistic approach (maybe helped by the fact that, in addition to her normal work, she is also a psychoanalyst . . .), the author simply exploits a well-known release mechanism: work to rule, or the zeal strike. Clinical practitioners involved in the work place and organisations are familiar with the idea that strict respect for the rules leads all organisations to failure.

What about protective groupings in all of this? Of course, their role is critical, and one could consider that union activity, in particular, protects against psychic imprisonment, at least through its dominant ideology. But it has become obvious that the different threats to employment, the increasing individualisation of assessment, and the fragmentation of organisations (networks, project groups, etc.), when added to the risks of psychic imprisonment described previously, contribute to a loosening sense of solidarity and a weakening union membership, at least in France, now one of the weakest in Europe. Perhaps if the unions were to take a greater interest in phenomena of social alienation, they might reach a wider audience.

Finally, to release oneself from the company's hold requires a form of "thirdness", the capacity to be within and without, inside and outside the system, or, as the Tavistock clinicians call it, "on the boundary". This kind of position undoubtedly requires a capacity to escape from the "illness of idealisation" (Chasseguet-Smirgel, 1985), more or less present in all of us, as well as a minimum of ontological security (Laing, 1960), which enables one to get a "well-tempered hold on oneself": that is, a hold that implies the intimacy of secrecy, which is the guardian of unconscious drives (Ferrant, 2003), as well as having recourse to the *Mètis* (Detienne & Vernant, 1974) to craft intelligence.

Nevertheless, such qualities, however useful they might be in these times of exacerbated social control, are not natural. They are, of course, related to potential space (Amado, 2009), without which anxiety would be unthinkable, as Winnicott (1965) would claim, and creativity would be inhibited. In the same way, a process of disillusionment cannot take place unless the illusion of having created the world, and a certain form of all-powerfulness, has existed. These ideas can provide useful insights into the difficult process of release from psychic imprisonment.

Of particular interest to us here are the social conditions that allow the potential space to be revived. In this respect, in addition to spontaneous transitional spaces, whether they are chance encounters, unplanned meetings, analysand events (Amado & Ambrose, 2001), or designed transitional spaces (Amado & Vansina, 2005), these can play an important role in achieving release from psychic imprisonment. A good illustration of this is Mendel and his colleagues' socio-psycho-analytical approach, based on homogenous groups (Prades, 2007), the aim of which is to develop people's "psychosocial personality" (Rueff-Escoubès, 2008), and enable them to recover power over their own acts within institutions. In the same spirit, we must take note of the growing concern for groups, which analyse their own practice and settings for psychosocial regulation, provided they avoid the "individualisation" of problems. The reaction of Renault's management after the series of suicides committed on the Guyancourt site in France is symptomatic of this kind of risk: they proposed stress management and free expression workshops in large cathartic meetings and smaller groups. Nothing meaningful was suggested to deal with the organisational processes that created psychic imprisonment and led to self-imprisonment.

It is not by chance, therefore, that the regulation processes, the working through, takes place outside institutions, given that employees are increasingly fearful of free expression.

To conclude, let us focus on the warning that Ricoeur (2004, pp. 156–157), the French philosopher, gave at the end of his life:

> The threats that reveal the fragility of individual or collective identity are not illusions; it is remarkable to see how the ideologies of power

undertake, with worrying success, to manipulate these fragile identities through the symbolic mediation of action. (Translated for this edition)

Is simple vigilance enough to counter that?

Notes

1. In the same way, Khan (1996), when talking of the maternal hold, underlines the fact that the idealisation of the over-good mother is due to the child's lack of early aggressive experiences.
2. Carrefour is a major French hypermarket chain.
3. Carrefour, the French hypermarket chain, is known for its advertising slogan orientated towards positive emotion.

References

Abraham, N., & Torok, M. (1978). *L'écorce et le noyau*. Paris: Aubier.

Amado, G. (1988). Cohésion organisationnelle et illusion collective. *Revue Française de Gestion*, 69: 37–43.

Amado, G. (1990). Identité psychique, crise et organisation: pour une théorie de la résonance. *Psychologie Clinique*, 3: 115–128.

Amado, G. (1994). La résonance psychosociale au coeur de la vie et de la mort. *Revue Internationale de Psychosociologie*, 1(1): 87–94.

Amado, G. (2004). Le coaching ou le retour de Narcisse. *Connexions*, 1: 43–51.

Amado, G. (2007). A vida psíquica na organização entre Thanatos e Eros' In: R. Facchin, T. Fisher, & J. F. Chanlat (Eds.), *Analisis das Organizaçoes, Perspectivas Latinas* (pp. 121–136). Rio Grande do Sul: URFGS Editoria.

Amado, G. (2009). Potential space: the threatened source of individual and collective creativity. In: B. Sievers (Ed.), *Psychoanalytic Studies of Organisations* (pp. 263–283). London: Karnac.

Amado, G., & Ambrose, A. (2001). *The Transitional Approach to Change*. London: Karnac.

Amado, G., & Vansina, L. (2005). *The Transitional Approach in Action*. London: Karnac.

Anzieu, D. (1984). *The Group and the Unconscious*. London: Routledge & Kegan Paul.

Avron, O. (1997). *La pensée scénique*. Toulouse: Erès.

Bellier, S., & Laroche, H. (2005). *Moi, Manager*. Paris: Dunod.

Bion, W. R. (1961). *Experiences in Groups*. London: Tavistock.

Boltanski, L., & Chiapello, E. (1999). *Le nouvel esprit du capitalisme*. Paris: Gallimard, coll. Essais.

Chanlat, J. F. (2002). Emotions, organisation et management: une réflexion critique sur la notion d'intelligence émotionnelle. *Travailler, 9*: 113–132.

Chasseguet-Smirgel, J. (1985). *The Ego Ideal: A Psychoanalytic Essay on the Malady of the Ideal*. London: Free Association Books.

Conroy, C. (1989). Suicide in the workplace: incidence victim characteristics and external cause of death. *Journal of Occupational Medicine, 31*: 847–851.

Correale, A. (2005). L'hypertrophie de la mémoire en tant que forme de pathologie institutionnelle' In: R. Kaës, J. P. Pinel, O. Kernberg, A. Correale, E. Diet, & B. Duez (Eds.), *Souffrance et Psychopathologie des Liens Institutionnels* (pp. 105–119). Paris: Dunod, coll. Inconscient et Culture.

Corrigan, P. (1999). *Shakespeare on Management*. Dover: Kogan Page.

Dalgleish, T., Mathews, A., & Wood, J. (1999). Inhibition processes in cognition and emotion: a special case? In: T. Dalgleish & M. J. Power (Eds.), *The Handbook of Cognition and Emotion* (pp. 243–266). Chichester: John Wiley.

De Gaulejac, V. (2005). *La société malade de la gestation.* Paris: Seuil.

Dejours, C. (2003). *L'Évaluation du Travail à L'Épreuve du Réel: Critique des Fondements de l'Evaluation*. Paris, INRA Editions.

Denning, S. (2005). *The Leader's Guide to Storytelling. Mastering the Art and Discipline of Business Narrative*. San Francisco, CA: Jossey-Bass.

Detienne, M., & Vernant, J. P. (1974). *Les ruses de l'intelligence, la Mètis des grecs*. Paris: Ed. Champ Flammarion.

Diet, E. (2005). Le thanatophore, travail de la mort et destructivité dans les institutions. In: R. Kaës, J. P. Pinel, O. Kernberg, A. Correale, E. Diet, & B. Duez (Eds.), *Souffrance et psychopathologie des liens institutionnels* (pp. 121–189). Paris: Dunod, coll.'Inconscient et Culture.

Dorey, R. (1981). La relation d'emprise. *Nouvelle Revue de Psychanalyse, 24*: 117–139.

Dorey, R. (1992). Le désir d'emprise. *Revue Française de Psychanalyse*, T-LVI, Congrès "De l'emprise à la perversion", 1424–1432.

Ehrenberg, A. (2000). *La fatigue d'être soi. Dépression et société*. Paris: Odile Jacob.

Eiguer, A. (1989). *Le pervers narcissique et son complice*. Paris: Dunod.

Eiguer, A. (1995). *Le cynisme pervers*. Paris: L'Harmattan.

Enriquez, E. (2007). *Clinique du pouvoir*. Paris: Erès.

Feist, G. J., & Barron, F. (1996). Emotional intelligence and academic intelligence in career life success. Paper presented to the Annual Convention of the American Psychological Society, San Francisco.

Ferrant, A. (2003). La honte et l'emprise. *Revue Française de Psychanalyse*, *67*: 1781–1787.

Foucault, M. (1975). *Surveiller et Punir*. Paris: Gallimard.

Freud, S. (1912–1913). *Totem and Taboo. S. E.*, *13*: 1162. London: Hogarth.

Freud, S. (1921c). *Group Psychology and the Analysis of the Ego. S. E.*, *18*: 69–134. London: Hogarth.

Goffman, E. (1968). *Asiles*. Paris: Ed. de Minuit.

Goleman, D. (1995). *Emotional Intelligence.* New York: Bantam.

Goleman, D., Boyatsis, R., & McKee, A. (2005). *L'Intelligence emotionnelle au travail*. Paris: Village Mondial.

Gori, R., & Le Coz, P. (2006). *L'empire des coachs*. Paris: Albin Michel.

Gournay, M., Laniece, F., & Kryvenac, I. (2004). Etude des suicides liés au travail en Basse Normandie. *Travailler*, *12*: 91–98.

Hirigoyen, M.-F. (1998). *Le harcèlement moral*. Paris: Syros.

Honneth, A. (2007). *La réification*. Paris: Gallimard.

Janis, I. L. (1972). *Victims of Groupthink*. Boston, MA: Houghton-Mifflin.

Johansson, U., & Woodilla, J. (2005). Irony. Its use and potential in organization theory. In: *Irony and Organizations* (pp. 25–50). Liner: Copenhagen Business School Press.

Kaës, R. (1980). *L'idéologie. Etudes psychanalytiques*. Paris: Dunod.

Kaës, R. (1989). Le pacte dénégatif dans les ensemble intersubjectifs. In: A. Missenard, G. Rosolato, & R. Kaës (Eds.), *Le négatif. Figures et modalités* (pp. 101–136). Paris: Dunod.

Kaës, R. (2009). *Les Alliances Inconscientes*. Paris: Dunod.

Khan, M. R. (1996). On symbiotic omnipotence. In: *The Privacy of the Self* (pp. 82–98). London: Karnac.

Kierkegaard, S. (1861). *The Concept of Irony*. Princeton, NJ: Princeton University Press, 1989.

Laing, R. D. (1960). *The Divided Self: An Existential Study in Sanity and Madness*. Harmondsworth: Penguin.

Le Bon, G. (1916). *Psychologie des foules*. Paris: Librairie Félix Alcan.

Lhuilier, D. (2002). *Placardisés, des exclus dans l'entreprise*. Paris: Seuil.

Lhuilier, D. (2006). *Cliniques du travail*. Toulouse: Erès.

Maier, C. (2004). *Bonjour paresse*. Paris: Ed. Michalon.

Marcuse, H. (1963). *Eros et civilisation*. Paris: Ed. de Minuit.

Mendel, G. (1998). *L'acte est une aventure*. Paris: La Découverte.

Moscovici, S. (1979). *Psychologie des minorités actives.* Paris: PUF.

Nothomb, A. (1999). *Stupeur et tremblements.* Paris: Albin Michel.

Orwell, G. (1949). *Nineteen Eighty-Four.* London: Secker & Warburg.

Pagès, M., Bonetti, M., De Gaulejac, V., & Descendre, D. (1979). *L'Emprise de l'organisation.* Paris: PUF.

Pinel, J. P. (1996). La déliaison pathologique des liens institutionnels. In: R. Kaës, J. P. Pinel, O. Kernberg, A. Correale, E. Diet, & B. Duez (Eds.), *Souffrance et psychopathologie des liens institutionnels* (pp. 51–79). Paris: Dunod.

Prades, J. L. (2007). *Intervention participative et travail social: un dispositif institutionnel pour le changement.* Paris: L'Harmattan.

Racamier, P. (1992). *Le génie et ses origines.* Paris: Payot.

Ranjard, P. (1972). Groupite et non-directivité. *Sociopsychanalyse,* 2: 209–238.

Ricoeur, P. (2004). *Parcours de la reconnaissance.* Paris: Stock.

Rouchy, J. C. (1998). *Le groupe, espace analytique.* Paris: Erès, coll. 'Transition'.

Rueff-Escoubès, C. (2008). *La sociopsychanalyse de Gérard Mendel.* Paris: La Découverte.

Salmon, C. (2007). *Storytelling.* Paris: La Découverte.

Salovey, P., & Mayer, J. (1990). Emotional intelligence. *Imagination, Cognition and Personality,* 9(3): 185–211.

Sirota, A. (2003). *Figures de la perversion sociale.* Paris: Editions EDK.

Stein, M. (2000). The risk taker as shadow: a psychoanalytic view of the collapse of Barings Bank. *Journal of Management Studies,* 37: 1215–1229.

Winnicott, D. W. (1965). *The Maturational Processes and the Facilitating Environment: Studies in the Theory of Emotional Development.* London: Hogarth Press.

CHAPTER TWO

Work, management, and psychic health

Dominique Lhuilier

I t is often noted that there is growing attention to the relationship between work and psychic health. This attention attempts to pursue an investigation of several core issues. Here, we will deal with two of them.

First of all, what is the nature of this relationship? How shall we put into perspective the transformations of work, new managerial practices, and the contemporary forms of psychopathology of work? Note that here the term "psychopathology" does not pertain to the classification of mental illness, but to the study of psychological mechanisms engaged in, individually and collectively, by subjects at work. The perspective is that of a "psychopathology of daily life" in the workplace. This perspective cannot be represented in a simplistic causal diagram in which the mental health of workers is determined by the stresses of work situations. That is, the model of physical occupational diseases resulting from physical–chemical–biological factors at the workplace cannot be applied here.

Between work-related stress and psychological problems is situated in an individual capable of understanding his situation, of reacting to it, and transforming it. So, here, the analysis of the transformations of work, which reflect the transformations of the framework of management, must include an analysis of the available resources, or resources that can be created, for organising, creating, and coping with the demands of the work situation.

Another angle of investigation would be to ask oneself to what extent the managerial controls, the discourse, and the systems put in place to "treat" suffering at work, actually guide the categorisation of subjective experiences and the demand. Psychologists are increasingly sought after in the workplace. Their credentials and practices are heterogeneous and need to be more widely discussed and clarified.

Contemporary forms of psychopathology of work

Here, we are not going to engage in a diagnosis of the world of work and its evolution. We will only note that there is a twofold process involving both an increase in workplace pressures and a decrease in availability of the means and resources needed to respond to them. Several reminders illustrate this process: job insecurity; internal and external flexibility; the intensification of work; the development of service activities; the amplification of contradictions between the customisation of service for quality improvement and the standardisation of work in order to increase productivity; increased indetermination concerning the means and ends of a given activity; as well as the inflated importance given to the procedures of control and evaluation . . .

These analyses have already been the subject of numerous commentaries, so, instead, we examine the evolution of the workplace against the backdrop of a broad spectrum of emerging pathologies.

Pathologies of "packaged" or "fragmented" and hindered activity

The situation of today's workers revolves around two symmetrical, yet opposing forces: overwork in the context of time pressure and competition, and under-employment, which translates into an ever-widening fringe pool of forced "part-timers", vulnerable and ignored, who are squeezed out of the space–time production routine.

High-stress, or packaged, activity is evidenced by the presence of pathologies of overwork or strain, notably musculo-skeletal disorders (MSDs). Physical strain, yet again, cannot be dissociated from psychological strain: the physical body exhibits evidence of forced rhythms of activity, and of what remains unarticulated, verbally unexpressed, which then self-accelerates as it serves to anaesthetise thought and affect. The calibration and intensification of movements contribute to an escalation of the psychological toll of work, which inhibits initiative and spontaneous activity. One might recall here the hard-hitting critical analysis of Taylorism proposed by Wallon (1976), which underscored that amputating an individual from his own initiative neutralises great portions of the individual's potential, which forces him into a deeper state of immobility, prolonging his stress. As this process of counter-investing (i.e., the inhibition of all initiative and spontaneous activity) is repeated, it constitutes an important part of the work experience and the fatigue associated with it.

The pathologies of prevented or stifled activity have been greatly emphasised in the analyses of Taylorian work. Today, some new dissociations are appearing, induced by management's attempts to solicit participation and initiative, while, at the same time, encouraging conformity and adherence to the corporate mission. Thus, to the dissociations of motion, at the same time demanded and discouraged by Taylorism, are added the psychological disconnections induced by simultaneously mobilising and stifling psychological energy, resulting in psychological tensions often ascribed to omnipresent stress (Aubert & Pagés, 1989), a general concept synonymous to frustration, fatigue, etc. Hindered activity refers here to activity proper or personal activity, as Tosquelles (2009) presents it:

> Activity differs from simple restlessness, and the same goes for action imposed or suggested by anyone other than oneself. The idea of activity, or activity proper, connotes self-initiation: personal and personalised, which finds inspiration and is rooted within each individual. (p. 25, translated for this edition)

Also, the apparent contrast between overwork and underemployment masks the same amputation of personal activity as a source and resource for the process of subjectification. This might take the form of an activity dissociated from the subject, ritualised and reduced to a simple mechanistic "operation", or it might take the form of repression of action, and of psychological mobilisation through forced inaction. In effect, the psychological toll and suffering linked to the inhibition of activity proper does not concern only the challenges encountered in the employee's work (in its modern "Taylorised" version prescribing not motion but subjectivity), but also applies to situations of forced idleness, or unemployment. Think here of both external unemployment and internal unemployment (in other words, workers who have been "sidelined" or laid off (Lhuilier, 2002). The lack of access to employment is, in effect, a relegation to a space–time apartheid. In addition, under-employment prohibits one from applying oneself in a functionally effective capacity. Without work, in the sense of activity, the subject cannot demonstrate to himself or others that he is capable. Without being challenged to produce, though constrained by limitation, but also availed of possibilities, those without work risk wavering between exaggerated feelings of inadequacy and grandiose illusions of power: between self-devaluation and escapist fantasies.

Work is not the domain in which one realises the expression of the desires of personal needs, or which permits the affirmation of self outside the imposed confines (of work). On the contrary, it is supposed to deal with that which is outside the "self", an activity, which will enlist his ability, direct and regulate his action, and the result will be recognised in the chain of collective activities. It is this realisation that characterises the work of simple occupations (the unemployed say "take care or you will be taken care of"). Work as a "function unique to the social being" (Meyerson, 1987) and of which the condition is usefulness to society, involves the principle of exchange. Without beneficiaries, the activity would break down, or collapse upon itself, and no longer serve the function of mediation between material and social reality.

Confronted by the symbolic violence of social obsolescence or oblivion, those without work experience a massive sense of loss: loss of the support system which bolsters self-awareness and sustains one's inner resilience; loss of the involvement in productive activity, which results in a type of "self amputation", or disconnection from oneself; deprived of purposeful connection with others: "disaffiliated", or disenfranchised (Castel, 1995), they are not only alone, but also isolated. They have lost their place. The workplace, both as it exists and as it is created, cannot be reduced to, or substituted by, one's origins in the sanctuary of the family hearth. The question is ontological in the sense that in all societies and at every age, each one searches for a place to belong, a place to make something of himself, trying to find with whom and with what to weave his story. The purpose of work is very much a necessary part of constructing the "self".

In a world which values efficiency and performance, responsibility and initiative, those without work represent a failure to live up to the norm. The unemployed worker is a repudiation of our norms of socialisation: unproductive, powerless, inadequate, and incapable. Condemned as having no useful purpose, he represents an undesirable element.

Hindrance or obstruction of activity causes ever deepening immobilisation of internal dynamics, all the more painful as energy previously invested in purposeful activity is diverted into a void and absorbed by internal contention, due to the powerlessness to act. The withdrawal from work undermines the satisfaction that comes from the exertion of body and mind. This psychological energy, lacking a constructive outlet, is substituted by irritability and discontent. This discontent can express itself in the form of psychosomatic decompensation, expressed in the form of new pathologies or the aggravation of chronic ailments heretofore manageable.

Hindered activity is, fundamentally, privation of the power to act, because work is not merely the discharging of assigned tasks, it is also a vehicle by which one makes a mark on one's corner of the world and the course of events. And the suffering that results from the want of work leads, in turn, to the diminished power to act. The experience of forced inactivity is very much that of a loss of a support system for the individual: a loss of material support, initiative is immured by the amputation of the power to act; and a loss of interpersonal support, relationships with others are abrogated due to isolation.

Gaining a perspective with regard to managerial practices and occupational health should take into account—and we want to remember here—not only the deleterious effects of new organisational models of work, but also the damage caused by what is essentially a "financial" or "virtual" economy. This unreal economy makes "human resources" susceptible to being discarded like consumable goods, and mere variables to be adjusted in the interest of competitiveness in a deregulated market. The focus on how work affects health tends to obscure work as an operative of health, and the output of scientific literature on the subject of health as a result of "non-work" is much less abundant. However, the history of the psychopathology of work has bequeathed to us a wealth of information, followed by the clinical studies on the social and psychological functions of work in terms of restoring and developing psychic health. This body of information provides a bounty of guides for thinking about work as an instrument for developing health, and avoids reducing the problem of work and health resulting from degradation, "fragilisation", mutilation, etc.

Pathologies of loneliness and ambiguity of work

These pathologies are the flip-side of individualisation in "human resources management": the individualisation of remuneration, hours, work rhythms, careers, training programmes, performance evaluation, etc., but also of the precariousness of work collectives for the benefit of a network organisation or group projects, and of the dilution of relationships, union memberships, and guilds, all for the sake of emphasising the value of versatility and adaptability.

Parallel to these developments, another theme concerns the tendency towards greater ambivalence regarding the goals and means of action. This is particularly vivid in the widely expanding area of service activities. By definition, service is work performed for, and in direct relation with, individuals. And "for" can be imperceptibly transformed into "on" or "to", undergoing a major alteration resulting in modifications of the officially designated outcomes. "If there is in place at least a clear general agreement in the factory concerning the object of production, a similar agreement is often absent in institutions where one does things for, or to, others" (Hugues, 1996, p. 67, translated for this edition). In effect, all work accomplished for others faces the complex trade-offs between what is just and what is unjust, good or bad, true or false: a complication distorted by the intensification of work.

Faced with an array of questions and uncertainties raised within, and at the time of, the activity, the individual is now more and more alone in coming to terms with, and deciding, what is just and good, what should be done and how.

The increasing isolation of work is added to the problems arising from the recognition of failings in the workplace, the topic of recurrent complaints. In effect, beyond the operative connection with the purpose of work persists the question of the symbolic relationship between individuals, which authorises the validation of practices and social recognition. Still, the catalogue of complaints occupies the fore-front of the landscape: What do they reveal?

All work implies judgements in terms of value and prestige. Furthermore, all discussion of work involves a narrative of self-worth and of recognition, which is filtered through the social hierarchy of professions and activities, whether valued or not, unrecognised or widely esteemed. Indeed,

> an individual's profession is one of the factors taken into account in forming an opinion of someone and, certainly, one of the factors that has the most influence on how he judges himself. A human being's occupation is one of the most important components of one's social identity, of his self and even his destiny within his own unique existence. (Hugues, 1996, p. 67, translated for this edition)

Also, one can comprehend that the division of labour, synonymous with the moral and psychological division of labour, creates a type of categorisation of professions and activities that do not (necessarily) provide equal narcissistic or ego validation in terms of social recognition.

However, and I wish to emphasise this point, today this division of labour tends to be generalised, and it is the group of activities that seems to fall into the category of "grunt work", that is, at the bottom of the hierarchy of labour. The difficulty in speaking of real work, the limitations encountered and the divergence in stated purposes, is growing. And the prevalence of work design by management (de Gaulejac, 2005) encourages a failure to appreciate "real-world" work situations.

The refusal to appreciate the facts is not so much due to lack of knowledge: indeed, there is enough well conceived information available. Rather, it demonstrates an active intention to know nothing, a refusal to acknowledge. Denial is one of the hallmarks of ignorance. It is the rejection of any perception that does not fit with the "theory" the subject has about reality. It requires knowledge, or a pre-existing worldview, prior to encountering something that contradicts what is assumed to be "already accepted". Thus, not only does this denial fail to alert the subject to the inadequacy of his knowledge, the complex of preconceptions is also very likely to resist "true" knowledge. These preconceptions encourage further entrenchment of erroneous knowledge to the extent that the subject is able to avoid cognitive dissonance with the recognised system of knowledge, be it collective or individual. At issue here is the defensive function of the representations of work, like the mental representations of the relationship between work and health, which masks the element of reality likely to provoke anxiety, vulnerability, shame, and other disagreeable affects: in other words, that which could disappoint the illusion of being the master of one's own activity.

Today, the denial of work as a sphere of real conflict is being pursued in new directions. Major studies geared toward analysing activities are initiated to take stock of practices, assembling repertories of functions in order to produce "professional references". Therefore,

> the substantial dichotomy between what is real and what is preferred is followed by the substantial dichotomy between what is being written and what is being done. The gap resulting from this imposition persists. Reality remains twofold and therefore will be doubled: the order of concrete reality resists any full-scale integration with procedural order. (Dassa & Maillard, 1996, p. 35, translated for this edition)

Certifications and quality controls, as well as the traceability requirement that accompanies them, and the legal system associated with accountability, lurking threateningly in the periphery, increase pressure to create an idealised image of both the process and the results, while simultaneously increasing the workload.

The prescription requires the ideal (Dujarier, 2006), and imposes operational modes that are increasingly at odds with the reality of resources available in the work situation. Here, it is no longer only a question of performing productive tasks (or providing service): behaviour that passes for expected conformity to the rules and objectives begins to materialise, alongside deceptive behaviour in the guise of real work. This is all being done while creating a coherent semblance of compliance to the task, however increasingly unreal, and disguising the divergences and inconsistencies, reducing them to fiction. The resulting deception creates a misleading concept of work and, in turn, contributes to the denial of the reality of work and the deterioration of health in the workplace.

The intensive production of tasks reports, the assessment of tolls and indicators, the ratios and balances, curve graphs, pyramids, and other statistical illustrations are used as "management tools", serving to provide a competitive edge and to evaluate production units. It is less a question of assessing reality and more an attempt to assign coherence to discrete objectives.

From that point, the growing concern is not only with the disregard for social recognition, but also with the deficient understanding of work itself, and of the impossibility of recognising oneself in one's work. Indeed, how does one make sense of one's actions, of what one "does"? How does one evaluate the relevance, the value, the "quality" of what one does when there is no flexibility within which to debate the work or the criteria for one's activities?

At the basis of this intensification of work, of the efforts at "quality assurance" and the denial of the essential reality of work, a silent suffering takes hold, indicating the widening discrepancy between actual and imagined achievement—achievement that one had aspired to accomplish, but in the end goes unrealised. The repudiation of work well done has the crippling effect of a heavy psychological blow. Criticism of one's own activity creates a diffuse malaise, a general sense of being compelled to do "grunt work" (Lhuilier, 2005), and of being pushed to the point of humiliation, in particular in a number of professions involving close interpersonal contact (teachers, caregivers, social workers, ticket-takers, shop assistants . . .). However, the shame is not openly expressed. A hush is imposed on expressions of discontent and the individual is forced into isolation.

Pathologies of mistreatment and violence

The rise of violence in work situations is, yet again, a product of forces of social disintegration, as individuals find themselves in the grip of intersubjective interaction, without collective or institutional mediation as a third party. The necessity of adhesion, involvement, and accountability serves as a counterweight against the "deterioration of the work environment" (Chiapello & Boltanski, 1999), and exclusion increases in proportion to the pressure to integrate. As the pressure to integrate increases within the grip of a vision (or illusion) shared by a tightly-knit, homogenous organisation, the more the group identity solidifies against scapegoats, deemed culpable and/or deficient, and the more likely it is that they will be shunned and segregated from the group.

All organisations which prescribe uniformity of thought (*la pensée unique*) generate a silent and terrifying destructiveness and an erosion of common cause which dissolves the group into a mere collection of individuals, face to face in a state of isolation, and even destructive rivalry. Often, within such organisational contexts, relationships of influence take on overtones of "harassment": dual relationships, unmediated by institution, law, the professional community, or the collective influence of the workplace. The inadequacy of a framework designed to regulate and prevent these very abuses become a wedge in the relations between the professional and the user, as well as among the employee, his colleagues, and management. Here, internal and external violence (Debout, 1999, 2001), aggression, insults, harassment, mistreatment, and sidelining (Lhuilier, 2002) trigger post-trauma pathologies previously only thought to relate to workplace accidents.

Access to real work is never given or offered, not even to the originator himself, so incomplete is his understanding of the overall process, due to the difficulty of exposing the nature of, and obstacles to, action. However, here I want to emphasise these new conditions and processes, which construct a kind of ob-scenity ("off-scenity") of work, unrecognisable in its extreme abstraction.

The tendency of management to operate behind closed doors contributes to the diminishing effectiveness of its directions. This is fed by the illusion of a social environment, which combines individualisation, a cult of excellence, and a denial of limitations. The Taylorian model, serving the purpose of control of behaviour by imposing standardised procedures, draws upon a utopian normative which presents a version of reality which conforms to its directives. It is taken over today by the ideology of excellence, which calls for adherence to heroic ideals in order to out-perform oneself and confront challenges, in service to the combined interests of personnel development and the economic health of the company in turbulent markets. Illusion rests at the centre of the formation of these ideologies, which tend to obscure reality and spur mobilisation, the pathway to action. The inflation of imagination is a more powerful force than the disappearance of the social fabric with its symbolic patterns, and the increasing obscuration of reality. Today, the world of work reflects a process of symbolic reduction and of managerial practices increasingly disconnected from reality, and designed to conceal reality, to resist knowledge, know-how, technique, and mastery.

Institutional systems and controls

The clearer awareness of the connection between work and psychological health does not arise from just the sum of singular experiences. The interpretation of these subjective experiences in the work situation draws upon the formation of common meanings that each individual can appropriate for himself in order to give expression to what he experiences and feels. The range of meaning and the lexicon offered to explain and describe the *mal-être* (or distress) in the workplace is a product of social construction, which varies across periods of time and professional environments.

Today, the problem of psychological suffering at work appears to have attached itself electively to three axes, constituting the principal vectors of the demands of management: the question of violence and mistreatment or abuse in the workplace that I just mentioned, the problem of stress, and the issues of career disruption and transitions. Around each of these vectors emerge institutional systems, action plans, and intervention measures introduced by new professionals in the field.

On the first axis, we will explore the example the emerging notion of bullying, or psychological harassment, particularly revealing with regard to the deterioration of analyses and treatment of forms of abuse in the workplace. Evidently, the various forms of violence and abuse at work were not born with the publication of the work by Hirigoyen in 1998. Nevertheless, this work constituted a powerful revelation of the deterioration of situations and relationships in the work environment. Even though this book dealt with the dynamics of bullying in couples and within the family, in addition to harassment in the workplace, it was the analysis of harassment occurring in a place of business that drew the most attention. What should we make of this selective focus and what does it tell us?

Obviously, in reading some of these cases, the individual can find himself looking in a mirror, recognising his situation as it is presented in the descriptions and identifying it as "harassment", which gives meaning and coherence to a series of disparate and diverse or experiences, but always characterised by ambiguity and misunderstanding. The book offers an analytic framework, placing at its centre the dynamic of a destructive interpersonal relationship, and provides an escape from the prison of nonsense. It finally gives a name to what was locked away within the affect and imprisoned in silence. Articulation dissolves the ambiguity of discomfort. Even more so, the proposed explanatory framework identifies both the origin and mechanisms of the abuse: abuse is the product of a perverse individual who snares his prey in his net. This is, indeed, a matter of providing a meaning, a context, allowing the "victim" to localise and process what is happening to him.

Cause and accusation share a common etymology. The notion of causality makes use of the notion of evil to get a grip and a sense of control by accusing other or self ("hetero- or auto-accusation"). If the notion of bullying has received such ready acceptance, it is undoubtedly because it substitutes for self-deprecation and guilt a perspective which is narcissistically more gratifying: it is better to be a "victim" of wrongdoing than to be an accomplice or perpetrator. The targets of the bullying, as well as their social environment, blinded in the face of "perverse" violence, are doubly relieved—of both the weight of silence and of the burden of responsibility. Also, taking on the role of a victim is even more acceptable now that it has gained a real status, confirmed by law, thanks to the proliferation of stories in the media. The scale of media attention to these cases of harassment assuages the guilt that every victim experiences (in response to any type of harm) and offers reassurance, in the form of the social and judicial legitimacy, to the expression of this kind of workplace suffering. Thus, a public forum is made available where each can express what he is feeling internally: referring to harassment through the use of metaphor and euphemism allows one to condense the pain and other distress.

The acceptance of this notion of harassment is essentially congruent with current analyses and the contemporary view of social relationships as interpersonal relationships. It allows us to recognise and understand what is already out there, waiting to be understood, matching the imaginary essence of our mental representation. The link between work and domination transcends history, while the link between work-based and interpersonal relationships is contemporary with the concept of the "erosion of the wage-earner's society" (Castel, 1995).

From the beginning, the promotion of the concept of harassment and its inclusion in the legislative framework have been placed within the landscape of the workplace: prior to the acknowledgement of "psychological harassment", the law has penalised, since 1992, work-place sexual harassment. And the issue shifts and expands through-out the same prism, that of the interpersonal relation between the dominant and the dominated, with the same dual concealment: the obscuration of productive activity and of the social and organisational contexts of this activity. The diffusion of the psychological culture, combined with a process of massive de-institutionalisation, con-tributes to the shaping of a world vision dominated by psychology—yes, even psychopathology.

Psychologism draws upon a contemporary rationality, which compels the subject to explain what happens to him under the auspices of subjective appropriation: to understand the causality of experiences and their facilitators is to explore one's inner self. The generalisation of the "internality norm" (Beauvois, 1994) shapes the development of personal responsibility and the individual as the initiator of his own life, for better or worse. Psychoanalysism prolongs this discourse by directing the investigation, focusing on childhood events, and the wanderings of transference and countertransference, driven by repetition. Psychopathologism constitutes a more danger-ous weapon in that it is always engaged in the process of causal attri-bution. It essentially serves to shut down exploration through placing blame. Thus, the "victim" of harassment is often characterised as hys-terical, paranoid, disturbed, and the harasser is diagnosed as perverse. The French law of 27 January 2002, by employing this concept in the official body of legislation, reproduces the accepted dichotomy of criminality (a culprit . . . a victim), and, at the same time, makes it easier to avoid an analysis of the contexts of work while reinforcing the authority of outside jurisdiction over relationships at work, thereby removing the treatment of symptoms outside of the scope of the organisation.

The psychotraumatology used by management and applied to the treatment of "victims" of harassment is employed against a back-ground of concealment of the links between violence and work. Psy-chological intervention is understood as mental health care to treat the psychic suffering of the victim, or victims, or as a measure to prevent the development of traumatic neurosis. These approaches originate within the practice of psychiatry: it was a military psychiatrist who identified this neurosis during wartime. The intervention called "defusing" aims to disarm or diminish the effects of psychological trauma in order to prevent its further deterioration into full-scale psychotraumatic pathologies. The "debriefing" focuses on intervention during the time period immediately following the event: it consists of encouraging, individually or collectively, the verbalisation of the experience that was endured, an exercise as much cognitive as emotional. These interventions, with varying protocols, aim universally at "tempering emotional volatility and restoring the ability to resume functioning effectively" (Crocq, 2004, p. 159, translated for this edition).

Although there is no denying that professional practice is capable of pinpointing potentially traumatic experiences, the approaches aimed at treating "victims" still desperately seek to understand the exact significance of work and its context. Centred on the individual, these protocols hinder both analysis and intervention in the organisation of work, ensuring that the eruption or occurrence of violence at work will be as inevitable as an earthquake or a tsunami.

> Yet, the escalation of violence on the part of the aggressors, and more generally, workplace violence, both hetero and autoaggressive, as well as typical workplace-type accidents, raises a number of questions concerning the organisational nature of work and social relationships in the workplace. The principal motivation for the prevention of violence at work has, without a doubt, more to do with preserving and facilitating the exchange of resources, the limitations of individual and group activity, occurrences of problematic situations, and the exploring of the scope of possibilities on the subject of treatment. Victimology, based on psychopathology that disregards the work situation, does not support an analysis of work, its conditions and its organisation. Victimology is a therapeutic approach dealing with symptoms rather than aetiology. (Dejours, 2007, p. 94, translated for this edition)

On the second axis, one discovers numerous tools, products of the cognitive–behavioural approach, offered by professional consulting firms specialising in "stress management". The first studies on the psychology of stress were followed by copious amounts of research and controversy: approaches to the field based on context, by personal tendencies, transactional definitions, objectification according to symptoms or "perceived stress", measured in tests. The semantic ambiguities within the concept of stress persist in spite of the distinctions between factors and determinants (specifically, "stressors"), mechanisms of regulation (physiological, psychological, or social), and effects (biological, psychological, pathological, or otherwise). Today, the two dominant models for defining, and also measuring, "stress" are the "job demand–control model", by Karasek and Theorell (1990), and the effort–reward model, by Siegrist (1996). The first is based on the hypothesis that a work situation characterised by a combination of elevated psychological pressure and a low level of decision-making autonomy increases the risk of developing physical or psychological problems. The second model addresses the relation between the extrinsic efforts (forced work) and intrinsic efforts (investment, commitment to the work), and compensation (e.g., salary, recognition, job security). The success of these models and their widespread implementation is due, no doubt, to the fact that they provide a quantitative approach to evaluating stress. Quantification supposes to be an essential resource for objectifying the subjective aspects of work, for eliciting acknowledgement of the difficulties associated with contemporary developments of work, and providing guidance on the matter of prevention (Neboit & Vézina, 2002). The demand for a quantitative method of measuring the tedium of work is increasing, as if the vagueness of the new category of risks referred to as "psychosocial" would be mitigated by quantitative objectification: as if the definition of that which is measured can be provided by the measurement itself. Quantophrenia reached into all social spheres. French politics set the tone with the report by Nasse and Légeron (2008), which recommends constructing a global indicator for observing psychosocial risks. The report in question did not include a single reference to previous studies on the psychopathology of work. Focused exclusively on stress, this report inventories the limits of existing instruments of measurement while emphasising the need to harmonise the diverse European methods of evaluation, which, in turn, draw essentially upon North American sources. The advancement of the notion of measuring stress is as popular with management as with the consultants involved in the lucrative market of "stress management" and cannot be explained only by the seductive promises of quantitative objectification of the subjective experience of work. It adheres to the dominant adaptive perspective in all models of stress, introduced by Selye (1956), who defined it as a "reaction of an organism faced with change, demands, requirements . . . in its environment, for the purpose of adapting itself to them" (p. 62), until Légeron's work

(2008), which ranks adaptation to the environment among the larger functions of the human being (such as respiration, digestion, reproduction). The adaptation to the demands of work is, thus, the focus of enquiry. This runs the gamut from the reinforcement of what is referred to as "perceived control", which consists of believing (or convincing to believe) that we make use of our personal resources, and enabling us to confront and master situations, to a focus on the use of adjustment strategies called "coping", such as managing emotions in the work situation (Lhuilier, 2006b).

Nevertheless, stress is primarily a category of common sense, and its extensive usage demonstrates that it has become a privileged point of entry from which to identify the modalities that shape both the problem and its methods of treatment. The significance of this reference to stress in the world of work reveals, without doubt, the growing disparity between the swelling demands of work and the dwindling means for responding to them: the challenges of work are not the stressors, but, rather, the impossibility of overcoming them. The accompanying distress results from a hindered progression, or an amputation, of the power to act (Clot, 1999). However, the majority of recommended measures for preventing stress favour a transactional approach (Lazarus & Folkman, 1984), which relates essentially to the evaluation of a situation faced by the subject and adaptive strategies based on the personal resources of the individual. In this perspective, the relevance of the organisation of work is underestimated in favour of strategies focused on the determinants of the individual's adaptation. Cognitive–behavioural techniques are implemented to work with the mental representations around the demands of work, in an effort to mitigate emotional reverberations, thereby helping the individual with better management of their levels of stress.

A comparative study on institutional strategies for "stress management" (Buscatto, Loriol, & Weller, 2008) revealed their common traits, such as their variations according to traditions and organisational "cultures". These mechanisms operate at the level of the selection of personnel (interviews and tests aimed at evaluating the degree of emotional control), at the level of initial or ongoing training (relaxation techniques, stress reduction methods), as well as at the level of psychological support (support groups, etc.).

Finally, the third vector of expression of the problem of psychological health and work must be addressed, even if its manifestations belong essentially to the field of public health or social work. Indeed, behind this growing sensitivity to the debilitating effects of work on psychological health, and the proliferation of scientific work pertaining to the suffering, stress, and burnout, another, less obvious, trend must be addressed. This concerns the beneficial effects on health of returning to work or safeguarding employment experienced by the most "vulnerable", those who have been displaced or are at risk of losing their jobs.

Here, we cannot ignore people living with a chronic condition or a disability (Blanc, 1995; Celerier, 2007; Lhuilier, Amado, Brugeilles, & Rolland, 2007), those released from psychiatric hospitals, those recently ensnared in a chronically marginalised state (Brétécher & Hersant, 2005), or all those old and new poor, sequestered in the margins of the working world and subjected to all strategies aimed at reintegration. Here, the question no longer concerns the potentially pathogenic effects of work: on the contrary, the promotion of work is understood as access to financial resources, liberation from dependence on assistance, restoration of self-esteem, and connection to others. The return to work represents a "return to normal", a promise of better health and a better quality of life.

Employment is not to be confused with its substance, activity. Similarly, health cannot be reduced to, or defined as, "normality". And we must take care to avoid two recurring pitfalls here: the over-valuation of returning to, or maintaining, employment, at the risk of underestimating the compatibility of tasks (the requirements of the task, work conditions) with the individual and collective resources of the subjects. We must be careful, in other words, not to reduce the relationship between work and mental health to simply an issue of loss of quality and degradation. It is necessary for us to recognise the psychological consequences of hindered professional activity, and to watch the conditions that allow for, or lead to, unemployment or idleness in activity.

Today, psychologists are more and more sought after across every field of intervention. Their practices are heterogeneous, as much as are their frames of reference. They include a diversity of all sub-disciplines: the psychology of individual differences, clinical psychology, social psychology, psychology of health, psychology of work. All fields are necessarily confronted with a series of questions that they cannot avoid without the risk of compromising deontological issues.

These mainly concern the growing excesses from popular psychology leading to "empowering" of employees to "self-manage" their professional lives, the obscuring of issues that have to do with the organisation of work in favour of a focus on "personal issues" of employees, reinforcing their vulnerability or "coping strategies", the ambiguity of work coaching of which it is unclear if it serves the individual or the organisation, the development of "psychological infusions" (such as discussion groups, individual coaching, listening lines for suffering at work, and, recently, the new service called "psych vouchers") proposing to improve the individual's ability to manage workplace situations considered at risk of deterioration, and the resurgence of "hygienism" that promises less suffering at work through the use of "best practices", and recipes for a better "quality of life" (play sports, watch your diet, your sleep, stress "control" . . .).

The clinical psychology of work opens up alternative paths (Clot & Lhuilier, 2006; Lhuilier, 2006a). Faced with the changes in the workplace and the forms in which psychological interventions present themselves, the clinical psychology of work provides a framework for theoretical and methodological reflections that support their practices and ethical issues.

The aim here is not to achieve the "best fit" to the requirements and limitations of the work, but, rather, to empower professionals to act both on the work environment and on their own behalf: to help them break out of impasses, and invent new ways of thinking and doing. This implies a collaborative effort towards a reconception of the subjective experience of work. The guiding vision here is not so much about taking care of the "victim" as it is about "taking care" of work: restoring the community of work wherein the work itself, as well as methods of implementation, are reorganised. Restoring the work community allows individuals to realise that the difficulties they encounter are not unique to them, but, rather, that these difficulties require a larger response on the part of the profession, in terms of finding new ways to transform together.

Conclusions

The investigation of the relationships between health and work requires, in the end, a clarification of concepts of health. Health is not the absence of disease, and neither is it a "state of complete physical, mental and social well-being" (definition by the World Health Organisation). Health is less a living state of being closed off from external forces than an evolving process: health is the expression of "polarised activity of a dialogue with the environment, which is perceived as either normal or not, according to what one perceives as normative or 'non-normative'" (Canguilhem, 1966). Health is not "normal" in the sense of conforming to social norms. In order to emphasise this point, we may even refer to these normopathies as forms of compliant submission ("false self", Winnicott) to the environment. Health refers more to the normativity of the subject: a subject who negotiates with his environment and with himself to establish equilibrium and a zone of personal security, An individual who can calculate his room to manoeuvre and is aware of his capabilities within his environment can employ them to redesign his environment for the better, in order to understand the problems it presents and the answers it can provide, because health has less to do with the ability to adapt to his environment than with the power to create the environment he desires.

From this perspective, "pathological" problems are seen as an inability to negotiate with himself and the environment, impeding his development. These pathological problems are indicated by mechanisms of regression, fixation, repetition, and inhibition of thought and/or affect, which make the subject a prisoner of his past, accepting his environment as a given, something non-transformable, even threatening. Here, we glimpse the close connection between health and creativity, on the condition that we do not define "creativity" so narrowly that it cannot be either realised or recognised. Far from the concept or a vision of adaptation, health refers to the ability to respond creatively to obstacles and limitations. We can recall Winnicott (1986) here, when he defines what is understood by inventiveness or creativity and its connection to health:

> Whatever definition we arrive at, it must include the idea that life is worth living or not, according to whether creativity is or not a part of an individual's experience. To be creative a person must exist and have a feeling of existing, not in conscious awareness, but as a basic place to operate from. Creativity is then the doing that arises out of being. Creativity, then, is the retention throughout life of something that belongs properly to infant experience: the ability to create the world. (pp. 39–40)

48 HUMANNESS IN ORGANISATIONS

References

Aubert, N., & Pagés, M. (1989). *Le stress professionnel*. Paris: Klincksieck.
Beauvois, J.-L. (1994). *Traité de la servitude libérale*. Paris: Dunod.
Blanc, A. (1995). *Les handicapés au travail*. Paris: Dunod.
Brétécher, P., & Hersant, C. (2005). Sortir du désœuvrement. In: M. Joubert & C. Louzoun (Eds.), *Répondre à la souffrance sociale* (pp. 35–45). Toulouse: Erès.
Buscatto, M., Loriol, M., & Weller, J. M. (2008). *Au de-là du stress au travail*. Toulouse: Erés.
Canguilhem, G. (1966). *Le normal et le pathologique*. Paris: PUF.
Castel, R. (1995). *Les métamorphoses de la question sociale. Une chronique du salariat*. Paris: Fayard.
Célérier, S. (2007). L'activité professionnelle des malades: risques non compris. *Colloque Santé-Travail-Sciences Humaines*, Université de Rouen.
Chiapello, E., & Boltanski, L. (1999). *Le nouvel esprit du capitalisme*. Paris: Gallimard.
Clot, Y. (1999). *La fonction psychologique du travail*. Paris: PUF.
Clot, Y., & Lhuilier, D. (2006). Perspectives en clinique du travail. *Nouvelle Revue de Psychosociologie, 1*.
Crocq, L. (2004). L'intervention psychologique auprès des victimes. In: C. Castro (Ed.), *Les interventions psychologiques dans les organisation* (pp. 141–175). Paris: Dunod.
Dassa, S., & Maillard, D. (1999). Exigences de qualité et nouvelles formes d'aliénation. *Actes de la recherche en sciences sociales, 115*: 27–37.
Debout, M. (1999). *Travail, violences et environnement*. Rapport du Conseil Economique et Social, Paris: Les Editions des Journaux Officiels.
Debout, M. (2001). *Le harcèlement moral au travail*. Rapport du Conseil Economique et Social, Paris: Les Editions des Journaux Officiels.
De Gaulejac, V. (2005). *La société malade de la gestion*. Paris: Seuil.
Dejours, C. (2007). *Conjurer la violence*. Paris: Payot.
Dujarier, M.-A. (2006). *L'idéal au travail*. Paris: PUF.
Hirigoyen, M.-F. (1998). *Le harcèlement moral. Violence perverse au quotidien*. Paris: Syros.
Hugues, E. C. (1996). *Le regard sociologique*. Paris: Ed. de l'EHESS.
Karasek, R., & Theorell, T. (1990). *Healthy Work, Stress Productivity and the Reconstruction of Working Life*. New York: Basic Books.
Lazarus, R., & Folkman, S. (1984). *Stress, Appraisal and Coping*. New York: Springer.

Légeron, P. (2008). *La prévention du stress dans l'entreprise. Rencontre nucléaire et santé.* Paris.

Lhuilier, D. (2002). *Placardisés: des exclus dans l'entreprise.* Paris: Le Seuil.

Lhuilier, D. (2005). Le "sale boulot". *Travailler, 14*: 73–98.

Lhuilier, D. (2006a). *Cliniques du travail.* Toulouse: Erès.

Lhuilier, D. (2006b). Compétences émotionnelles: de la proscription à la prescription des émotions au travail. *Psychologie du travail et des organisations, 12*: 91–103.

Lhuilier, D., Amado, S., Brugeilles, F., & Rolland, D. (2007). Vivre et travailler avec une maladie chronique. *Nouvelle Revue de Psycho-sociologie, 4*: 123–143.

Meyerson, I. (1987). *Ecrits 1920–1983.* Paris:PUF.

Nasse, P., & Légeron, P. (2008). *La détermination, la mesure et le suivi des risques psychosociaux.* Rapport remis au ministère du travail. Paris, mars.

Neboit, M., & Vézina, M. (2002). *Stress au travail et santé psychique.* Toulouse: Octarès.

Selye, H. (1956). *The Stress of Life.* New York: McGraw-Hill.

Siegrist, J. 1996). Adverse health effects of high effort/low reward conditions. *Journal of Occupational Health Psychology, 1*: 27–41.

Tosquelles, F. (2009). *Le travail thérapeutique à l'hôpital, 1967–1972.* Paris: Ed. du Scarabée.

Wallon, H. (1976). *Lecture d'Henri Wallon. Choix de textes, 1932–1976.* Paris: Editions Sociales.

Winnicott, D. W. (1986). Living creatively. In: C. Winnicott, R. Shepherd, & M. Davis (Eds.), *Home Is Where We Start From* (pp. 39–54). London: Penguin.

CHAPTER THREE

Approaching twenty-first century, information-based organisations

James Krantz

Introduction

Circumambulation is the act of moving around an object, often a sacred object, and looking at it from different vantage points. This chapter is a kind of circumambulation. It attempts to look at the intersection between systems psychodynamic thinking and emerging twenty-first century organisations from a series of perspectives. It arises from a set of interlinked issues that I have been thinking about in connection with the profound social, organisational, and economic transitions that accompany the shift into the Information Age. At one level, it involves the question of what the systems psychodynamic tradition has to contribute to our understanding of the information society and, in particular, whether its concepts and tools will be relevant to the organisational forms that are emerging, or whether it will become obsolete, alongside so many other time-bound organisational concepts and frameworks. On another level, it is concerned with the meaning and nature of social defences in the newly emerging organisational forms. Many of the containing structures and practices that reinforced integrated thought and functioning are disappearing, leaving people with less support for depressive position functioning and more vulnerable to regression to paranoid–schizoid states of mind[1] in relation to their work and their institutions.

Systems psychodynamic theory has represented a creative and powerful approach to understanding organisations since its origins in the 1950s. The history of this tradition (some say the religion it consecrates) is an amalgam of systems and psychodynamic theories. It has evolved as organisations have evolved. Originally developed in relation to industrial organisations, the approach was applied to the service orientated and knowledge-based organisations that emerged with what came to be described as post-industrial economic conditions.

Now we are in the midst of another transition, of equal if not greater magnitude, that is defined by the shift to an information-based society. In my view, we are just beginning to experience and understand the profound changes that are arising from the digital revolution. One of my preoccupations centres on the question of how systems psychodynamic thinking needs to adapt to these new circumstances, similar to how it has done so previously. Exploring this leads to the question of what are the essential concepts necessary for the theory to retain its identity as systems psychodynamics. What is absolutely core, without which it is no longer systems psychodynamic theory? My belief is that adapting to the information age entails maintaining a central focus on *the relationship between people and their technologies within the context of shared tasks.*

Origins and historical context

It might seem paradoxical to start a chapter about the future by looking backwards. My reason for turning to the origins of the tradition is to consider what I regard as an absolutely central element in the tradition of thought—an element that exists at the metaphorical level of its DNA. I am not suggesting that the relationship of task and sentience is the only fundamental building block, but I am proposing that it is an indispensable element in efforts to bring systems psychodynamics into meaningful relationship with emerging organisations.

The origins of the theory are often traced to the seminal study (Trist & Bamforth, 1951) of a newly introduced technology for coal mining, called the longwall method because new machinery allowed for a longer expanse of the coalface to be removed at once. The results, however, were disappointing. Increased absenteeism and industrial accidents, disappointing production, and other indicators of dysfunction were the surprising result of what had been touted as an exciting new innovation.

Trist and Bamforth realised that the introduction of the new three-shift longwall cycle had resulted in a breakdown of the traditional social system that had developed underground in the mines. The social system that functioned underground, with the prior shortwall technology, had provided many qualities that contributed to both worker safety and productivity, including flexibility, managed interdependence, and sophisticated collaboration. The new technology, while more capable on one level, rendered the prior social system unworkable. They devised a solution that jointly addressed the needs of both technical and social subsystems, the "modified longwall method".

This germinated the development of socio-technical systems theory, which put forward the idea that understanding either the formal (technological in a broad sense, not just machinery) or the informal (comprising people) sub-systems was insufficient—they had to be understood jointly, in relation to one another. Before this integration, there were generally two competing perspectives on organisational analysis. One emphasised getting the formal organisation right—structures, technologies, job design, etc. Proponents of the structuralist viewpoint argued that what mattered, from the broadest level to the minute details of job design, was structure. The alternative perspective saw the key to success as the texture of human relations in the work environment. What really mattered, in the human relations tradition, is the quality of relationships.

The Tavistock researchers realised that while both perspectives were essential, neither was adequate. Linking the two enabled them to move beyond a polarised view that had formed around the two perspectives. The socio-technical approach recognised that performance requires both a technological organisation (machinery, work plans, structures, etc.) and a social system for those who use the technological organisation to carry out the institution's tasks. While the technological organisation is an important constraint on the performance, the social system has social and psychological properties that serve as an equally important constraint. These two systems exert their influence independently and are best considered in tandem when organising institutional work (Emery & Trist, 1960).

Extending the "dual focus" approach to a broader range of organisations, Miller and Rice (1967) reframed the social and technical sub-systems as task and sentient systems. Through this refinement, they were able to address the service intensive, knowledge-based, client/customer-centred organisations that were characteristic of the increasingly turbulent environments. Whereas for Trist and his colleagues socio-technical intervention was a matter of organisational design, for Miller and Rice it became an ongoing management process. Task and sentient systems rarely coincided in the emerging organisations.

Socio-technical theory was addressed to situations, such as coal mines or manufacturing plants, in which the two sub-systems were co-located. But for airlines, service enterprises, and other organisations that depended upon greater flexibility or geographic dispersion, the conceptualisation needed to evolve accordingly. Since then, the interaction between task and sentient systems has been extensively examined in a wide variety of turbulent, post-industrial settings. Nevertheless, what remained at the core was a theoretical construct that focused on the relationship between the human and technological dimensions as it occurred in the context of shared task.

The Tavistock researchers also recognised that each sub-system unfolds according to a fundamentally different logic. Technology refers to the tools, processes, and systems humans discover and develop to get things done, whether it is fire, the wheel, computers, or nanotechnology. The word comes from the Greek word τεχνολογια (*technología*); from τεχνη (*téchnē*), meaning "art, skill, craft", and from -λογια (*-logía*), meaning "study of". Technical sub-systems comprise the entire range of non-human elements in an institution, including organisational structure, methods, practices, techniques of work, policies, etc. It conforms to impersonal and rational factors.

Social systems, on the other hand, are seen through the lens of human functioning and are based on an understanding of human functioning that reflects Klein's psychoanalytic theory (1959) and Bion's (1961) group theories. They are characteristic of how the paranoid–schizoid and depressive positions come to be expressed as group processes. The theory illustrates how elements of the emotional situation are so closely allied to "phantasies" of the earliest anxieties that the group is compelled, when the pressure of anxiety becomes too great, to take defensive action. The psychotic anxieties that can be stimulated involve splitting and projective identification.

The DNA of systems psychodynamics

Also central to the history of Tavistock-related research is the effort to understand and confront novel conditions as they emerge in the social, technological and economic spheres. Trist and Bamforth's (1951) early work, for example, invented ways to take advantage of new technologies while, at the same time, addressing the needs of workers. Others devised social technologies and methods of helping organisations create more effective fit—"joint sub-optimisation", in technical terms—between the two sub-systems. Developing ways of creating and maintaining robust social systems was a major advance.

One of my questions is, what will be the twenty-first century corollary to the "modified longwall method"? Many organisations now appear to be shaped entirely around the dictates of new information technologies, with the resulting emergence of paranoid–schizoid environments.

The governance and regulation of these organisations, socially and psychologically, often display forms of connection in which there is a paucity of stable relationships. Similar to the traditional social organisation of the coal mines (the longwall form of organisation), emerging social systems that are designed and configured to animate new technologies that foster global integration often create debilitating paranoid–schizoid environments which are increasingly dysfunctional. As such, I view these current corporate arrangements as transitional: forms that will ultimately be superseded by something that provides more beneficial social and psychological conditions, both with regard to task performance and psychological well-being.

Requisite sentience and social defences

The fundamental premise is that relationships, when harnessed to task, create organisational capacity. With this comes the idea that there is a degree or quality of sentient relationships that optimally supports task performance. A balance is to be achieved. This, in turn, suggests a concept that is analogous to Ashby's (1958) idea of "requisite variety", which states that in order adapt successfully, systems must contain within themselves variety that is requisite to the complexity in the surrounding environment. Looking over the arc of theorising and practice in the systems psychodynamic tradition, it appears there is an underlying parallel idea, an idea that might be described as "requisite sentience". It speaks to the importance, in systems psychodynamic thinking, of creating social systems that are simultaneously matched to new technologies while providing conditions in which people could work in a more integrated, depressive position state (Klein, 1940). Organisations lacking requisite sentience can be expected to exhibit dysfunction. As in the Trist and Bamforth example, the first adaptation to the longwall method failed because it did not allow for an adequate social system to form. The modified longwall method, however, benefited from the newer extraction technologies while simultaneously enabling the miners to establish an effective constellation of social and collaborative relations.

I believe that the transition to information age systems is often characterised by misalignment between the task and sentient systems, creating, in consequence, a form of dysfunction parallel to that originally discovered by Trist and his colleagues. It is distinctive in scope and scale, reflecting the character of many of large, global, industrial enterprises—environments created in a particular type of organisation that has emerged in the past ten years. As with the imposition of longwall mining, it appears that many organisations are fashioned solely according to the dictates of the technological system with little regard to the social systems and, in particular, to the importance of sentient relationships for supporting realistic connections.

Social defences and information technology

Menzies Lyth's nursing study (1960) built upon and extended Jaques's (1953) work on how social systems function as a defence against persecutory and depressive anxiety. While, for Jaques, the system was essentially a fantasy, an invention, for Menzies Lyth, it is more than a reflection of unconscious dynamics. It has real, enduring, and impersonal qualities. These elements of organisational life—structures, practices, policies, technologies, methods of working, patterns of decision making, the distribution of authority, and so on—are the "stuff" of social defences. While these aspects of organisational life exist to facilitate work, they also come to be utilised for the additional purpose of helping people manage anxiety. These features of organisation she named "social defences". Thus, the relationship between social and technical systems reappears.

What makes social defences so effective is that either they eliminate situations that expose people to anxiety-provoking activity altogether, or they insulate people from the consequences of their actions. The nursing service Menzies Lyth described was an ideal setting to illustrate the concept. Its approach to scheduling, decision making, and work assignment created a depersonalised and fragmented pattern of care. Coupled with infantilising management practices, the system promoted dependency, ritualistic work, impersonal relationships with patients, and other characteristics that had the effect of shielding nurses from the painful anxieties stimulated by close and intimate contact with patients and their families.

The ineffectiveness of the nursing service led to insights about the secondary effects of social defence systems. Heightened turnover, disaffection of the most talented nursing students, and other aspects of low morale revealed the corrosive effect of rigid social defences on task accomplishment and, as a consequence, a negative impact on the developmental potential contained in effective work arrangements. Ineffective, unsatisfying, and dispiriting work practices were maintained because these same organisational "building blocks" had come to be unconsciously used for the added purpose of managing primitive emotion rather than for facilitating competent work.

The ongoing vitality of systems psychodynamic thinking is closely related to whether we can understand how social defences operate in the novel conditions with which we are increasingly faced—network-based organisations and the reliance on networks and organisational ecosystems rather than hierarchical entities.

The dimension of globalisation complicates questions of developing appropriate social defence systems to contain the anxieties inherent in new organisations. The rapid advances in information technologies have made possible the vast dispersion of activities across the globe, which, in turn, has modification in the conditions within which people work. Among the effects of this change is that traditional forms of social relations and community life are increasingly nullified by the supra-national entities. The new ability to quickly relocate people and investments creates rapid change, flux, and uncertainty, where employees lose a traditional sense of place. The anxiety created by the volatile evolving markets and newly flexible labour processes leads to the additional uncertainty created by the need for geographical mobility.

Psychic life is fragmented by the loss of a sense of place and community as people face the dissolution of traditional support systems. The weakening of the sense of belonging to a collectivity has left the individual with little to mediate between innate desires and the larger organisational and social context. At its root, globalisation is about "delocalisation"—the uprooting of activities and relationships from local origins and cultures. It entails displacing activities that were previously local into networks of connectivity whose reach is distant or worldwide. In the words of Giddens, "Globalization can be defined as intensification of worldwide social relations which link distant realities in such a way that local happenings are shaped by events occurring many miles away and vice versa" (1991, p. 178).

In consequence, for example, domestic prices and managerial decisions are less governed by local and national conditions. Multinational corporations disaggregate the chain of production and relocate links in different areas around the world, depending on economic criteria (e.g., massive, shifting outsourcing, to take advantage of less expensive labour markets). Products are less and less identified with nations. Globalisation lifts social activities out of local knowledge and places them in networks in which they are conditioned by worldwide events.

These aspects of globalisation are captured succinctly and presciently by Schumpter (1942, p. 368), "Capitalism, while economically stable, and even gaining in stability, creates, by rationalizing the human mind, a mentality and a style of life incompatible with its own fundamental conditions, motives and social institutions". Following systems psychodynamic theory, social defence systems will be established to contain and manage the considerable anxieties stimulated as a result. Will these social defence systems support integrated, depressive-position functioning, or will they enshrine and reinforce the tendency toward paranoid–schizoid functioning? About this, I believe systems psychodynamics has a lot to say.

Futures we are in

Emery's *Futures We Are In* (1974) discusses how "leading elements" of the future that already exist in the present make it possible to discern the outlines of emerging systems. Early detection of emergent processes that lie concealed in existing systems, with which they share parts, creates opportunities to adapt and even shape the future. These emergent processes also stimulate primitive anxieties associated with invasion and, as a result, can debilitate existing systems.

With post-industrialism in the latter part of the twentieth century, the world moved toward a constant change gradient resulting in a state of continuous transition. The state I believe we are now entering is one in which the gradient of change, largely due to information technology, is shifting from linear to exponential. The changes we are now facing and will continue to face much more ferociously are of such magnitude that survival will depend on the ability of people to work through the psychological effects of this fragmentation and destabilisation on many levels of personality.

Clearly, a co-evolution of humanity and technology is under way. One common narrative is that we are facing increasing complexity and uncertainty in the world, information overload, distraction, shallowness of critical thought, and a lack of foresight. For those focused on the "silver lining", we have a massive, untapped supply of creativity and imagination, sufficient to change the world and our crumbling systems if we can figure out how to unlock and unleash it from our billions of—now interconnected—minds. (As with the mine operators, many assume that "solutions" are to be found in technology alone, depending on better algorithms and mining "big data".)

A recent presentation about a large architectural firm, which has twenty-six offices across the globe, further illustrated some of these dilemmas. The firm was "run" by a management committee consisting of a CEO, CMO, CIO, Administrative Director, and head of HR. Two of them lived and worked in the same city, others were widely dispersed. There were also fifty "market leaders", experts in specialised areas who provided leadership in client-facing, vertical market areas, five firm-wide "initiative leads" (such as in the area of sustainability), and numerous "marketing section leaders" in different offices.

The idea of applying traditional concepts of hierarchical leadership and authority was clearly inadequate. Although certain elements of bureaucratic hierarchy were present, in terms of understanding the governance, management, or the social and psychological dynamics of this complex system, other concepts were needed. What we were dealing with was more of an ecosystem than an enterprise. Familiar institutions and practices are in disarray. Contemporary organisations are often unstable, chaotic, turbulent, and sometimes unmanageable.

Twenty-five years of social, economic, industrial, and technological upheaval have left us, in many respects, with a fragmented, shocked society with people searching for connection, hope, and lost meaning, often turning to evangelism and fundamentalism to provide lost security or familiarity. Symbol systems involving family, social, and political authority, sexuality, birth, death, and the ordering of the life cycle are in disarray. Repeated betrayal by organisations, failed dependency, massive social trauma, and fragmentation of the self have stimulated a deep yearning for renewal in the midst of a catastrophic loss of reliable, containing structures.

Turquet's (1974) description of the loss of a sense of identity in large groups provides a vivid illustration of this basic situation, against which the idealisation of leaders, group regression, activation of primitive object relations, primitive defensive operations, and primitive aggression all emerge readily. Dynamics that take place in a large group, enmity occupies a pivotal role. A perennial and important manoeuvre is to designate an enemy, as is splitting into subgroups and splinter systems.

Specifically, the hypothesis is that the factors noted above have a common theme: the rise of technologically driven organisations and the disinvestment in sentience or social systems. Technologically driven arrangements, not modulated by ongoing sentient relatedness, have come to dominate the interpersonal landscape, which, in turn, provides a fertile ground for persecutory fantasies, and psychologically regressed relations. What is difficult to achieve or understand is the nature of a *sentient* culture of cohesiveness, gratification, and reality testing that fosters integrated functioning. Reflective, more balanced, integrated and "nuanced" processes associated with *depressive position* states of mind are considerably diminished to the detriment of robust, organisational functioning. One of the major challenges of systems psychodynamic thinking is to bring that same focus, one that relates the human system and the technological system in relation to a common task, to bear on twenty-first century organisations.

Networks and groups: the dissolution of familiar boundaries

Among the mainstay concepts that have been key building blocks that are becoming outmoded is the role of stable, bounded small groups as the primary mediating structure between the individual and the larger context. Of course, networks are not new. We are all part of networks: our families, schools, and social circles, for example. One vital difference now, as pointed out by Shirky (2008) is that the socio-emotional presence of networks is pervasive:

> we are living in the Golden Age of network theory, where sociology, math, computer science and software engineering are all combining to allow the average user to visualize, understand, and most importantly, rely on the social and business networks that are part of their lives. (p. 28)

A remarkable assortment of new tools and technologies—from free conference calls and emails to blogs, wikis, tags, texts, and tweets—are changing the way we communicate and connect.

Many argue that the new technologies and the move from groups to networks is inherently regressive from a psychodynamic standpoint. It is possible to hear a chorus of worried voices concerned about how new technologies will diminish the Self. Does it provide, for example, an easy avenue for avoiding meaningful relationship and the reparative aspect of authentic experience? The illusion of proximity in time and space might distort how we relate to the world. How do the technologies affect our ability to tolerate the frustrations of reality? For example, whether being able to "know" things instantaneously, instead of having to tolerate the discomfort of not knowing, impairs thinking. Others have argued that it constitute a breakdown of the authority of reality, resulting in less repression, diminished ability to cope with reality, and reduced sublimation.

Yet, this line of thinking does little to shed light on the role that information technology will play in shaping social defences in work organisations. It would be tantamount to saying that the solution to the mining problems would have been to preserve the shortwall method and abandon technological advances. And, of course, all new technologies are bemoaned by those least comfortable with the new. That new technologies enable organisations to mobilise the most valuable intangible resources—minds and relationships—has been clearly demonstrated. At the same time, the overwhelming complexity and fragmentation that have accompanied these changes inevitably entail anxieties. Social defence analysis raises the question of how the same technologies that potentiate such enormous productive capabilities also are used to help people defend against the anxieties embedded in the tasks and animating the enterprises.

From the systems psychodynamic standpoint, our conceptual tools, so well honed for twentieth century organisations, need to be renewed and sharpened for the twenty-first. There are hints of where support for the depressive position in network arrangements can be found in some contemporary thinking. The most important shift goes beyond the technologies themselves. The real transformation is in the way that people are using the tools to change how they think, form groups, and do their work. There are containing features of networks, especially when they are made explicit. Social network maps shift people's mental models so that they can appreciate the density of their links to others; seeing social networks helps people understand their connections to others in new ways and to take action based on that knowledge. The maps identify leverage points for helping networks produce better outcomes, building a sense of connection and shared purpose across networks, and assessing changes in collaborative conditions over time.

The new tools facilitate rapid sharing and co-creation of new knowledge. In *The Wisdom of Crowds* (2005), Surowiecki described the capacities that are unleashed by technologically sophisticated networks. This has all of the characteristics of Bion's sophisticated work group and has all the hallmarks of social defence systems that supported depressive position functioning. For example, he chronicled the global collaboration that found the cause of SARS. When the epidemic broke out in 2003, the World Health Organisation set up a network of eleven research laboratories around the world in a massive collaborative effort to find and analyse the cause of the disease. The labs each pursued what they believed to be promising lines of investigation, but were able to co-ordinate what they were learning and share data and information in real time, conferencing daily over the phone and on the web. One week after the project began, the team of labs had isolated a candidate virus. Within a month, the labs proved that the virus was the cause of SARS, sequenced the virus, and developed several diagnostic tests. Four months after the first outbreak outside of China, the epidemic was successfully contained, due in large part to this unprecedented international collaboration and co-operation.

Theoretically, there is a close, though unexplicated, relationship between Bion's Work Group and the Kleinian idea of depressive position functioning. The capacity to work well, creatively, and effectively is one of the most important gratifications of adult life and source of personal development. Under certain circumstances, networks contain new potential for bringing about such affirming and developmental environments. Among the qualities these networks have to create and foster productive enterprise are:

- overcoming barriers to collaboration to find others who share specific passions and to take on larger projects that would have previously been unthinkable;
- accessing knowledge, leadership, and expertise in places that were once beyond their reach;
- sharing information quickly and with little effort, making more resources available and enabling people to easily build on the work of others;
- coming together and disassembling as needed to achieve goals.

Relationship and relatedness

I want to include this systems psychodynamic distinction in my circumambulation because it brings us closer, I believe, to understanding an important feature of the shift I am trying to explore. The conceptual distinction between relationship and relatedness opened a field of vision through which we can understand different forms of connection between the individual and the organisation. Relationship is the direct interpersonal contact between people and rests in psychodynamic terms, ultimately, on the cycle of projection and introjection.

Relatedness, on the other hand, refers to the internalised mental representation of an institution, its roles, structures, and meaning in the larger world. Relatedness is a matter, in psychodynamic terms, of internalisation. It is an image of the organisation and/or institution that binds people outside of their work roles. Existing only in the mind, relatedness refers to the quality of largely unconscious connection between individuals or groups: they share a common organisation even if no relationship is to be discovered. Relatedness is a way of seeing and making sense of context. Awareness of relatedness might enhance the value of personal relationships and increase their range because it cultivates respect based on shared experience of working together. But it is also more than simply perceptual, because it also shapes the mutual engagement that derives from the experience of membership.

A useful illustration of the distinction can be found in Shapiro and Carr (1991, pp. 83–84):

> The president and the floor sweeper can scarcely be described as "in a relationship". But they each have ideas about the enterprise in which they participate and so each is "related to" it and through that to each other. As persons, they are not particularly important to each other; but the roles that each occupies significantly affect each other's behavior, albeit unwittingly. Thus even when no discernible relationship exists, significant shared relatedness exists. And since the company, like the family, does not exists in isolation, we may further discern relatedness between people and many other enterprises with which they have no direct connection.

Increasingly, people are contained in shared organisations or networks where they have no relationships with one another, or perhaps only glancing ones. Diminished relationship and sentience raises the question of what binds people and gives them shared meaning. My hypothesis is that a form of relatedness is, as a result, becoming more important, something I think of as a kind of citizenship in an institution, and that this form of relatedness is becoming increasingly important in response to the fragmented, dispersed, attenuated, globalised situations in which people increasingly find themselves.

The citizen role, in contrast to the work role, emphasises the centrality of the institution rather than the organisation. Organisations consist of the building blocks of productive enterprise: objectives, strategies, tasks, work roles, boundaries, practices, accountability, and success or failure within an enterprise. The idea of the "organisation-in-the-mind" is addressed to the emotional experience of these aspects of the enterprise and the meaning they carry for participants (Hutton, 1997). The institution, in contrast, is about the meaning and purposes of an enterprise. It refers to the values, ideals, hopes, beliefs, and symbols that underlie the purposes for which these entities are created. "Institution-in-the-mind" refers to the emotional experience of these aspects of the enterprise (Armstrong, 1997).

Organisational citizenship, as a form of relatedness, connects people with the fundamental emotional dynamics that shape the meaning and experience of specific institutions. Hutton (1997) offers a concise illustration of the difference through the example of the nuclear family. "Nuclear" describes the organisation-in-the-mind, and "family" the institution-in-the-mind. Work role involves an experience of these relationships as well, but, as discussed below, organisational citizenship is organised primarily around the meaning of the "institution" while work role is grounded in the experience of others in an "organisation".

The idea that people are related to the enterprise outside of their specific work roles was first discussed by Miller (1993) in connection with an intervention in a manufacturing company. A series of large group discussions he had organised led him to recognise a different way of relating to, and influencing, the wider system. He came to think that in order to fully exercise their authority, people had to bear some responsibility for the outer boundaries of the enterprise as well as those pertaining to their specific roles, labelling this aspect of relatedness as "organisational citizenship". His notion, however, was centred on relatedness to the organisation rather than to the institution.

The hypothesis that the "organisational citizen" role is becoming increasingly predominant while organisational role is receding in centrality is clearly related to the earlier discussion of how boundaries and structures that have traditionally given organisational roles meaning are dissolving or fragmenting. As a result, they carry less meaning for people as a source of identity, as a container for anxiety, and as a point of reference for understanding the wider system.

Organisational citizenship provides an opportunity for people to participate in, and influence, ownership of the enterprise at that level. Organisational politics are becoming increasingly central as they have become increasingly unstable. In homogenous settings, the political philosophy of an organisation can be taken for granted, a mirror of the established political arrangements in its wider context. With globalisation, organisational politics becomes both unstable and increasingly critical. Political controversies evoked in multi-cultural environments pose major challenges to creating the unified action required in productive enterprises. Already existing anxieties, related to tasks and hierarchies, can be greatly exacerbated by the mistrust and projective identification that can readily characterise multi-cultural environments.

Organisations must accommodate these differences in ways of seeing, doing, and thinking. Relatedness is not a set of formal rules governing relationships between individuals and the enterprise, but a set of social relationships, sentient ties where relations are negotiated and fluid. I am suggesting that the role of "organisational citizen", which is premised on the idea of relatedness, is an important container of political arrangements, one that provides people with the opportunity to have an impact on the character of the enterprise and through which people participate in the negotiated resolution of different viewpoints. Organisational citizenship speaks to the political dimension of the "institution-in-the-mind" and its power relations.

Human resources (HR) as a defence against the loss of sentient relationships

These ideas lead to a consideration of the role of HR in such organisations, and how it is mobilised to mediate the social sphere in the absence of sufficiently rich relationships and the containing function they serve. What often emanates from HR is a prescriptive, normative notion about correct behaviour, the management of feelings, and the creation of "proper" attitudes. The premise that appears frequently to underlie contemporary human resource organisations is that culture can be treated like software, something analogous to what has been referred to in the social media circles as "culture hacking".

I see this as representing a form of social defence against the anxieties associated with the anomic experience of excessive detachment, together with the diffusion and attenuation of more authentic relationships. *Prescriptive relatedness* functions to mediate when a rich web of relationships are both missing and missed. I would hypothesise that HR has increasingly become an instrument that unconsciously fosters a humanising veneer. One trend that supports such outcomes is the extensive, almost ubiquitous, use of 360° feedback mechanisms, which result in another way of reinforcing (and enforcing) a culture of *prescriptive relatedness*, based as it is on consensus, adjusting oneself to the views of others, and "getting alongness" as dominant behavioural values. Such trends represent the creation of the mass customisation of behaviour.

Another example is the massive proliferation of psychological and behavioural training programmes; in part, they represent a more general societal trend to "normalise" and regulate relationships. A striking analogue is the increased (and dehumanising) effect of "manualised" psychotherapy, which appears to be based on the assumption that psychotherapists should not try to understand their patients' experience, help them face painful realities, and come to an acceptance of their limitations, etc., but, rather, they should be trying to medicate, manage, re-educate, control, and correct the irrational behaviour of people whose suffering is inconvenient to the family, the organisation, and the larger culture. This undermines and undercuts the development of meaningful connections, or assisting them to make meaningful connections with and to their experience. In sharp contrast to the "manualised" psychotherapy movement, the various forms of more traditional psychodynamic psychotherapy foster a sense of authenticity, vitality, agency, creativity, and the capacity for enjoyment, as well as the ability to tolerate grief and limitation, whether or not the behaviour is unconventional or inconvenient according to cultural norms.

Manualised psychotherapy has an obvious parallel in HR-driven organisational human relations training. It amounts to the promotion of *prescriptive relatedness*, in contrast to fostering authentic and often messy relationships.

Conclusion

As I hope will be clearer as a result of my circumambulatory journey around the intersection of systems psychodynamics and twenty-first century information-based organisations, many mainstay concepts that have been important building blocks are becoming outmoded, such as the role of stable, bounded small groups as the primary mediating structure between the individual and the larger context. New systems, tools, processes, and structures designed to cultivate the expression of the authentic self, liberate collective creativity and imagination, and foster the expansion of universal human capacity are required in the Information Age.

Systems psychodynamics has a great deal to contribute to the development of new social systems as people will, inevitably, have to confront the impact of unconscious life and irrationality. To make this contribution, we will need to adapt our theories, concepts, and practices accordingly and, in particular, learn how the new organisations can foster depressive functioning without reliance on stable boundaries, well-defined task systems, and direct human contact.

Note

1. The notions "paranoid–schizoid" and "depressive position" were introduced by Klein.

> The paranoid–schizoid position is characterized by not perceiving persons as complex entities, but seem to equate individuals with each individual function that people perform for them. The dominant anxiety is of a paranoid nature, and splitting mechanism are preferred defences. The depressive position is marked by the recognition of whole persons. Persons that are recognized as performing different functions in different ways at different moments. This supposes the activity of integrative functions, and introduces feelings of ambivalence, depressive anxiety and guilt about anger and hate one might feel towards loved ones. At all times people may oscillate between the two positions. (Vansina & Vansina-Cobbaert, 2008, pp. 422–423)

References

Armstrong, D. (1997). The 'institution in the mind': reflections on the relation of psychoanalysis to work with institutions. *Free Associations*, 41(7): 1–14.

Ashby, W. R. (1958). Requisite variety and its implications for the control of complex systems. *Cybernetic*, 1(2): 83–99.

Bion, W. R. (1961). *Experiences in Groups*. London: Basic Books.

Emery, F. E. (1974). *Futures We Are In*. Canberra: Centre for Continuing Education, Australian National University.

Emery, F. E., & Trist, E. L. (1960). Socio-technical systems. In: C. W. Churchman (Ed.), *Management Science, Models and Techniques* (Vol. 2) (pp. 83–97). London: Pergamon Press.

Giddens, A. (1991). *Modernity and Self-Identity: Self and Society in the Late Modern Age*. Stanford, CA: Stanford University Press.

Hutton, J. (1997). Re-imaging the organization of an institution: management in human service institutions. In: E. Smith (Ed.), Integrity *and Change: Mental Health in the Market Place* (pp. 127–129). London: Routledge.

Jaques, E. (1953). On the dynamics of social structure: a contribution to the psycho-analytical study of social phenomena. *Human Relations*, 6: 3–24.

Klein, M. (1940). Mourning and its relation to manic-depressive states. In: *The Writings of Melanie Klein Vol. 1: Love, Guilt and Reparation*. London: Hogarth Press.

Klein, M. (1959). Our adult world and its roots in infancy. *Human Relations*, 12: 291–303.

Menzies Lyth, I. (1960). Social systems as a defence against anxiety. *Human Relations*, 13: 95–121.

Miller, E. J. (1993). An intervention in a manufacturing company: In: *From Dependency to Autonomy: Studies in Organization and Change* (pp. 195–216). London: Free Association Books.

Miller, E. J., & Rice, A. K. (1967). *Systems of Organization*. London: Tavistock.

Schumpter, J. (1942). *Capitalism, Socialism and Democracy*. New York: HarperCollins.

Shapiro, E., & Carr, W. (1991). *Lost in Familiar Places: Creating New Connections Between the Individual and Society*. New Haven, CT: Yale University Press.

Shirky, C. (2008). *Here Comes Everybody: The Power of Organizing Without Organization*. London: Penguin.

Surowiecki, J. (2005). *The Wisdom of Crowds: Why the Many Are Smarter than the Few*. New York: Anchor.

Trist, E. L., & Bamforth, K. W. (1951). Some social and psychological consequences of the longwall method of coal getting. *Human Relations*, 4: 3–38.

Turquet, P. M. (1974). Leadership: the individual and the group. In: G. S. Gibbard, J. J. Hartmann, & R. D. Mann (Eds.), *Analysis of Groups* (pp. 337–371). San Francisco, CA: Jossey-Bass.

Vansina, L., & Vansina-Cobbaert, M. J. (2008). *Psychodynamics for Consultants and Managers*. Chichester: Wiley-Blackwell.

CHAPTER FOUR

Are we losing the group in the study of group dynamics? Three illustrations

Sandra G. L. Schruijer

Introduction

The systematic study of groups and their dynamics was stimulated by the Second World War and its aftermath. Kurt Lewin, an émigré from Nazi Germany, was a main factor in these developments (Marrow, 1969). He founded the Research Center of Group Dynamics at MIT that became very active in group research. Programmes in social psychology and group dynamics, grounded in sociology and psychology, were initiated by prestigious American universities (Oishi, Kesebir, & Snyder, 2009; Sewell, 1989). For the burgeoning discipline of organisation development, with Kurt Lewin again as pioneer, working with groups constituted a main building block; hence, the understanding of groups was important. In the field of training, the National Training Laboratories (NTL) was a powerful player. It offered training for managers, often using T-groups as a methodology (something that emerged from Lewin's work). In Europe, the Tavistock Institute of Human Relations (THIR), with people like Eric Trist and Wilfred Bion as pioneers, likewise was very influential (e.g., Fraher, 2004). The TIHR studied group and organisational dynamics in actual work settings, from a systems psychodynamic perspective. Within the context of TIHR, social technical systems theory was developed, a (re)design philosophy of groups and organisations, based on the premise that the technical system needs to be jointly optimised with the social system (Trist & Murray, 1990, 1993; Trist, Murray, & Emery, 1997). Other European institutes that can be mentioned in this context are the European Institute for Transnational Studies in Group- and Organisational Development (EIT), and the Association pour la Recherche et l'Intervention Psychosociologique (ARIP) in France (Vansina, 1970).

Through the work done by these pioneers and institutes, much was learned about the dynamics of groups. Group dynamics were, especially in Europe, understood as an expression of emotional processes that are a consequence of the demands of group work, such as the group's demand partly to give up one's individuality in order to become a group member and to work, as a group of interdependent individuals, on the group task. In order to engage in productive work, groups need time to form, as group members need to work through tensions regarding belonging and freedom, regarding dependency and autonomy. Given these tensions and the tendency of human beings to avoid them, the emotional life of groups is a key factor in understanding their dynamics and working with them in order to achieve group effectiveness. In this tradition, much of the research on, and training in, group dynamics has been done with real groups, working on real tasks. Furthermore, Lewin showed that group dynamics can be studied experimentally without reducing the group level of analysis to that of individuals (Lewin, Lippitt, & White, 1939).

More than sixty years have passed since the start of the golden era for group dynamics, social psychology, socio-technical systems theory, and organisational development. During that period, psychoanalytic thinking became less influential, group research more experimental and less social, and the demand for quick fixes overwhelming. The word "team" seems to have replaced the word "group" and the activity of team building seems to have replaced the experiential learning of group dynamics. In this chapter, I want to provide three illustrations of the demise of the tradition that studies and works with group dynamics in the world of training, research, and education, by looking into its language and practice. I start with an exploration of the use of the terms "group", "team", "group dynamics", and "team building", in the general and in the academic literature. Then, based on anecdotal evidence, I look critically at the tendency to equate workshops around, for example, Belbin's Team Role Inventory (Belbin, 1981) with learning about group dynamics. Subsequently, I focus on how developments within the discipline of social psychology has provided a context for the relative neglect of group dynamics. Finally, I formulate my conclusions and make a comment on the potential role business schools could play in reanimating the study of group dynamics.

The language of groups and teams

Language reflects trends in society, yet, in turn, also influences perception, thinking, and feeling. The language around groups and its study, therefore, can be informative if one wants to understand thought and practice regarding groups and changes therein. It often seems to me that the word "team" has become more popular in the past years at the expense of the term "group". At least, I observe myself systemically questioning every use of the word "team" I encounter in my colleagues' work or my students' papers. Why "team" and not "group", what is wrong with "group"? I am invariably told that a group is simply a collection of individuals, whereas a team stands for a group of interdependent people who work towards a shared goal.

However, the original social psychological meaning of "group" included interdependence. For example, Lewin wrote, "conceiving of a group as a dynamic whole should include a definition of group which is based on interdependence of the members (or better, of the subparts of the group)" (Lewin, 1951, p. 146). Shaw, who wrote a classic textbook on group dynamics, defined a group as "two or more persons who are interacting with one another in such a manner that each person influences and is influenced by each other person" (Shaw, 1981, p. 8). And Forsyth, still one of the most used classics in the domain of group dynamics, conceives of groups as "two or more interdependent individuals who influence one another through social interaction" with, as common features, interaction, group structure, variations in size, shared common goals, and change in these features over time (Forsyth, 1990, pp. 22–23). Thus, originally, the term "group" implied interdependence and not simply an assemblage or a category. And since work groups, study groups, etc. were investigated, the concept of task or goals around which interdependence existed was natural. Did the word "team" then become a necessity as the study of groups evolved into studying a group of individuals without a task?

To find out about how the terms "group" and "team" have been used with different intensity over time, I consulted the browser Ngram (http://books.google.com/ngrams/). This browser claims to examine word frequency as featured in 5.2 million books (which is four per cent of all books published, including academic, literary, and other books), that have been published in the last two hundred years (Michel et al., 2010). I checked developments in the usage of the words "group" and "team" in the English language since the beginnings of the systematic interest in group dynamics, so, since the Second World War. The results are shown in Figure 4.1.

What can be concluded is that the term "group" is still used much more frequently in day-to-day language than the word "team" (although dropping from 0.031% to 0.023%). However, the word "team" is on the rise (from 0.002% to 0.008%).

The latter search embodied all books that mentions "group" or "team" and, thus, can include all kinds of texts. To narrow the search down to terms more likely to be related to the social sciences in general and the study of groups in particular, I also consulted Ngram for changes in usage of the words "group effectiveness", "team effectiveness", "group performance", and "team performance", as predicting group effectiveness or group performance has always been an important research theme in the study of group dynamics. The results are presented in Figures 4.2 and 4.3, respectively.

It appears that the terms "team performance" and "team effectiveness" have taken over from "group performance" and "group effec-

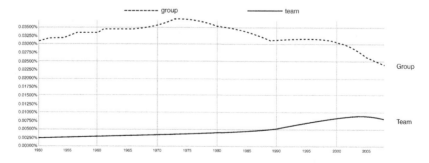

Figure 4. 1. Frequency of the words "group" and "team" in published books in English.

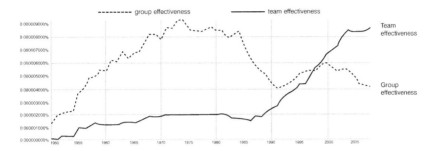

Figure 4.2. Frequency of the words "group effectiveness" and "team effectiveness" in published books in English.

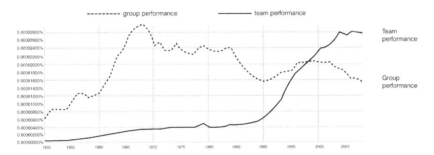

Figure 4.3. Frequency of the words "group performance" and "team performance" in published books in English.

tiveness" towards the year 2000, with a steep rise in these "team" constructs from 1990 onwards. The terms "group effectiveness" and "group performance" have slowly levelled off since the early 1970s, while having exhibited a similar steep rise (as the "team" constructs since 2000) since the 1950s.

Finally, I observed the trends in the usage of the terms "group dynamics" and "team building", the results of which are shown in Figure 4.4.

The term "team building", non-existent in the 1950s, is clearly on the rise, approaching the frequency with which the term "group dynamics" is used. The frequency of the term "group dynamics", still higher than that of "team building", is on a slow decline since the beginning of the 1970s, exactly the same time that the term "team building" makes its entrance and from which time it is becoming increasingly popular.

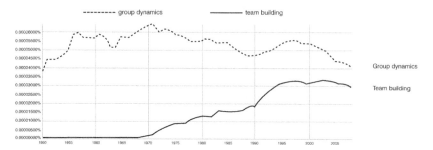

Figure 4.4. Frequency of the words "group dynamics" and "team building" in published books in English.

The question is now whether similar shifts can be observed in the academic literature. First, I compared two social psychological journals. Social psychology has been the academic discipline that does, and has done, most research on groups. The two journals chosen have been in existence the longest and are also the most important mainstream journals in social psychology in the USA and in Europe: the *Journal of Experimental Social Psychology* (*JESP*) and *the European Journal of Social Psychology* (*EJSP*). I started the analysis (and comparison) from 1971, as that is the year that *EJSP* was founded. I counted per decade how often the term "group" or "team" featured in the title of an article. The results are shown in Table 4.1.

What can be learnt from this table is that both social psychological journals have not succumbed to a "team" rhetoric, that the topic of groups is on the rise, at least as reflected in the titles of articles, and that *EJSP* has a longer history in studying groups, but that *JESP* is latching on quickly. It is striking, though, that the term "group" does not feature during the 1970s (and for *JESP* in the 1980s, too), inconsis-

Table 4.1. Frequency of the use of the terms "group" and "team" in the titles of articles published in *JESP* and *EJSP*, 1971–2010.

	JESP		EJSP	
	Group	Team	Group	Team
1971–1980	0	0	0	0
1981–1990	0	0	23	0
1991–2000	25	0	60	1
2001–2010	88	2	94	1

tent with the claim that social psychology has been the harbouring discipline of the study of groups.

One can imagine that the term "team" is more likely to emerge in applied journals, especially those that focus on groups in particular, for example *Small Group Research* (*SGR*) and *Group and Organization Management* (*GOM*). Further, it would be interesting to find out how *Human Relations* (*HR*), an applied journal in the domain of social and organisational psychology, jointly founded by Lewin and Trist, can be positioned regarding the "group or team" discourse. Table 4.2 reflects a similar analysis as above, but now for *HR*, *SGR* and *GOM*.

It is obvious that, for all three journals, the term "team" is on the rise at the expense of the word "group". Interestingly, also, *HR*, a journal that has a history in Lewinian and Bionian group dynamics, has fallen for the "team" discourse. The rise of the word "team" is the largest in the past decade (2001–2010).

A second type of analysis I performed was checking the frequency with which the terms "group effectiveness", "team effectiveness", "group performance", and "team performance" appeared in the title in any article published in an academic journal in psychology since 1950. I searched the digital journals, classified as psychology, using the library of Utrecht University. I created two categories, before 2001 and from 2001 onwards, in view of the steep increase found earlier around the year 2000. The results are displayed in Tables 4.3 and 4.4, respectively.

The results confirm the earlier analyses: the word "team" has become popular in psychology, especially in the past decade, at the

Table 4.2. Frequency of the use of the terms "group" and "team" in the titles of articles published in *HR*, *SGR*, and *GOM*, 1971–2010.

	HR		SGR		GOM	
	Group	Team	Group	Team	Group	Team
1951–1960	79	1				
1961–1970	44	1				
1971–1980	60	6	194	2		
1981–1990	42	4	224	1	31	10
1991–2000	26	9	166	15	16	13
2001–2010	13	18	150	85	24	30

Table 4.3. Frequency of the use of the terms "group effectiveness" and "team effectiveness" in the titles of articles published in psychology journals since 1950.

	Up until 2000	2001 and beyond
Group effectiveness	9	5
Team effectiveness	7	29

χ^2: $p = 0.0053$.

Table 4.4: Frequency of the use of the terms "group performance" and "team performance" in the titles of articles published in psychology journals since 1950.

	Up until 2000	2001 and beyond
Group performance	22	36
Team performance	12	62

χ^2: p = 0.0054.

expense of the word "group". Chi squared calculations demonstrate that the shift is highly significant. Mainstream social psychology journals, by the way, are relatively well represented in the category of "group performance", but not in the others. Specialised journals in the domains of group, organisation, or management research do use the terms "team performance" and "team effectiveness". Finally, when searching for the terms "group dynamics" and "team building" the following table emerges (Table 4.5).

Both the terms of "group dynamics" and "team building" are not very popular in the psychological literature, with team building even less popular than group dynamics. At least, they are not so important

Table 4.5. Frequency of the use of the terms "group dynamics" and "team building" in the titles of articles published in psychology journals since 1950.

	Up until 2000	2001 and beyond
Group dynamics	16	18
Team building	4	8

χ^2: p = 0.5086.

as to appear in the title. There is hardly any difference between the number of publications before and after 2001.

On the whole, it can be stated that the language of group dynamics has changed dramatically over the past ten to fifteen years. The term "team" is replacing the term "group" in the general and psychological literature, especially in the specialised journals on groups, organisation, and management. A quick glance at the use of the word "team" in the titles published in economic journals results in a frequency of more than 500. The word "team" might well have infiltrated from the economic and business discourse into the general language and into psychology. This might provide an explanatory context for the increased frequency of the word "team" in *HR*: an economic discourse has entered *HR* at the expense of a psychodynamic one (Loveridge, Willman, & Deery, 2007), and with it the "team" discourse could have entered, too. Mainstream social psychology journals, by the way, have stayed away from the term "team". Regarding the use of the terms "group dynamics" and "team building", we have seen that in the general literature the latter is becoming more and more popular, a trend which is not evident in the academic literature of psychology, perhaps since team building is clearly associated with the practitioner world of training and coaching.

In Old English, the word "team" stands for (among other meanings, such as offspring) a "set of draft beasts"; it is derived from the Dutch word "toom" (which means "check", as in "keeping in check", or "bridle") (*The Random House Dictionary of the English Language*, 1987). One meaning of the verb "team" is "to harness in a team" (*Merriam-Webster's Collegiate Dictionary*, 1983). The term "team", thus, has an association with control. The question is, whose control—who is doing the harnessing and checking? Team adepts say that teams are about empowerment and autonomy. Yet, is it true or illusory autonomy, as in the word "empowerment"? If I can empower you, I may take it back when it suits me. Many concepts have changed over the past few decades. Organisational development became the management of change, industrial relations became human resources management, social dynamics became organisational behaviour. In all these instances the change in terminology went together with an individualisation and instrumentalisation of the social.

Still, it is not clear what the language shift means exactly. Maybe the language change does not, or only to a limited extent, reflect a change in practice, and might not even in the direction I suggested. In the next section, I present some anecdotal evidence regarding the substitution of learning about group dynamics with measuring and discussing individual differences, that does imply a shift for the worse.

Group dynamics or individual differences?

Often, I ask my mature manager-students at the business school whether they have engaged in experiential learning regarding group dynamics. A most peculiar answer I regularly receive is, "Yes, we do! We have done Belbin!", or, "Yes, we have done MBTI!" (Myers-Briggs Type Indicator). Such answers can also be obtained from trainers and human resources directors. It seems that for quite a few, learning about group dynamics has become reduced to measuring individual differences. For me it always comes as a shock that people, who can be expected to be intelligent and experienced managers, seem to be satisfied with discussing certain individual styles or dispositions, irrespective of how relevant these might be to the task at hand, and to think that now they understand the dynamics of groups.

Working with Belbin's model (1981) or with MBTI (Myers-Briggs, 1980) has been consistently popular in the world of training and development over the past two or three decades. The same applies to other inventories that, one way or the other, measure individual predispositions, styles, or inclinations, for example, Hersey and Blanchard's leadership styles (1988) or Quinn's management roles (1988). Whether such exercises are helpful, for whom, and for what purpose, is not always clear. The effectiveness, efficiency, and ethics of some practices can be questioned. For example, is the individual difference variable under consideration relevant to the work context and to the tasks that people are expected to fulfil? Who determines that, and on what basis? What is the theoretical robustness of the individual constructs under consideration and what are the psychometric properties of the instruments that are used to examine them? How is the information obtained handled? Are people expected to share their test scores with the total group of trainees, often their direct colleagues? Are the test results interpreted by individuals who have been properly trained to do so? Are people free to say "no" to completing those instruments that tap information that belongs to the private domain, for example, when dealing with personality types, such as in MBTI? Are they, in principle, free to say "no", yet do they feel coerced into taking part due to group (or management) pressure? And so on.

When it comes to using such instruments while pretending to learn about group dynamics, my objections multiply. Interestingly, after sharing my objections with my students, they still maintain it was worth the effort and the money: "It was interesting anyhow, you know, we learned a lot from doing the exercise. At least we understand now that people differ". As if they did not know that people differ! And why would managers not be concerned whether their (financial and emotional) investments brought them what they needed? Let me first list my objections against individual differences instruments, such as Belbin, when the learning need involves group dynamics. Although I focus on Belbin or MBTI, my objections pertain to all individual differences instruments that are used only to measure and then create awareness of the fact that individuals have different inclinations.

As a first objection, I would like to point to the psychometric weaknesses when it concerns the vast majority of instruments that are used in management training, including Belbin. Belbin's instrument has hardly been researched and, in so far as it has, the results have not been very supportive: quite the contrary (e.g., Furnham , Steele, & Pendleton, 1993) . The psychometrics of the scales used to determine people's preferred roles are questionable, to say the least, implying that one cannot reliably predict group performance based on (any combination of) these roles. How come that, despite the limited credentials of Belbin's model, it remains widely used by practitioners and, I suspect, taught at business schools? What about all the other scales and tests that are in vogue, yet were given no research attention at all; what is the validity and reliability of these scales? Why is it so seductive for people to receive their scores on any so-called "key competence", whether that variable makes sense or not?

Even if the psychometric properties were in order, what is the use of being aware of individual differences when aiming to understand group dynamics? Individuals differ in a multitude of dimensions, dimensions that might or might not be relevant for understanding group dynamics. The whole idea of learning about groups and their dynamics pertains to understanding how the dynamics that are inherent to working in groups have an impact on individuals and the way they work together in accomplishing a group task. For example, the dynamics that result from an unavoidable conflict between wanting to become a group member while aiming to maintain one's individuality. Such dynamics are part and parcel of any group and affect all group members, irrespective of their individual inclinations. What is needed henceforth is a group level of analysis. Rather than making an inventory of individual differences, key is how a group works with its diversity.

In administering questionnaires that tap individual styles, dispositions, or preferences, it is more or less assumed that the impact of such an individual characteristic is constant across different groups, working at different tasks and operating in different contexts. Yet, group dynamics, again, involves understanding how the social processes can affect different (types of) individuals alike: almost anyone, given the right circumstances, can fall victim to obedience or conformity. Not only, therefore, is focusing on individual level dynamics misleading when one wants to understand groups, it might also damage individuals. Regularly, individuals report that, after having shared their individual questionnaire results in public, they have felt (unjustly and incessantly) stereotyped by their colleagues as if the only behaviour they could exhibit was in terms of the individual characteristic (as in Belbin's or Quinn's role), as if they were stuck for life with that characteristic and as if they were incapable of exhibiting any other behaviour.

The next objection concerns the relevance of the individual characteristic studied in view of the task at hand. Individuals may differ on a number of dimensions and attributes, for example, regarding their personality, attitudes, demographics, and role. Differences are tapped so as to become aware of them, as well as to help trainees value the differences, as if any heterogeneity will benefit task accomplishment. Yet, whether heterogeneity or homogeneity will further the task and what type of heterogeneity would be beneficial, depends on the requirements of the group task. For example, one can question whether organisations need to internationalise their management teams when they intend to serve national markets only.

Then there is the type of learning that is induced when one uses questionnaires only, measuring and reflecting on an individual attribute rather than experiencing how these differences manifest themselves while working on an actual group task and learning from a real experience (and from joint reflection afterwards). It remains an exercise in which one's emotional involvement is low. Further, how working with differences (assuming one focuses on relevant differences) evolves over time and affects performance remains unexplored. It is as if a group consists of static individuals and as if a group only gathers at a specific moment in time and then disperses. When one has been a member of a group, one knows that nothing is further from the truth.

How can one understand the continuing popularity of Belbin and other instruments when aiming to learn about group dynamics? There is a long tradition of teaching and researching group dynamics, so one cannot maintain that there is nothing else available. In the next section, I describe the developments within the research and education practices of the university-based discipline of social psychology since the Second World War, which provides yet another example of the growing neglect of group dynamics and which also might provide a context for understanding the above.

The asocialisation of social psychology

Social psychology, the academic discipline that has been most involved in small group research, has grown considerably over the past six decades in terms of its number of departments worldwide, academics, its societies, its literature, and its academic status. In the USA, a strong confidence was invested in psychology; it was seen as a discipline that would help build society and support the Cold War effort (Schruijer, 2008). The financial investments in social psychological research at the time were huge; investments that also benefited the European social psychologists (Moscovici & Marková, 2006). The early generations of social psychologists, both in the USA and Europe, wanted to develop a discipline that was research orientated, yet also contributed to society's well-being (Rodrigues & Levine, 1999). In the beginning, social psychology was a discipline that was close to sociology and was interested in applied issues. Experimentation was but one of the research methods adopted.

Over the years, experimentation became the norm of what was considered good social psychological research: to be more precise, laboratory experimentation (Danziger, 2000). With it, social psychology individualised. Over the years, the study of group dynamics has largely been reduced to studying individual behaviour in a group context—a context that, more often than not, is imaginary rather than real. Such concerns were already voiced in the 1970s (e.g., Steiner, 1974) and did not quiet down (Greenwood, 2004). Still, practices did not change. The individualisation of mainstream social psychology was further reinforced by its increasing cognitive orientation, while nowadays a biological route is being chosen. The initial close collaboration with sociology in a so-called "sociological social psychology" has disappeared, while a "psychological social psychology" by now is well established (Good, 2000). It is separated from sociology. Recently, it allowed its boundaries to be permeated by the neurosciences (Cacioppo, Visser, & Picket, 2006).

Mid-1960s European social psychologists founded their own society, the European Association of Experimental Social Psychology (EAESP), which was intended to be less individualistic than their American counterpart. The pioneers aimed at studying the human being as a social agent, embedded in social context. They further wanted a social psychology that was of applied value, and it did not rely solely on the laboratory experiment (Jaspars, 1986). Moreover, they wanted to establish social psychology as a research-based academic discipline at European universities. Almost fifty years later, we can safely say that the latter aim has been fulfilled: EAESP flourishes and social psychology has been firmly established in Europe. However, it also has succumbed to the individualised American social psychology it wanted to compensate for (Schruijer, 2012). Over the years, laboratory experiments with undergraduate students have predominated the research practice (at odds with the recent deletion of the word "experimental" from the association's name).

The psychodynamic perspective on group dynamics has also vanished from social psychology. Bion (1961) is the main representative of the psychodynamic tradition that wants to fathom group life (French & Simpson, 2010; McLeod & Kettner-Polley, 2004). Although his ideas were considered to be very promising for a social psychological understanding of groups (Hall & Lindzey, 1954), a recent chapter on the history of small group research (Levine & Moreland, 2011) does not even refer to Bion's classic *Experiences in Groups* (1961). An analysis of the citation history of that classic book (Schruijer & Curseu,

2013) shows that social psychologists hardly ever refer to it. Those academics who do work with Bion's ideas are investigating the world of work and health. Although a deeper analysis of how ideas from the psychodynamic tradition may have entered group research is required, this citation analysis is yet another illustration of how the meaning of the term "group dynamics" has changed.

These developments are likely to have affected the teaching of group dynamics, too. In the 1960s and 1970s, for example, T-group training did feature in the social sciences curriculum of universities (Vansina, 1970). Nowadays, courses in group dynamics still exist, but the experiential learning dimension seems missing unless one counts the so-called skill-labs as such, in which simple exercises and role-plays are conducted which can hardly substitute for the rich and deep learning that normally results from taking part in, for example, T-groups, or learning groups. I have made an inventory of which Dutch universities offer a group dynamics course as a part of a bachelor degree in psychology and if so, what that course entails, by consulting their online study guides. Table 4.6 provides a summary of the type of course offered (lectures or a practicum), the reading that is required, and the number of ECTS (European Credit Transfer System) it results in.

Table 4.6. The current teaching of group dynamics as part of the BA-degree in psychology at Dutch universities.

	RUG[1]	UU	TU	VU	RU	LU	MU	UvA
Course for BA[2]	3	1	1	1	—	1[3]	1	1
Lectures	1	0.5	0	1	—	1	0	1
Practicum	2	0.5	1	0	—	0	1[4]	0
Total ECTS[5]	11	7.5	2	6	0	5	6	6

[1]RUG = University of Groningen; UU = Utrecht University; TU = Tilburg University; VU = Free University (Amsterdam); RU = Radboud University (Nijmegen); LU = Leiden University; MU = Maastricht University; UvA = University of Amsterdam.

[2] The course is either compulsory for all BA students or a course as part of a specialisation in social psychology or work and organisational psychology.

[4]"Problem based learning" is the didactic philosophy of Maastricht University.

[5]European Credit Transfer System.

The University of Groningen is most active in teaching group dynamics, while Radboud University offers nothing at BA level. On the whole, time is equally divided between lectures and practicums. As far as I could retrieve, these practicums are of short duration and consist of exercises and role-plays. Regarding the Masters level: all universities offer a Masters degree with specialisations in social psychology and/or in organisational psychology). There are no Masters courses in group dynamics at the universities of Groningen, Utrecht, Nijmegen, Maastricht or the University of Amsterdam. The remaining universities offer teaching at Masters level, in the form of one course varying from six to ten ECTS, consisting of lectures and debates, on the topic of processes in organisations, in groups, and between groups. There was only one specific group dynamics course ("group psychology", as it is called) in Tilburg (six ECTS, yet only two-hour sessions with lectures and discussion).

Further study is required to find out what exactly is being done in these courses, but one can imagine that the new generations of academics will have had insufficient background in group dynamics to appreciate its importance in full and perhaps to give it a stronger presence in a future curriculum. Similarly, those who enter the field might need quite a bit of extra training in group dynamics, although it is not clear where they will find it. There are still institutes and organisations, generally separate from universities, that offer experiential training programmes in group dynamics, but my impression is that many practitioners and their employers favour short programmes that are cognitive in nature: they want it short and fast.

Conclusion

In this chapter, I have offered three illustrations that suggest a tendency of instrumentalisation and individualisation of the study of group dynamics. The equation of group dynamics training with measuring individual differences is a clear example of reducing group dynamics to the individual level. It also is a literate example of instrumentalisation by relying on a simple instrument, and a more figurative example, as it gives the illusion of clarity, understanding, and control. The developments in the academic study of group dynamics also demonstrate such individualisation, as groups are hardly studied at the group level of analysis any more. Rather than supporting a team rhetoric and practices like MBTI, Belbin, or team building, the social psychological study of groups has withdrawn into the ivory tower and has become more cognitive and biological. Academic teaching is following suit.

The changes in the study of group dynamics and the practice of helping groups and organisations to work with them need to be seen in the light of larger trends in institutions and society. Social psychology wanted to be seen as a science and, to this end, modelled the natural sciences while rejecting psychodynamic thinking (Schruijer, 2012; Schruijer & Curseu, 2013). In turn, systems psychodynamics theorists and practitioners tended to operate independently (Farr, 1996) or in competition (Fraher, 2004) and did not seem to be very interested in social psychology. Competition between universities stimulates a "publish or perish" ideology, which favours experimentation, as data can be collected and published quickly. Such competition takes place in a society that advocates global competition, in which processes of individualisation seem to know no limits, in which everyone strives to be number one and thinks s/he can be, in which anything can be fixed (quickly) and in which everyone has a right to be happy or, if not, can hold others responsible.

The changing discourse from "group" to "team" may be signalling such shifts when it involves the dynamics of groups. Yet more research needs to be done in order to corroborate my speculations. For example, researchers in the field of socio-technical systems theory also talk about teams. I expect these researchers to be critical regarding cheap rhetoric and quick (illusory) fixes. So why, then, did they change from the language of autonomous and semi-autonomous groups to teamwork (e.g., Rolfsen & Langeland, 2012)? We need to find out more and take a more systematic look at the developments within psychology and in which contexts they have taken place. Further, it might be worthwhile to study the actual practices of trainers and consultants to a greater degree and gain a contextual understanding of the changes therein.

Business schools might be the place where group dynamics can be revived. They are ideally positioned in between academic research and the actual practice organisations and managers bring. Rather than developing isolated courses, I think of group training and of process consultation around coursework, as I know does happen at some

business schools. Also, complex simulations can be (further) introduced in business schools and not only computer-modelled exercises.
However, there needs to be a willingness to dig deeper rather than
immediately offering what the customer thinks s/he wants. It needs
courage to be less "business" and more "school", but I truly believe
that in the end work done well pays off.

References

Belbin, M. (1981). *Management Teams: Why They Succeed or Fail*. Oxford:
Heinemann.

Bion, W. R. (1961). *Experiences in Groups and Other Papers*. London: Tavistock.

Cacioppo, J., Visser, P., & Picket, C. (2006). *Social Neuroscience: People
Thinking about Thinking People*. Cambridge, MA: MIT Press.

Danziger, K. (2000). Making social psychology experimental: a conceptual
history, 1920–1970. *Journal of the History of the Behavioral Sciences, 36*:
329–347.

Farr, R. (1996). *The Roots of Modern Social Psychology*. Oxford: Oxford
University Press.

Forsyth, D. (1990). *Group Dynamics* (2nd edn). Belmont, CA: Wadsworth.

Fraher, A. (2004). *A History of Group Study and Psychodynamic Organizations*. London: Free Association Books.

French, R., & Simpson, P. (2010). The 'work group': redressing the balance
in Bion's Experiences in Groups. *Human Relations, 63*: 1859–1878.

Furnham, A., Steele, H., & Pendleton, D. (1993). A psychometric assessment of the Belbin Team-Role Self-Perception Inventory. *Journal of
Occupational and Organizational Psychology, 66*: 245–257.

Good, J. (2000). Disciplining social psychology: a case of the boundary
relations in the history of the human sciences. *Journal of the History of
the Behavioral Sciences, 36*: 383–403.

Greenwood, J. (2004). *The Disappearance of the Social in American Social
Psychology*. New York: Cambridge University Press.

Hall, C., & Lindzey, G. (1954). Psychoanalytic theory and its applications
in the social sciences. In: G. Lindzey (Ed.), *Handbook of Social Psychology. Volume 1: Theory and Method* (pp. 143–180). Cambridge, MA:
Addison-Wesley .

Hersey, P., & Blanchard, K. (1988). *Management and Organizational
Behavior*. Englewood Cliffs, NJ: Prentice-Hall.

Jaspars, J. (1986). Forum and focus: a personal view of European social psychology. *European Journal of Social Psychology, 16*: 3–15.

Levine, J., & Moreland, R. (2011). A history of small group research. In: A. Kruglanski & W. Stroebe (Eds.), *Handbook of the History of Social Psychology* (pp. 233–255). New York: Psychology Press.

Lewin, K. (1951). *Field Theory in Social Science*. New York: Harper.

Lewin, K., Lippitt, R., & White, R. (1939). Patterns of aggressive behavior in experimentally created social climates. *Journal of Social Psychology, 10*: 271–279.

Loveridge, R., Willman, P., & Deery, S. (2007). 60 years of *Human Relations*. *Human Relations, 60*: 1873–1888.

Marrow, A. (1969). *The Practical Theorist: The Life and Work of Kurt Lewin*. New York: Basic Books.

McLeod, P., & Kettner-Polley, R. (2004). Contributions of psychodynamic theories to understanding small groups. *Small Group Research, 35*: 333–361.

Merriam-Webster's Collegiate Dictionary (1983). 9th edn. Springfield, MA: Merriam-Webster.

Michel, J.-B., Kui Shen, Y., Presser Aiden, A., Veres, A., Gray, M. K., The Google Books Team, Pickett, J. P., Hoiberg, D., Clancy, D., Norvig, P., Orwant, J., Pinker, S., Nowak, M. A., & Aiden, E. L. (2011). Quantitative analysis of culture using millions of digitized books. *Science, 331*(6014): 176–182.

Moscovici, S., & Marková, I. (2006). *The Making of Modern Social Psychology: The Hidden Story of how an International Social Science Was Created*. Cambridge: Polity Press.

Myers-Briggs, I. (1980). *Gift Differing: Understanding Personality Type*. Mountain View, CA: Davies-Black.

Oishi, S., Kesebir, S., & Snyder, B. (2009). Sociology: a lost connection in social psychology. *Personality and Social Psychology Review, 13*: 334–353.

Quinn, R. (1988). *Beyond Rational Management*. San Francisco, CA: Jossey-Bass.

Random House Dictionary of the English Language (1987). 2nd edn, S. B. Flexner (Ed.). New York: Random House.

Rodrigues, A., & Levine, R. (1999). *Reflections on 100 Years of Experimental Social Psychology*. New York: Basic Books.

Rolfsen, M., & Langeland, C. (2012). Successful maintenance practice through team autonomy. *Employee Relations, 34*: 306–321.

Schruijer, S. (2008). Is the EAESP a Cold War baby? An investigation into the political context of its formation. Paper presented to the conference

"Divided Dreamworlds – The Cultural Cold War East and West", Utrecht University, the Netherlands, 26–27 September.

Schruijer, S. (2012). Whatever happened to the term 'European' in European social psychology? A study of the ambitions in founding the European Association of Experimental Social Psychology. *History of the Human Sciences*, 25: 88–107.

Schruijer, S., & Curseu, P. (2013). *A Historical Perspective on the Gap between the Social Psychological and Psychodynamic Perspectives on Group Dynamics* (submitted manuscript).

Sewell, W. (1989). Some reflections on the golden age of interdisciplinary social psychology. *Annual Review of Sociology*, 15: 1–16.

Shaw, M. (1981). *Group Dynamics* (3rd edn). New York: McGraw-Hill.

Steiner, I. (1974). Whatever happened to the group in social psychology? *Journal of Experimental Social Psychology*, 10: 93–108.

Trist, E., & Murray, H. (Eds.) (1990). *The Social Engagement of Social Science. A Tavistock Anthology, Vol. 1: The Socio-Psychological Perspective*. Philadelphia, PA: University of Pennsylvania Press.

Trist, E., & Murray, H. (Eds.) (1993). *The Social Engagement of Social Science. A Tavistock Anthology, Vol. 2: The Socio-Technical Perspective*. Philadelphia, PA: University of Pennsylvania Press.

Trist, E., Murray, H., & Emery, F. (Eds.) (1997). *The Social Engagement of Social Science. A Tavistock Anthology, Vol. 3: A Socio-Ecological Perspective*. Philadelphia, PA: University of Pennsylvania Press.

Vansina, L. (1970). Sensitivity training or laboratory methodology in Western Europe. In: S. Mailick (Ed.), *Newer Techniques on Training* (pp. 56–62). New York: United Nations Institute for Training and Research.

CHAPTER FIVE

Notes towards a model of organisational therapy

Edgar H. Schein

Background and introduction

In this brief chapter, I lay out some thoughts and propositions about the concept of organisational therapy (ORTH). What many of us in organisation development find ourselves doing can best be described as organisational *therapy*, though the client systems would strongly resist this terminology because of its implications of pathology.

The paradox, or the thing I have the hardest time getting across in my process consultation workshops, is that we have the consultation model pretty well worked through for dealing with an individual or a team, but we have very few models for how to do stress reduction or therapy with larger systems that consist of complex subsystems. We can sit down with individual executives and counsel them. We sort of know how to do that. However, in dealing therapeutically with a larger system, an organisation, we use individual or small group models and then are surprised when we can only improve the functioning of the individual or the small team. The larger system does not improve. So, let us look at some large system characteristics and the dilemmas of working with them therapeutically.

Some propositions about organisational therapy (ORTH)

I will address three questions: (1) What distinguished organisational therapy from individual, group, or family therapy? (2) What are the major determinants of organisational health and pathology in organisations? (3) How does one define therapeutic goals and the role of the therapist when dealing with organisations?

The goal of ORTH is organisational (systemic) health, not individual, group, or departmental health *per se*.

Organisations as systems exist within larger systems, such as communities and nations, so the consultant/therapist (CT) must be clear in his or her own mind what the boundaries of the system are. That point implies that the needs of the larger system might be in conflict with individual or group sub-systems. There might arise situations where the health of the organisation is, in fact, not in the best interests of some members of the organisation. The CT must be clear in his/her mind who the client system is on whose behalf the therapy is conducted. The CT must, therefore, have a value system that is congruent with the concept that organisations have value, even if they sometimes disadvantage certain individuals. The concept of "client" or "patient" in ORTH is, therefore, a complex and moving "target" that evolves over the course of the "treatment" once one gets above the level of the individual or small group. This becomes especially problematic because one is often dealing with individuals in *roles* that make them representatives of larger units.

One must distinguish "contact clients", who first bring a problem to the CT, from "primary clients", who ultimately own and pay for the therapy, and from various categories of "ultimate clients" who are parts of the organisation but not necessarily aware of the therapeutic process that is going on. Some of these might oppose the therapeutic process *if* they were aware of it (Schein, 1999).

Hierarchies, status systems, interpersonal and intergroup power dynamics are intrinsic to all organisational systems and must, therefore, be taken into account in the consideration of any ORTH process. The CT must both build a trusting relationship with the primary client and be able to identify the power dynamics operating around him or her, and be able to determine at what level in an organisational hierarchy it is optimal to intervene further.

Diagnostic and remedial interventions that are aimed at social units, roles, groups, inter-groups and total systems require intervention models and technologies that are systemic in nature. The kinds of interventions that work at different levels of complexity require different skills on the part of the CT. Curing a "role conflict", or an "inter-group conflict", or a total system pathology requires different interventions.

How do we define organisational health and/or pathology?

Basic health criteria

Bennis (1962), following the lead of others defining mental health in general, proposed the following four criteria of organisational health:

- *adaptability*: capacity to identify and solve problems in a changing environment;
- *sense of identity*: insight on the part of organisational members as to their mission, goals and means;
- *capacity to test reality*: ability to perceive and correctly interpret outer and inner states and processes;
- *integration*: the sub-systems of the total system are working in alignment and co-ordination to achieve the mission.

This definition focuses on the "state" of the system at a given point in time and might lend itself to diagnostic assessment. It does not, however, emphasise ongoing processes of healthful coping. The value of having a complex, multi-faceted criterion of health is that it enables us to work with the client on which elements need attention and makes the client aware of the complexity of the concept of a "healthy organisation" as an abstraction.

Adaptive coping cycle

Schein (1965) following the lead of information theorists working on "systems health", identified an "adaptive coping cycle" which consists of the following stages or processes:

- sensing a change in some part of the internal or external environment (ability to perceive);

- getting the relevant information to those parts of the system that can interpret it, digest it, and act on it (ability to communicate internally);
- modifying internal processes as needed without creating undesirable side effects (behavioural flexibility);
- exporting new "products" as needed for survival and growth of the system (ability to act and communicate externally);
- obtaining feedback on whether or not the new products achieve the goals intended, which starts a new sensing cycle (ability to perceive results of own action non-defensively).

Pathology can now be classified according to which process is failing or working sub-optimally. Is the organisation unable to perceive what is going on, is the relevant information failing to get to the right places in the organisation, is the organisation incapable of acting on the information because of rigidities in its current processes (culture), is the organisation failing to export (market) its new products, and/or is the organisation failing to obtain accurate feedback on whether its coping efforts are working or not?

A shorthand way of encapsulating these points is to note that adaptive health has two fundamental components: (a) the ability to perceive and think and feel "accurately" in terms of the available data, and (b) the capacity/ability to respond flexibly to the changing demands that are perceived. Health can be thought of as "the ability to rise to the occasion", which implies, of course, the ability to perceive accurately what the occasion demands. Pathology can be defined as inability to perceive accurately what the occasion demands and/or lack of flexibility to respond.

Pathology and/or health at the systemic level are fundamentally different from individual health

One of the paradoxes of ORTH is that systemic pathology can be created by "healthy" individuals and groups that are not aligned or co-ordinated to achieve total systems goals. An individual employee helping his product group to win out over another product group is behaving in an individually healthy, expected fashion, yet his or her efforts might be so effective that the other group is destroyed, even though it has the better product. A psychologically "healthy" executive might create an incentive system that pits organisational units against each other in such a way that the organisation cannot cope effectively.

Unfortunately, we often confuse the two concepts of health and come to believe that if we cure the individual or the sub-group this will cure the organisation. That formulation ignores what we know about the impact of role pressures, group norms, and organisational culture. Misperception, misinterpretation, defensive thinking, and miscommunication based on cultural assumptions cannot be solved *by* working with individuals who are only part of the system that holds those assumptions.

Organisational culture and organisational defences, that is, any set of role definitions, group norms or cultural assumptions that were learnt originally to solve the organisation's problems of external survival and internal integration can become maladaptive as external and internal conditions change (Schein, 2003, 2009, 2010)

Because these elements were learnt as solutions to prior problems, they become taken for granted and begin to function as "organisational defences" in the sense that they will create misperception, defensive thinking, and miscommunication. Such defences serve the individual members of the organisation very well in supplying meaning and predictability on a daily basis, but their collective impact can put the organisation into great jeopardy (Schein, 1996, 2003).

The CT must, therefore, balance what might be the perceived need for people to retain a stable sense-making system against unfreezing the system by creating or taking advantage of widespread disconfirmation. This usually happens through scandals or disasters that have a collective impact. Lewin called this process "unfreezing" the system, and can be thought of as consisting of three further processes that I identified in various change cases: (1) disconfirmation; (2) creation of anxiety and/or guilt; (3) creation of psychological safety (Schein, 2009).

Reference groups and membership groups can be sources of pathology

All members of any given organisation will have a complex set of identifications with various reference and membership groups. We know that the daily behaviour of individuals is very much a function of their group identifications, and that group relations can lead to blocked or inaccurate communication between groups (especially under conditions of inter-group competition). The patterns of identification and the structural relations between groups are, thus, a potential source of health or pathology.

In particular, group norms not only affect how members perceive reality, but also limit the behavioural options of the members. For example, the organisation would be healthier if all sources of safety hazards were clearly identified *by* employees, but group norms at the employee level are very clear that one does not report to management safety infractions that a fellow employee is committing. The norm of "not ratting on your colleagues" will be stronger than any amount of management emphasis on "open communication" in the interests of safety.

How does one define therapeutic goals, methods. and the role of the therapist?

ORTH differs from other forms of therapy in that the "problem definition" evolves not only over time as one works with the client, but also evolves through the sequential contact with the various parts of the client system, especially as one moves from contact to primary clients.

Process consultation. The primary implication of this sequential unfolding of goals and problem definitions is that the role of the therapist has to be built on the philosophy of "Process consultation" (Schein, 1969, 1987, 1999).

The essence of this philosophy, for purposes of ORTH, is that from the very first contact with the client system both diagnostic processes and remedial processes have to be seen as interventions and have to be jointly owned by the CT and the contact client. In other words, everything the CT does is an intervention that has both diagnostic and remedial consequences. The concept of "diagnosis" as a stage prior to intervention disappears, because diagnostic processes themselves have potentially huge and unknown consequences for the client system. A senior executive asking a consultant to interview his subordinates to "diagnose" what might be malfunctioning in the organisation has already influenced his relationship to those subordinates in unknown ways. If the consultant goes ahead, he or she is further influencing the system in unknown ways by stimulating individual thought and group communication among those subordinates.

A second philosophical principle of process consultation is that clients and consultants must jointly own all interventions. The CT's main job, then, is to build a relationship with each part of the client system, so that they take ownership of further interventions together. To build such relationships, the consultant must have a model or theory of what is going on that makes sense to the client. What this usually means is that the CT must be able to articulate his or her model of how organisations work in language that is understandable *by* the client system. The group therapist who told his training group "now the group is trying to castrate me" could better have said, "*I* observe that whatever suggestions *I* make are consistently ignored and undermined *by* the group members."

A third philosophical principle is that expert advice, recommendations, or prescriptions have limited use because the CT will rarely know enough about the culture of the client system to know unilaterally what is relevant and what will work. In this sense, the *CT role* is completely different from the traditional consultant role. On the other hand, the CT must be expert in managing process so that an appropriate helping relationship can be built with each part of the client system as the ORTH process evolves.

The multiple roles of the CT

If every intervention must be *owned jointly* by the *CT* and the *part of the client system* he or she is working with at that moment, it follows that the role itself will evolve as the client system produces more data, both about its perceptions of reality and its flexibility of response. As will be seen below, when we classify different types of interventions, the CT must have a repertory that includes the ability to work with:

- individuals in organisational roles;
- small groups, teams, committees, task forces that are basically "family groups" from one organisational unit;
- small groups that are made up of representatives of different units, which might be in co-operative, competitive, or neutral relationships with each other;
- small groups that represent the tops of organisational units;

- "inter-groups" of various sorts where the client system is two or more groups at the same time;
- total organisational units, such as departments, product groups, marketing groups, functional groups, etc.;
- the entire organisation;
- "inter-organisations", such as mergers, joint ventures, partnerships, strategic alliances, etc.

It is the ability to respond flexibly to these various types of clients that defines effective behaviour on the part of the CT. Does such "flexibility" include ever giving recommendations and prescriptions to the organisation? This is a complex question for two reasons. First, it is a valid question in relation to *any* therapy. Under what conditions is it effective or desirable to tell an individual client what he or she should do, or how he or she should perceive, think about, or feel about a given set of circumstances?

Second, what are the chances that a CT would understand a given organisational system well enough to be able, with confidence, to make a recommendation, to tell the organisation what it should do or how it should perceive, think about, and feel about a given set of circumstances? The chance of an individual therapist understanding a given personality well enough to figure out what that person should do is much greater than the chance of a CT figuring out the roles, norms, and cultures of organisational sub-systems and the total system. A given personality remains more or less the same over time, but an organisation (and its sub-parts) is changing constantly as a function of changes in its personnel and leadership.

To make reliable recommendations to an organisation would, thus, require understanding not only the cultures and sub-cultures, but also the personalities of leaders and other influential figures in the total power structure. To gain such understanding would require so much diagnostic intervention over such a long time that one could not argue that one is making a recommendation to the same system that one started with.

What, then, is the role of "telling" or "recommending", *if any*? I believe it can be a form of "testing intervention" that can be useful as a way of gathering data about how the system will respond. It would fall into the same category as when an individual therapist makes an interpretation to the client in order to test the client's level of insight and, at the same time, based on the client's response, tests his or her own degree of understanding of what might be going on with the client. It fits Lewin's dictum that "in order to fully understand a system, you must try to change it". Some of the deepest dynamic characteristics of the system do not surface until it is perturbed by such an intervention. In other words, the function of the recommendation is to study the *system's reaction*, not to get it to accept the recommendation. The CT must, therefore, remain on hand to observe and to deal with the reaction. He or she cannot responsibly terminate the process with the recommendation.

Cultural definitions of consultation and therapy

All of what has been said above is coloured by broader cultural assumptions about the helping process. In some cultures, it is not acceptable to have problems and to seek help. In some cultures, therapy is defined in strict doctor–patient terms, where the doctor is an absolute authority expected to give prescriptions, which are expected to be followed. The comments and notes made here apply particularly to economically evolved industrial cultures of the West. In those cultures, for example, the USA, it is acceptable to have certain kinds of problems and to seek consultation, but the word "therapy" itself implies a level of pathology that is to be concealed from public view. Both at the individual and organisational level, having to "see a shrink" implies some loss of face.

ORTH and the CT role are, therefore, necessary, but not publicly acknowledged as such. The result is that we have multiple forms of "consultation", "coaching", "educational interventions", "personal and organisational development programmes", "organisational learning", and myriad other forms of helping, some of which qualify as ORTH and some of which do not. One of the purposes of this set of notes is to begin to unscramble what is ORTH and what is not ORTH, so that our client systems can make better choices as to what it is they need.

References

Bennis, W. G. (1962). Toward a "truly" scientific management: the concept of organizational health. *General Systems Yearbook, 7*: 269–282.

Schein, E. H. (1965). *Organizational Psychology*. Englewood Cliffs, NJ: Prentice-Hall.

Schein, E. H. (1969). *Process Consultation: Its Role in Organization Development*. Reading, MA: Addison-Wesley.

Schein, E. H. (1987). *Process Consultation. Vol. 2: Lessons for Managers and Consultants*. Reading, MA: Addison-Wesley.

Schein, E. H. (1996). Three cultures of management: the key to organizational learning. *Sloan Management Review*, 38(1): 9–20.

Schein, E. H. (1999). *Process Consultation Revisited: Building the Helping Relationship*. Englewood Cliffs, NJ: Prentice-Hall.

Schein, E. H. (2003). *DEC Is Dead, Long Live DEC: The Lasting Legacy of Digital Equipment Corporation*. San Francisco, CA: Berrett/Kohler.

Schein, E. H. (2009). *The Corporate Culture Survival Guide* (revised edn). San Francisco, CA: Jossey-Bass.

Schein, E. H. (2010). *Organizational Culture and Leadership* (4th edn). San Francisco, CA: Jossey-Bass.

PART II
THOUGHTS AND IDEAS
FOR THE PRACTICE

Introduction

Leopold Vansina

I n this part, we share some of our professional experiences that generated "actionable knowledge", at least for us. We hope they will inspire managers of private companies and business schools to rethink some of their policies and structures, in order to optimise economic objectives while taking technological opportunities and social requirements into account. Consultants and social scientists might find some ideas with with to enrich their interventions, or to encourage field studies and action research projects.

The presented approaches, methods, and ideas run somewhat counter to the more general culture of "avoiding inconveniences": no difficult personal talks, confrontations, and reflections, and quick, painless adaptations instead. Is that culture not present, not just in many organisations or client systems, but also within our own social science profession, in the form of fearing to negotiate the necessary conditions for doing valuable consulting work and relevant research?

The selected chapters discuss approaches and interventions that are not far removed from daily life. They are not so sophisticated that they require special expertise or additional training. Yet, they all create conditions that enable human beings, groups, or whole systems, to become *also* in contact with those "small" and often annoying "things" that cannot easily be accessed or discussed. These "small" elements in our lives, which shape the meaning of what we see around us, disturb the peace of our inner world and our genuine interactions with the outer world. They appear as fleeting images or thoughts, flashes of uncomfortable sentience, and perceptions that are spontaneously dismissed as inconvenient, too. However, they are important to understand the underlying dynamics of our human and social life. The challenge, then, is to create conditions that enable these small things to surface and to learn from them, in order to be free, more fully alive and present, and to act responsibly.

In Chapter Six, "Processing mental representations of roles: alternating written and face-to-face interactions", I describe an approach to (re)define roles within a structure of roles, to achieve strategic objectives. Organic growth, geographical spreading of resources, but also strategic restructuring projects, usually results in overlapping roles, gaps in responsibilities and accountability, and/or broken work relations that reduce effectiveness, and create a breeding ground for stressful misunderstandings.

A method and design is described by which the impact of "social suppression" is reduced, which was successfully applied in a fairly large distribution company. It enabled people to communicate freely about their mental representations. Subsequently, they were processed in direct interaction with the real role-holders. The outcome was a clearer and more accurate conception of one's core tasks and accountability within a structure of roles conceived to achieve strategic objectives.

Chapter Seven, "Facilitating transitional change", written by my colleague Sandra Schruijer and me, presents an approach to enable members of a community or organisation to co-create change and development. The approach grew out of an in-company training programme in group-dynamics, long before the notion of transitional objects, space, and change was introduced in the psychodynamic literature. Since the late 1960s, the approach has inspired some managers and consultants to introduce it as a vehicle to co-create organisational change.

A transitional space is created, often requiring the consent of the hierarchy, in which participants or employees can express their images about their actual and ideal selves or their "willed organisation" in a creative way. Inevitable changes are mentally dealt with in the process, possible consequences are explored, and steps are taken to control or eliminate undesirable consequences.

The quality of the approach is appreciated with our conceptual understanding of transitional change.

In Chapter Eight, "Feedback or reviewing: a conceptual attempt to clarify the differential impact on human beings and work systems", I make a conceptual attempt to elucidate the differential impact of two methods, "feedback" and "reviewing", on human beings and work systems.

In Part I, a French and an American social scientist already pointed at the negative impact of the often impersonalised social pressures of the popular 360° feedback practices. Here, a more extensive and deeper analysis is made of this approach, focusing exclusively on the individual, and then contrasted with a work systems approach: "Reviewing".

Reviewing is an activity in which all the members of a work system take part in creating a reflective appreciation of the way their system has been functioning, and, subsequently, in exploring what can be done to improve their system. It is assumed that all actors in the work system, including the manager, learn from the process, but the immeasurable advantage comes from gaining ownership of, and becoming committed to, executing their improvement actions.

In Chapter Nine, "Conversations on work", Kenneth Eisold describes in simple terms his way of helping individuals grappling with their own career incidents and deeper expectations. Three major principles guide the rather informal and interpersonal quality of work conversations: tactfulness, sensitivity, and focus.

These guard us from presuming that we know or understand more than we actually do, and from introducing clichés or unfounded opinions into our conversations with clients or others.

This chapter is inserted after the critical analysis of impersonal feedback procedures, because it highlights the importance of personal conversations. Furthermore, it leads us to explore the organisational conditions and procedures under which such conversations on work can be introduced into the work setting itself and replace or complement the computer-guided career planning procedures of employees. Would it not give human resource managers a human function, and an excellent opportunity to get a feel for what lives in the organisation?

In Chapter Ten, "Enacting one's way to new thinking: using critical incidents to vitalise authentic collaboration and learning", Tom Gilmore and Nora Grasselli present a thoughtful method of working through participant critical incidents that enrich learning in both class settings and in coaching, or team preparation for forthcoming challenging encounters. Rather than using prepared business cases, with their overemphasis on analysis and clever strategies, the focus is on enacting key moments in their real cases.

The established case teaching methods teach students about interactions with employees, managers, clients, groups, whole systems, strategic management, you name it, as if all these subjects exist out there simply as an object for objective study or for a technique to be applied to others. This frame neglects, or even denies, personal involvement of the participant—willing or unwilling—in the real situation. It leaves them, in any case, unprepared to face the reality of their own involvement and sensitivities in working with human and social systems, much of which is hidden to themselves, yet visible to others. In the dynamics of enactments, interpersonal, intrapersonal, and substantive issues are made more visible in the service of development.

CHAPTER SIX

Processing mental representations of roles: alternating written and face-to-face interactions

Leopold Vansina

An international distribution corporation asked Gilles Amado, Dominique Lhuilier, and myself to help them to clarify roles and strengthen role identities within the commercial function. The organisation enjoyed a steady growth with an entailing fuzziness in role definitions, for example, role overlaps, duplications, misunderstandings, and gaps. Seven roles within the commercial function were brought together (three to four role groups at a time) in residential workshops of three to four days' duration to exchange and define the core responsibilities within these roles. The structural relations between the roles of commercial director, regional manager, product sales manager, area manager, product sales merchandisers, chief of butchers, and store managers are graphically represented in Figure 6.1.

Mendel (1998), a French psychoanalyst, inspired us in the design of the residential workshops. Homogenous role groups met regularly at times to agree on the key responsibilities in their role and communicate these to other role groups, along with their experiences about the roles of these other role groups. All role-holders were asked to define the "key tasks" in *verbs* (Checkland, 1981). Describing key responsibilities in *verbs* encourages people to think about the kinds of

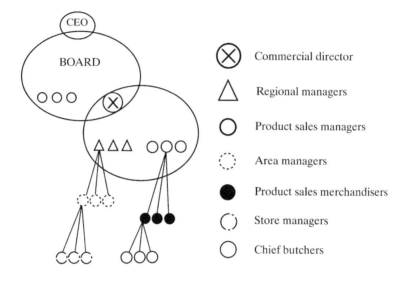

Figure 6.1. Graphic representation of roles involved.

activities that are needed to transform a given input into a desirable output. The emphasis, thereby, is on taking action to change/transform. Subsequently, the role groups studied these written messages and wrote a group reply to the various senders. The senders studied these replies and, as a group, formulated their responses in writing. Care was taken to eliminate (a) all actual hierarchical relations between the members of the role groups, and (b) face-to-face interaction. Only after two of the described rounds did the role groups meet in plenary to share and process their experiences. Subsequently, balanced mixed groups (equal number of role holders from the various role groups) were formed to discuss what could be done to facilitate collaboration between the different roles through adjusting responsibilities. Finally, the homogenous role groups defined their own roles, based on the acquired insights and requests from others in the structure of roles.

During the whole process, a facilitator was delegated to each homogenous and mixed group to assist them in dealing with psychosocial processes within their group that hindered work on the task.

The whole project lasted about a year. In the process, we found that (a) the different roles became defined in relation to the other roles, and

(b) they maintained their clarity and relative power position within that structure while strengthening role identities (Vansina & Amado, 2008).

So far, these are the essentials of the design needed as background for this chapter.

The purpose of this study is to explore the inherent processes and benefits of alternating written and face-to-face interactions between groups to enable the processing of partly *imagined* representations of roles. In addition, we wish generally to stimulate creative thinking in inventing "normal" ways for social systems to expose conscious and unconscious elements in their constructions of mental role representations, while enabling them to distinguish these from real key tasks in logical roles for achieving organisational objectives.

First, we describe the meaning of mental representations of roles in relation to the much broader and widely known notion of the "organisation-in-mind". Second, we explore the advantages of written communications over face-to-face interactions in attenuating social suppression. Finally, we focus on the processes of sorting out and working through "irrational" and emotional elements in mental representations and inter-role relations in redefining the key tasks in roles requisite for implementing organisational strategy.

Mental representations of roles

Twenty-four male college students volunteered to take part in the well-known Stanford Prison study (Haney, Banks, & Zimbardo, 1973). They were randomly assigned to take the roles of prison guards and prisoners in a mock prison in the basement of a Stanford University building. No one had any previous experience, either as a guard or as a prisoner. The day before the start of the simulation, the guards received a *minimal* briefing of their roles: they should do no physical harm to the prisoners, but were allowed to induce feelings of boredom, a sense of fear to some degree, a notion of arbitrariness that their life is totally controlled, and they will have no privacy, no individuality, no power . . . The mock prison was made to look real, with prison cells, proper uniforms and dress. Very rapidly, the students *internalised* their roles and the prisoners started behaving like real prisoners, terrorised and humiliated by their guards. Faced with the inhuman behaviour and some mental breakdowns, the experiment was terminated after six days of the planned two weeks.

The researchers explain the brutal results in terms of the importance of situational rather than dispositional attributions, such as
personality traits or past experiences.

It is not our intent to speculate on the similarities between life in
organisations of any kind and state prisons. What is relevant for our
study is that situational factors have a marked influence on how
people behave and the role they carve out for themselves based on
what they *imagine or are told* is expected from them.

We define *mental representations of roles* as the mental construction
of roles based on (a) explicit, implicit, and imagined expectations of
other role-holders (e.g., bosses, peers, and clients constituting the
social situation), (b) past experiences, and (c) one's subjective understanding of one's position in a constellation of other roles. The less
expressive the situational variables (e.g., machinery, position in relation to clients, work dress) and the more ambiguous the role expectations, the more role representations will contain personal, subjective
elements. The elements vary widely from subjective understanding,
interpretation, and preferences for key tasks to emotionally charged
or personal gratifications, frustrations, and defensive responses. However, one also finds in role representations a blend of aspired to and
existing relations with other roles and career prospects. When homogenous role groups are asked to define the essential tasks of their roles
in verbs, these imagined representations become moulded into a
unanimous, acceptable, but largely *self-constructed role*.

When the same homogenous role groups describe the *roles of others*
based on past experiences and observations, but without any opportunity to check their reality base, their individual representations
become *shared constructed representations*. These *shared constructed
representations* are likely to differ from largely *self-constructed roles.*
They are largely based on direct and indirect subjective experiences
with the role holders and tend to be made coherent with assumed
intentions and projections.

Whenever the differences between the self-constructed role and the
shared constructed representations of that same role by other role holders are substantial, they become a source of tensions, frustrations, and
conflicts in inter-role collaboration, thereby reducing the overall efficiency and effectiveness of the organisation. Other people in the organisation come to rely on others to take responsibility for key tasks, while
these might not be included in the self-constructed role. Reporting and

information lines, evaluations and accountability, control and areas of discretion, goals, targets, and ways of role execution are likely to become scrambled, providing opportunities for defensive actions, but also for constructive self-initiatives and reparation. The aim, therefore, is to arrive at a good enough shared understanding of the roles and their relative position in the structure. I believe that this can be achieved best by including, in the processing of rational data, irrational, emotional, and consciously and unconsciously imagined material. By involving a larger part of the whole person in mutual role clarification, we can expect to facilitate collaboration and increase efficiency and effectiveness in realising the company's strategy. Arriving at perfectly synchronised roles that fit in a finely designed structure, like cogs in a well-oiled machine, is an impossible goal. Furthermore, it would be highly undesirable from the human and organisational point of view. It would sap out all flexibility, obstruct role identification, constrain initiative, and freeze creative responses to changing conditions.

Loosening social suppression in describing mental representations of roles

First, written communications make it possible to eliminate the *visual presence* of the addressed person from the process. Under this condition, the influence of the everyday or normal *social suppression* is being reduced, thereby making it possible for the persons involved to express themselves more freely.

Social suppression is an ongoing process by which human beings *learn* how to behave, what may be said or not in specific contexts, what may be thought or felt, how and under what conditions human needs may be satisfied in socially acceptable ways, and how to control emotional and bodily expression. The learning can take place through (a) approval (rewards) and disapproval (punishments), mostly induced in social conversation (Billig, 1999); (b) through identification with persons one likes, admires or aspires to become; (c) through efforts to gain or enhance membership in groups. It is part of a life-long learning process.

As human beings, we are very sensitive to the affective quality and emotional climate in our social interactions with others. Subtle cues are picked up and one learns what is socially acceptable or unacceptable, usually without being aware of what one is learning, or why. The suppressed elements are stored in that broad area between the conscious and the unconscious, without us being clearly aware of the fact that they were ever conscious.

Social suppression differs fundamentally from the Freudian notion of *repression*. The latter refers to a process that is *automatically* triggered by *anxiety*, although it might be related to some fear of not being accepted (Vansina-Cobbaert & Vansina, 2008, pp. 76–77). The latter, however, is not a necessary condition, since repression can and does already take place before the other is recognised as a distinct human being. Overwhelming hunger, a lightning strike and exploding thunder, for example, can be a trigger. In this study, we deal with the normal learning process of social suppression.

The consequences of that normal learning process potentially are both positive and negative. On the positive side, we note that human beings only become human when raised in a human environment. Social suppression helps us to become "civilised citizens" of a community. In other words, a culture is passed on about what to do and not to do *to belong*, to maintain *social harmony* within that community, and to avoid *exclusion*. It also makes us feel at home with people sharing the same etiquette, habits of communication, and behaviour.

On the negative side, social suppression entraps our thoughts, feelings, spontaneous actions, expressions, and reactions. Maintaining social harmony might become a goal in its own right, while different responses to changing conditions and proactive innovations might be required. Social suppression, indeed, might fuel the confusion in organisations between maintaining social harmony by avoiding interpersonal frictions or conflicts, on the one hand, and, on the other, engaging in task conflicts whenever needed to secure survival and effectiveness of the social system. Finally, social suppression often dampens authenticity and freedom in self-expression, in particular when it implies taking a deviant position or confronting others perceived to be in a more powerful position (Crossan, Maurer, & White, 2011). Recently, one has started to investigate a more conscious expression of social suppression, called "implicit voices" (Detert & Edmondson, 2011). *Implicit voices* refer to a form of self-censorship that regulates verbal interactions: to speak up or to remain silent.

Social suppression is the outcome of a lifelong learning process. As such, it should be distinguished from complying, consciously or unconsciously, to *actual* social pressures from a group or a domineering person. Such behaviour we have come to know as "false consent", "withholding dissent or deviant information" from the dominant or preferred line of thinking and choice, or what we now call "victims of groupthink" (Janis, 1972, 1992). These responses are not necessary *learnt responses*, but compliance to *actual* social pressures. As a matter of fact, actual physical or observable social pressure is not a necessary condition for yielding to learned social suppression. It is sufficient that persons *imagine* or *anticipate* that a deviant or unpleasant response might lead to disapproval, rejection, or ostracism, as described in the Abilene paradox (Harvey, 1974). In daily life, this distinction, although theoretically correct, is often blurred by the unconscious blending of imagined and real threats or pressures. In fact, it is more correct to speak of more or less partially real and more or less partially imagined pressures. The latter are also a blend of what we have learnt to expect and what we imagine will happen when we "disturb" social harmony, in particular when it implies persons in powerful positions.

The *absence of self-reflection* (with or without a mirror reflecting the actor), or the *physical absence* of other persons, attenuates social suppression. Children left waiting individually in front of a bowl of biscuits are more reluctant to pick some when they can see themselves in a mirror than when they cannot observe themselves in the act. The person of the actor disappears in the absence of a *seeing face* or *being seen*. The actor might conceal his/her face through wearing a mask, operating from a distance, or shielding himself behind the anonymity of a group. This phenomenon has found its expression in our common language as "talking behind someone's back". In the case of our study, the absence of the addressed persons whose role was being described made it possible for the writers to express themselves more frankly and with less social constraints. This is by far not the outcome of a calculated decision. It just happens without us being fully aware.

Seeing a human face and being seen or not being seen can be manipulated to protect the actors' emotional involvement, empathy, compassion, or guilt. Whenever we cannot any longer *see the human being* in our enemies, prisoners, patients, employees, or role holders, we tend to lose our capacity to treat them in a civilised, human way.

It is well known that individuals who have a higher degree of self-awareness or self-monitoring are known to be more careful in their expressions and ways of presenting themselves whenever they experience being noticed or identified as a person. These self-monitoring persons are greatly concerned about social appropriateness. The person is "particularly sensitive to the expression and self-representation of others in social situations and uses these cues as guidelines for monitoring his own self-representation" (Snyder, 1974, p. 528).

In our project, written communications have a second benefit, as they trigger irrational and emotional responses *by the reader*, the recipient of the message, besides rational ones.

Written communication is an impoverished way to transmit accurately emotionally loaded content such as attitudes, emotional states, personality, and rapport in comparison to face-to-face interactions (e.g., Ekman & Friesen, 1980; Grahe & Bernieri, 1999). In the absence of non-verbal cues (facial and body expressions), tone, and the possibility to get in touch with the *emotional quality* of the developing relation between sender and receiver, one is left with just understanding words, sentences, and, occasionally, the handwriting. However, much of their meaning is lost when one is unable to get in touch with the emotional quality of interactions and the whole setting. The writer might carefully pack the meaning in words to convey the message, or might equally carefully select words and phrases that obscure the content, or, indeed, he or she might defy the addressed. Although the intentional stances of honesty may be stated explicitly, his or her messages might still be suspected. Deceitfulness and defiance, however, has to be deducted from the text. Consequently, the reader is left with the task of discovering the meaning of the written communication. There is ample room for the reader to make sense or interpret the message. Empathising with the writers becomes very difficult, in particular when the communication is written by a group (in our case, a homogenous role group) whose members one does not know personally. Some groups did send their raw text with all the corrections still visible: for example, changed words or rephrasing to the addressed group. Others carefully rewrote their message on a clean sheet before sending it out, removing all traces of internal discussions to arrive at a proper, unanimously agreed role representation. The message then becomes like a Rorschach test. In an attempt to understand and make sense of the meaning, it is attributed and projected on to the text as a mixture of attempted empathy with the writers, and past and partial experiences with people in similar roles. The reader is bound to inject quite a bit of his/her inner world that, in turn, will affect the written response. It is somewhat similar to reading a book and seeing the film. While a book liberates our imagination, a film holds it.

In order to clarify this point, I will give one example of the responses of the "boss group" to the self-constructed role of a "subordinate group" and their shared role representations of their boss. The "boss group" responded to the first message by returning the received sheet crossed over in red ink with "do it all over again!" The sheet describing the assumed key tasks of the "boss group" was subsequently returned with crossed words, equally in red ink, and words in bigger capitals! The message of superiority and disapproval was quite clear, but the receiving group could only guess *why* the "boss group" was so dismissive, triggering a similar rejection.

As such, the written exchanges generated rich messages about the relation between the self-conceived boss role and the boss role assumed and described by the subordinate role group.

The psychic difficulties of dealing with messages like this are well described by Trist (2001[1987], pp. xxiii–xxiv):

> One has to sense all this and so to begin to make sense of it—to make an appreciation of it, as Vickers (1965) would say—in emotional as well as cognitive terms. One cannot do this (especially when constrained by time) unless one can, to a considerable extent, internalize the new material, which is apt to be ambiguous and value-laden, and allow it to come in contact with what is already in oneself. This takes us already into a transitional area. If one's defences are too rigid, one is not going to allow this to happen, so the novelty is likely to be screened out. . . . As regards working through, one is not going to have much to work on if one has not let very much in. But beyond this, working through entails the painful process of tolerating all the emotional upheaval that is consequent on coming to realize that one's old familiar world is not going to see one through, that one's security base and the very foundation of one's identity are being challenged . . .

On top of all these psychic difficulties proper to processing new information, the impoverished nature of written communications further entices the reader to interpret, to give meaning to the message. In the process, the reader is bound to expose in his or her subsequent responses more of his or her inner world: unverified assumptions, emotions, fantasies, and projections.

Some other factors

In the design of the project, we had two other factors favouring the expression of the inner worlds: the task itself, and the anonymity of unanimity.

The task itself. The given task requires that the members recall, process, and build on their recollections of experiences with their own role and other role holders. It turns the attention away from role holders towards their own inner worlds, for example, recalled expectations, memories of incidents, personal experiences, and ideas of appropriate and inappropriate role behaviour within their organisation. The opportunities to check and verify their constructions of the key tasks are confined to comparing the "experiences" of the members within the homogenous role group. Consequently, one may expect a variety of conscious as well as unconscious elements to become mixed in the description of the own role and the roles of others. *The role constructions are produced in consent.* This instruction turns the group into a self-protecting shield of unanimous anonymity. Fear of retaliation, of offending others, or anticipated guilt, easily fade into the background. Furthermore, the fact that each role group had to define in consensus their own and other roles made it easier to express oneself in more categorical wordings. Indeed, the required consensus creates conditions that increase the influence of colleagues on the individual member and facilitate *group-attitude polarisation.* This is likely to occur when an initial tendency of individual group members towards a given direction is enhanced following group discussions (Myers, 1986). In other words, the role definitions and messages tend to become more extreme after discussion in the homogenous groups than the original proclivity of an individual group member. This is even more likely to be the case for addressed messages when the argumentations and recalled experiences with the roles of other groups are less factual, and more of an interpretative nature (Isenberg, 1986).

We may summarise and conclude that the attenuation of social suppression by the absence of the visual presence of the addressed, the nature of written communications, the task itself, and the anonymity of unanimity, facilitate the exposure of mental role representations. These representations include, besides factual experiences, insights, and rational constructions of roles, subjective desired and/or detested elements in role tasks, accountabilities, and relations of a conscious and unconscious nature. These elements are, furthermore, conceived in reference to their own self-constructed role within an experienced structure of roles. Part of the data is on the table in a written form, but a much larger part has become activated in the minds and psyche of the persons involved. Together, they provide a rich palette of factual date, images, emotions, impressions, interpretations, projections, and conceptions to be processed before roles can become realistically defined and serve as a base for role identities (Vansina & Amado, 2008).

Processing in face-to-face interactions

The human face has a particular psychological quality. Exposing one's face and being seen by another human being makes us a *person* and/or a *member* of a group. The distinction between the two is of psychological importance. The latter is revealed in the question: "Are you talking for yourself or for the group?" The answer reframes one's understanding of the message and the way we respond to the person in his own right or as a member of the group. At least, in our Western culture, we seem to be more careful not to hurt or offend an individual than a member of a group, although the latter risks triggering a more threatening hostile group response.

Face-to-face interactions add non-verbal cues to the palette of words about the persons engaged in a communication. Their assumed meaning (emotional and cognitive) can be explored directly ("Did I offend you?"), or indirectly through subsequent interactions ("Why were you surprised when I said this? What would you have wished or expected me to say?"). Assumptions can also be held in suspension for later explorations. In verbal interactions, one can carefully introduce a painful message ("It may not be pleasant, but I have to tell you . . .") and/or qualify or accentuate it according to the non-verbal reactions of the listener. Noticing the non-verbal expressions, exploring them, and adjusting one's way of formulating the message all imply a capacity to be *present*, *to be attentive to the other*, and *to understand the context*.

This richness of face-to-face interactions enables human beings to compare in a conscious or more unconscious way one's mental representations (partly expressed in writing) with the role holders in person. The statement, "The data is on the table!" carries two meanings. First, what has been written has become more easily discussable. It is no longer secret or suppressed. In a way, it has already been communicated. Second, the representations of the writers and readers have largely become activated in the minds of all involved; they have become more accessible for elaboration. Furthermore, the authors of the written messages get a (group) face, become alive, and one is enabled to compare "shared mental representations" and "mental, self-constructed roles", discuss and discover patterns of correspondence and discrepancies. Comparison might generate new questions, even uncertainties, but they can be explored and checked, as human beings do to stay in touch with reality. For example, "Why do you think this was one of our key tasks? Who told you so?"

This basic human drive to find out and test reality has allowed the human race to survive dramatic changes in the environment and to learn. These processes of testing reality take here the form of sharing, comparing of impressions and representations to find out what makes sense, what is real enough as a basis for role work. They take place without much direct assistance of the members of staff. The major part of their role is to help them understand the method and put it into practice. As Gilles Amado said, "the method opens itself". Furthermore, the mere presence of a member of staff served to contain tensions and create space conducive to "sharing, comparing, and finding out". In that space, we find *active* interactions, as implied in the three verbs (sharing, comparing, and finding out), but also *time and silence* to reflect and allow for insights. The more "time and silence" is eliminated by frenzied exchanges or disputes, the more people tend to transgress to automatic and habitual behaviour unrelated to the task, closing doors for reflection, reality testing, and insights. The reflective silence needs to be distinguished from "unresponsive silence". The meaning of the latter is hard to distinguish from the manifest conscious or unconscious withholding of information or the inability to relate. In these instances, some extra effort to initiate exploration or to question its foreclosure might be called for.

A second task consists of monitoring the interactions to allow for clarifications of the underlying logic and of the fit of key role tasks in the overall structure of roles to facilitate an effective collaboration.

In the earlier mentioned consulting project (Vansina & Amado, 2008), we organised three different face-to-face settings to facilitate the processing of mental role representations. In a first setting, the homogenous role groups (and its member of staff) were seated around separate tables arranged to provide optimal visibility to the other groups. After the two rounds of written exchanges, the role groups could interact, explore, and process their experiences, assumptions, frustrations, and implied relations. Subsequently, balanced groups consisting of two members of each role group could explore their understanding of the roles (on rational and emotional grounds) and redefine the roles to improve collaborative efforts and organisational effectiveness. Finally, the homogenous role groups met (a) to share— from the balanced role groups—their experiences and understanding of roles within a structure of roles, and (b) to finalise the adjustments in their self-defined roles.

Homogenous role-groups interact in plenum

The intergroup setting encourages people to speak as role-group members. The homogenous role groups are visibly seated around separate tables. On the one hand, this seating arrangement enables power and other relations to emerge in the felt frustrations and humiliations, the disagreements and misinterpretations of the written messages. Everyone can see, feel, react, and explore real or assumed power relations implicit in the mental representations or the ways in which the written exchanges took place. On the other hand, the presence of all role-group members makes it easier to raise delicate power issues. One feels the support of the group. Comparing these power relations with those legitimately derived from the role position within the structure of roles takes place privately and often openly. "You are our boss but you can't ask us to do your work!" "I thought you were our boss, but you aren't. Stop asking us to police for you!" are statements questioning the felt, and even expressed, power relations in the mental representations. However, the issues themselves might not be resolved in that setting. Rational exploration and adjustment of role tasks and work relations require another composition of the groups.

Balanced mixed role groups

In balanced mixed role groups, two members of each role group within the studied structure of roles are brought together. By balancing the roles in the group, possible power differences stemming from the size of the representation are evened out in order to create a suitable space for checking and correcting role representations. In the mixed groups, the structure of roles is visibly present and accessible. The mental representations and work relations can be explored face-to-face and also checked against the logic of the distribution of key tasks to implement an assumed, an explicit, strategic choice. The purpose is to arrive at considered suggestions about the definition or redefinition and distribution or redistribution of the key tasks of the represented roles in order to facilitate collaboration. Collaboration is not a goal in itself, but a necessity within the structure of roles to achieve strategic organisational goals in efficient and effective ways. It implies the elimination of overlap, duplication, and neglect of key tasks. All this can be done in an explorative mood in the knowledge that the final redefinition of roles will take place in homogenous role groups.

Homogenous role groups

Each role group can now process the deliberations of three to four different mixed groups to build a more realistic base of mental representations and a more effective fit in the structure of roles. Nevertheless, the groups are counselled not to jump into a more quantitative search for commonalities in the proposed definition/redefinition of key tasks by the mixed groups, but to engage in exploring the rational grounds and anticipated cost–benefits of the proposed redistribution and redefinition of key tasks (and entailed changes in work relations), to create a coherent, logical, functioning whole. In this way, rational and logical thinking are brought together with the well-known, healthy, psychic processes of worrying and working through (Vansina, 2008, pp. 134–135). The refined role definitions are written down to be shared and checked with the other role groups. In the project, briefly described at the beginning of this chapter, the role definitions were subsequently handed over to senior management for approval and the commercial strategy was updated. The proposed distribution of key tasks within the structure of roles was largely approved.

Concluding comments

No unusual methods are required to activate, expose, and process partially conscious and partially unconscious elements in mental role representations. Alternating written with face-to-face interactions is largely sufficient to make the undiscussable discussable.

Mental role representations contain elements of preferred and satisfying activities, assumptions about appropriateness, efficiency, and effectiveness, experiences and expectations alive in the inner world of human beings. These elements of our inner worlds become intertwined with rational considerations. Together, they form the basis from which one actualises one's role representations in taking or not taking actions, and in the way this is done.

Allowing the homogenous role group to collect its thoughts has the double impact of putting more weight behind its common view, and making it more stable by writing it up. Deprived of the "presence of the other", one may expect to gain more honesty in the expression of mental representations.

Roles become defined in relation to other roles. It is, therefore, essential to create time and space to clarify and adjust mental representations of roles in a face-to-face setting where all the roles within a structure of roles are present. In that space, the role holders are enabled to compare, clarify, and adjust their mental representations with the logic of the distribution of key tasks within a structure of roles to achieve strategic objectives.

These clarifications and adjustments of mental role representations are the outcomes of an ongoing process of comparing what is assumed with what is rationally required within a structure of roles. At the same time, healthy mental processes of worrying and working through become activated in anticipation of changes in roles, even role identities. Thus, not only are roles clarified, but also the persons involved develop a more accurate picture of the functioning of the structure of roles and its implications for implementing strategic choices. In short, the method discussed here enables the creation of shared systems of meaning.

Genuine processing of mental role representations might gain more relevance in times of change. In particular, when employees are no longer assumed to carry out a neatly described set of activities in a robot-like manner, but are expected to identify with key tasks (transformation processes whose operational qualities could become modified by changing conditions) and to commit themselves to strategic objectives. To enable the employees to identify with their roles, management needs to provide a minimal amount of freedom in defining their roles, so that they can feel challenged and comfortable with their key tasks. Such a role definition needs to be realised within a setting, comprising the relevant structure of roles along with the given strategic objectives. Alternating written and face-to-face exchanges seems to be a useful way to process mental role representations and make them more compatible with what is required to be effective and efficient.

References

Billig, M. (1999). *Freudian Repression: Conversations Creating the Unconscious*. Cambridge: Cambridge University Press.

Checkland, P. (1981). *Systems Thinking, Systems Practice*. Chichester: Wiley.

Crossan, M. M., Maurer, C. C., & White, R. E. (2011). Reflections on the 2003 AMR decade award: do we have a theory of organizational learning? *Academy of Management Review, 36*(3): 446–460.

Detert, J. R., & Edmondson, A. C. (2011). Implicit voice theories: taken-for-granted rules of self-censorship at work. *Academy of Management Journal, 54*(3): 461–488.

Ekman, P., & Friesen, W. V. (1980). Relative importance of face, body, and speech in judgements of personality and affect. *Journal of Personality and Social Psychology, 18*(7): 270–277.

Grahe, J. E., & Bernieri, F. J. (1999). The importance of non-verbal cues in judging rapport. *Journal of Non-verbal Behaviour, 23*(4): 253–268.

Haney, C., Banks, W., & Zimbardo, P. (1973). Interpersonal dynamics in a simulated prison. *International Journal of Criminology and Penology, 1*: 69–97.

Harvey, J. B. (1974). The Abilene paradox: the management of agreement. *Organizational Dynamics*, Summer: 63–80.

Isenberg, D. J. (1986). Group polarization: a critical review and meta-analysis. *Journal of Personality and Social Psychology, 50*(6): 1141–1151.

Janis, I. L. (1972). *Victims of Groupthink: A Psychological Study of Foreign-Policy Decisions and Fiascos*. Boston, MA: Houghton Mifflin.

Janis, I. L. (1992). Causes and consequences of defective policy-making: a new theoretical analysis. In: F. Heller (Ed.), *Decision-Making and Leadership* (pp. 11–45). Cambridge: Cambridge University Press.

Mendel, G. (1998). *L'acte est une aventure*. Paris: La Découverte.

Myers, D. G. (1986). Discussion induced attitude polarization. *Human Relations, 28*: 699–714.

Snyder, M. (1974). Self-monitoring of expressive behaviour. *Journal of Personality and Social Psychology, 30*: 526–537.

Trist, E. (1987). Discussion paper of Harold Bridger's: To explore the unconscious dynamics of transition as it affects the interdependence of individual, group and organisational aims in paradigm change. Published as "Prologue" in: G. Amado, & A. Ambrose (Eds.) (2001). *The Transitional Approach to Change*. London: Karnac.

Vansina, L. (2008). Psychodynamics: a field of study and an approach. In: L. Vansina & M.-J. Vansina-Cobbaert (Eds.), *Psychodynamics for Consultants and Managers* (pp. 108–155). Chichester: Wiley-Blackwell.

Vansina, L., & Amado, G. (2008). Understanding and working with organizational dynamics: coping with organizational growth. In: L. Vansina & M.-J. Vansina-Cobbaert (Eds.), *Psychodynamics for Consultants and Managers* (pp. 273–320). Chichester: Wiley-Blackwell.

Vansina-Cobbaert, M.-J., & Vansina, L. (2008). Defensive processes and behaviour. In: L. Vansina & M.-J. Vansina-Cobbaert (Eds.), *Psychodynamics for Consultants and Managers* (pp. 68–87). Chichester: Wiley-Blackwell.

Vickers, G. (1965). *The Art of Judgement*. London: Chapman & Hall.

CHAPTER SEVEN

Facilitating transitional change

Leopold Vansina and Sandra G. L. Schruijer

I n the 1960s of the past century, many social scientists strongly believed that they could better society, build more humane organ-isations, and improve racial and interpersonal relations, and even life in general, through group dynamics and experiential learning. The optimism and dedication released a lot of creativity in developing training methods and consulting interventions that, however, awaited research and further conceptualisation. Training in group dynamics was introduced in open management development conferences. Some companies even introduced T-group training in their in-company training programmes, for example, IBM's International Executive Development Programme, Blaricum, the Netherlands, and in a Danish shipping company (Hjelholt, 1963). However, not all companies were pleased with the outcomes. The experiences of Swiss Air, for example with their in-company T-group training, were not at all encouraging. Swiss Air decided to stop that kind of training all together, because the employees became more interested in interpersonal and group relations than in getting the work done.

During that period, the general manager of a family owned, small distribution firm asked the first author to design and organise T-group programmes for his employees. He himself had taken part in an open T-group conference and had benefited so much from that experience that he wanted to offer his colleagues a similar learning opportunity.

Being warned of, and familiar with, the potential difficulties associated with in-company T-groups, we carefully set up some structural conditions (Vansina, 1971). The most important ones being that

- a couple of the general managers and directors would first take part in an open T-group programme to provide a broader base of understanding of the method;
- the general manager and some of his directors would take part in the T-group programme as regular members (allowing for what we now would call "leadership in learning");
- the T-groups would be composed of diagonal slices of participants, thereby avoiding direct hierarchical relations within the T-groups;
- the programme was open only to volunteers, screened by the first author in an effort to prevent breakdowns;
- management would not be informed why certain employees were advised not to attend the programme;
- after attendance, the participants would be allowed to experiment with improving their work systems;
- thee months later, in a follow-up meeting, management and participants were to review and appreciate the outcomes of their experiments for management to decide to either stop or to formalise the changes in the work systems.

During these seven-day residential T-group programmes, we observed that certain members were handicapped in expressing their experiences in words. Several of them had not had an equivalent to a high school education and lacked some verbal agility. Inspired by existing projective techniques, we tried out group drawings and paintings. They allowed for expressions of inner states, partly conscious, partly unconscious, which were subsequently commented on, again in words. However, our instructions did not allow the individual member to express him/herself in relation to their T-group and the wider community, including the other T-group(s). So, the idea emerged to build a "village".

The village

In the middle of one particular programme, when the T-groups had already made some group paintings and felt comfortable in sharing experiences in verbal and non-verbal ways, we asked each member, staff included, to build something three-dimensional that had *a function* in a village and that expressed how they *experienced themselves* in the programme–community at that very moment.

A big white sheet of paper with only the outline of a stream and a railway track was placed in the middle of the room. A broad variety of material was provided: clay, colour markers, paper, old magazines, scissors, knives, glue, sheets of cardboard of different colours, pipe cleaners, staplers, tape. Everyone was free to go outside and pick some material from the surrounding environments that could help their self-expression.

The members were encouraged to take time and find a place where they could reflect before building something that expressed their state of being in the programme. When they returned to the plenary room, they selected an individual space for creating their piece. Members could ask for assistance if they came across some unexpected difficulty in their construction. After about forty-five minutes, when everyone was ready, a staff member gave a signal and every member could at that moment put their construction on the white sheet that represented the landscape of the village. A long silence came over the group of participants that had sat down in a wide circle and stared at their village. Taking turns, the members talked about their creation while keeping their eyes on their piece. When a person had finished, the other members were free to comment, share their evoked experiences, point at what seemed to be missing in that piece, or features that were not talked about, and ask questions: why, for example, the house was so big, with only windows wide open, but the door firmly closed. Some talked about what they had hoped to find in that piece, some kind of clue, a sign of personal insight or development. Others took it a step further by saying something like: "Maybe you might come to leave the door ajar, so that we can come in and we don't have to wait until you make your comments from your open windows. Maybe, you might still like to work on this during the coming days!" Or, "Wouldn't it be nice if someone was sitting on that bench near that lonely tree?" Still others explored the meaning behind the position of that tree, way out of the village. The members became highly involved, interested in each other's pieces and the comments of others. They were moved emotionally: feeling the inner joy by hearing the authenticity in some revelations, not infrequently tears appeared, or one became uneasy because of not having been fully honest. Once the village was created, no one was allowed to touch the pieces, modify them, or change their position.

The pieces in the village helped members to express themselves, while allowing others to share their experiences. Members who had difficulties before in putting their observations and experiences into words found it easier to talk about their own constructions (or that of the others) in the village, in front of them. We, in the staff, gradually realised that the creative activity of building a village and discussing it together had led to better images of the members as to where they were in their developments and in the village, and to hopeful and aspiring symbolisations of the members and the village, which they could work on during the rest of the programme, or in their everyday situations.

We kept the village in the middle of the room for every one to see until the last day of the programme. Some members modified their piece in between some sessions. Some explained in the group why they did it, or talked about it in a more comfortable setting of friends. Still others waited until the community session of the last evening. At that session, the whole community gathered around their village and could, if they wished, change their piece and position. Some members spontaneously explained why they modified their personal creation, others responded to the instigation of other members. Most members were very careful in changing their pieces. While some tore parts of it and drew these away, still others felt they were not ready yet to change anything, or were happy with their representation as it was.

One member of the staff asked, "How would we like the village, the community, to be?" There was some hesitation; could we move our pieces from how we experience ourselves in the village to represent how we would like the community to be? The participant who was the general manager got up and shoved his statue from the outskirts towards the centre of the village, where most of the pieces had been put. It did trigger some hectic actions of replacing one's piece, putting it closer to the one of the general manager. Some members could not do this, because their boat needed to be in the river, for example. A few just moved closer to a colleague, even if it meant being further away from the boss.

A few minutes of silence pointed to a new experience. The village was no longer *a nice place to live*: too cramped, too much togetherness, not enough space to breathe. "I wanted to be with the people to stay in touch with what is going on, rather than observe from a distance!" the manager explained. A most interesting discussion followed. How could one in real life be in touch with other people while doing one's work: driving a truck, moving the merchandise in the warehouse, sitting in an office away from where the action is, seeing the boss coming in and at times going out? And how can we tell our peers and spouses about our experiences which they have not been part of? The discussions of all these questions and concerns made the members think about their normal everyday situations and how one could create some of these experiences of openness, honesty, care, and understanding in the workplace while doing one's job.

The next day, in a final community session, the members dismantled the village. Each member could take his/her piece away. Some kept their pieces to take home to remember or to show their children; others left them to be taken to the bin. Did it serve its purpose?

In our understanding, it supported learning in several ways.

- The self-created, personal representation of each member facilitated the sharing of experiences and observations in images, while it allowed for the expression of parts of the self that could not be put into words.
- In the discussion of the pieces and experiences, tensions between the present state of being and an aspired state became activated, creating sketchy images of areas of development and learning for members to work on. These tensions had to remain as a motivational force.
- The village became the visual representation of the learning community. It contained not only the concerns and aspirations of the members, but also concomitant tensions. It seemed to allow the membership to do their work.
- The village also acquired a symbolic meaning. It came to represent the family company. Members' responses to "How would you like it to be?" directed the attention to the situation back home and what could be done to move forward, not just in the

conference, but in the company. What could realistically be done to reconcile or integrate humanness and task work in the workplace? Many of these questions were left open. They had to find answers in little experiments and trying things out.

- These thoughts about the future made a link to the follow-up, three months later, to appreciate and evaluate their changes introduced in the company. After reviewing their experiences, senior management decided, mostly on the spot, whether to continue, adjust, or stop the experimental changes.

The village became an integral part of the subsequent T-group training programmes for at least six years. The family company continued to grow, with the inevitable ups and downs. By now a new generation has taken over, built a family holding, and internationalised and diversified its activities. Currently, the group counts more than 21,000 employees and is still expanding.

The village is an integrated part of our open International Professional Development Programme: Leading Meaningful Change.

From building a village to jointly redesigning a care home

These principles of the village were used in a change process the second author was involved in. It concerned a home for the elderly that faced a negative inspection report by the governmental authorities and that had only limited time to correct the practices criticised. A decision was made by the local and regional management that a participative approach would be taken in which the relevant stakeholders would be involved in diagnosing and solving the organisational problems that were the underlying cause. As part of the change process, a series of one-day working conferences were designed in which all stakeholders took part: the local management, the regional board, the departmental managers, team leaders, nurses, medical staff, administrative and other staff, and the family council (for details see Schruijer, 2006). Initiatives that were developed during these working conferences were to be enacted in between the conferences and reported on during subsequent conference, reviewed, etc. The consultant (second author) helped to design and execute the four working conferences, each having its own theme.

The first working conference was intended to come to a shared understanding of the organisational difficulties and the potential causes (after the consultant had held a series of individual interviews throughout the organisation, the results of which were distributed to all employees before the first conference). The second conference was aimed at developing a joint vision for the future, the third one at developing action plans for how to get from where they were to the jointly formulated desired future, while the fourth one reviewed the experiences and the actions that had been taken thus far in the context of the change process.

The main activity of the second working conference, arriving at a shared definition of a desirable future, consisted of creating a three-dimensional home in which it was "good to live and good to work", to be created using clay, paper, tape, paint, and anything else that could be (legitimately) taken from the premises. This activity was to be executed in heterogeneous sub-groups. In the end, around ten homes were built. These homes were subsequently discussed in plenum, where the constructing group first listened to the observations, fantasies, and associations of the others, and after that were asked to provide their ideas, intentions, and wishes regarding their home of the future. The discussions were put into the formulation of a shared vision during that same working conference.

Initially, the sponsors had been sceptical regarding the use of creativity exercises during the whole change process ("You are not going to ask us to work with clay, are you . . .?"). Yet, they had consented to incorporating a village-like exercise. On the day itself, there were hesitations and laughter before the groups actually started doing the work. However, as the morning that was dedicated to this activity progressed, groups really got excited and worked very hard, with intense intra-group discussions, in building their pieces. The plenary discussion and the different elements put forward became part of the joint vision that was developed that same day. At the end of the working conference, the consultant naïvely thought of cleaning up and doing away with the constructions so as to leave the place clean for the conference premises. The participants came immediately to the rescue of their homes. They were carefully placed in their cars.

It was a great surprise for me to see them in the home the next time I visited them. They were all displayed in the main hall of the care home, for every staff member, resident, and family member to see.

Over time, notes with comments were added, photographs, and poems. They told me that visitors were escorted to the table and were being introduced to all the changes that were going to happen as they were building this new home, which was to be a nice place to work and live. They were not there yet, they explained, reflected in the differences between the constructed homes, but they were on their way. This comment, as well as the display, aired a sense of enthusiasm, pride, and also a sense of insecurity, as the future was not known.

Looking back at the exercise, it can be said that asking the participants to build something three-dimensionally helped individuals who were not so comfortable with putting ideas out into the open, maybe because they have different personalities, were less verbally inclined, had difficulties expressing their thoughts in a large group, or in a group where a regional director or the medical director was present. After initial hesitations, the members in the heterogeneous groups engaged in a "constructive" conversation across their functional and hierarchical boundaries. The plenary discussion was much more reflective and careful, yet provided a set of shared elements that were to be the basis of the joint vision. Some participants seemed surprised by what aspects the observers could pick up, aspects the building group was not conscious of at the time (while constructing), but appeared to be very pertinent. The fact that their constructions were meaningful to them became clear in the display of the houses in the central hall of their building. Over time, elements were added to the houses and visitors were shown around, all of which can be taken as indications that these homes referred to a joint and meaningful experience regarding their collective change process. It became a kind of reference point, while also allowing differences to exist and new thoughts to emerge, which could be added to the constructions.

Transitional change

Looking back at our experiences, we come to understand "the village" as a design to facilitate transitional change in people and their organisation.

In the 1980s, the late Harold Bridger introduced the notion of transitional change in his work with organisations. He came to see the relevance of the normal psychic processes, observed by Donald

Winnicott in children, for changes even in adult life. Later, Gilles Amado took a leading role in bringing the notion and processes under the attention of scholars in organisational behaviour and managers (Amado & Ambrose, 2001).

The notions of *transitional object* and *transitional phenomena* come from Winnicott (1951), a British psychoanalyst and paediatrician. He observed that very young children play with their special pet, a teddy bear, a rabbit, or a preferred toy. From his observations, he inferred that the special pet seemed to take on different representations and functions. The teddy bear could at one time be a comforter to soothe the baby to sleep, or bring some peace, and at another time the bear would be punished for bad behaviour, put in a corner to be picked up later and comforted, fed, or mothered. He conceptualised the teddy bear as a *transitional object* (it could as well be a special toy, a tune, or any other *special object*) that bridges and makes contact possible between the individual psyche and the external reality. Experiences, real and/or fantasised, become part of playing with that external object. In this way, the transitional object creates room for mental processes of becoming able to accept differences between "me" and "not me". The "me" fantasised as omnipotent (being hungry and being fed) and the "not me", that is, the outside world with an independent existence (the mother figure is not always around to provide immediate satisfaction). It also enabled the discovery of similarities in the "me" and the "not me": the joy of being cuddled and to cuddle, the need to be cared for and to care. In playing, the child could master in a way some of its experiences and fantasies, give up some omnipotent illusions in favour of learning to act, to do things that change the external world. In so doing, the child learns and develops as a human being.

Bridger recognised similar transitional phenomena among adults during organisation changes. He identified three different, but related, types of transitional processes:

- relinquishing earlier and dysfunctional, but still valued, roles, ideas, and practices;
- creating, finding, or discovering new, more adaptive and feasible ideas and ways of thinking and acting;
- coping with the instability of the changing conditions, both outside and within the organisational system, and with a sense of insecurity arising from it (Ambrose, 2001, p. 14; Bridger, 2001).

If such processes were prevented or did not take place, people seemed to face some serious difficulties. For example, illusory thinking overruled realistic thinking, making people believe that the old ways are still relevant, or the merging of managers and employees with the organisation, thereby making it difficult to separate the self from the "not me", e.g., the external world of the organisation (simply believing that if I, the manager, change my thinking, so will the organisation). The latter can only be affected through action, not wishful thinking. And last, a kind of loss of identity, as habitual practices that were successful in the past have to be given up.

Transitional space, then, came to refer to the *conditions* provided to enable human beings to work through the tensions of moving from the past to a future that is only partly known and largely imagined. As more studies, in various settings, became published, we were able to specify the most important, minimal conditions facilitating transitional processes of change (Amado & Vansina, 2005). It is important, however, to realise that one can create these minimal conditions, but one can never *make a person engage in transitional change processes.*

Minimal critical conditions enabling transitional change

First, a good enough *climate of safety* must be created to allow the inner world to emerge and reveal itself in thoughts, images, actions, artefacts, and words. Some of these elements of the inner self might be quite conscious; the meaning of others might escape awareness.

Second, some minimal structures that provide *time and space* for reflection, insight, and discovery while checking reality as it reveals itself in intersubjective exchanges and objective data. In other words, time and space to reconcile the inner and the outer world.

Third, the presence of the *time dimension* in the issues under discussion to enable the persons involved to work through the *tensions* in the present between the past (e.g., partial and whole experiences, learnt responses, gratifications, and mental frames) and the future (partially known, largely imagined, anticipated, or "willed"). Working through is often done in reviewing ways of working in the past and exploring and inventing new ways of functioning that are thought to improve the performance of the system and the life of those involved. It includes processes of giving up some advantages and benefits enjoyed in the past for anticipated benefits in the future and accepting unavoidable, anticipated costs for oneself and significant others.

Fourth, the provision of a *good enough cover*, or a vehicle with an external *raison d'être* (a possible transitional object), to make it easier for the persons concerned to reveal their inner feelings, fears, negative fantasies, silly and valued gratifications. At times, a kind of "playfulness" is displayed as boundaries between fantasies and reality become blurred.

In the process of reorganising General Motors Antwerp from a highly hierarchical and functionally differentiated organisation to a structure encouraging team work, we faced endless debates. Not so much about the socio-technical changes, but about the reduction of the number of restaurants (one for managers, one for white-collar employees, and one for blue-collar workers) and the standardisation of various forms of work dress (each distinguishing various categories of specialists). Beneath these discussions, we could recognise working through processes of the deeper anticipated problems in working with less social status and fewer functional identities. The restaurants and the work dress had become a vehicle (transitional object) to facilitate healthy psychic work (Vansina, 2008, pp. 133–134).

These minimal conditions facilitate transitional change to take place. The transitional change processes are *not created* by these conditions, but *enabled*. The processes themselves are operative in that broad space between consciousness and unconsciousness. There is no need to bring transitional phenomena to awareness; in fact, such interventions hinder and might even stop these healthy processes.

Let us take another look at the design of our self-expression exercise.

"The village" can be seen as both a transitional space and a transitional object. A *transitional space* to the extent that it offered a set of conditions as "time and space" to reflect and express oneself, exposing the tensions between how one experienced oneself and one's aspired being in the community, and the time provided to bring the two closer together: in other words, to reconcile one's inner and outer world. The "village" also became a *transitional object*. The concept of a village itself triggers twilight images, tatters of a romantic place of togetherness and peace, and/or a confining situation of rules and rituals. It is an imagined community. It came to represent the community of the training programme and, in a symbolic way, the desired or willed family-owned company. The latter was still a blend of aspirations, intentions, and imagined states of being and working, yet had been awakened to some impossibilities of working together in that way. However, some steps were spotted that would enable the move from the past to a more satisfying future, a future for them to realise in their everyday situations.

The individual, self-created representations can be seen as transitional objects, allowing members to express themselves more freely, even those things that could not be put in words, and to learn about themselves, their inner wishes and fears. The care members devoted to making and handling their object, the feelings with which their objects were eventually modified and taken away, and the way the members talked about their object and those of others are a clear indication that the self-created representations had become a part of them—not their whole self, but neither simply a lump of clay, or a piece of cardboard.

In working through the inevitable tensions between the past and the aspired future, the consultants had to pay attention to maintaining the constructive tensions for realising a willed future, bringing shortcuts (such as just removing the door of the house without any elaboration) and easy escapes in a non-real world to awareness. The end of the programme often strengthens such tendencies by the wish to "end in beauty". However, life in the real world goes on.

Finally, "the village" was and is not a magic exercise. It enables transitional phenomena to emerge, but it does not create them. The context in which transitional space is created may not be underestimated. If people do not feel safe enough to expose themselves, or openness is considered a weakness, the minimal critical conditions are insufficient. Furthermore, management might not even grant permission to try to create them.

References

Amado, G., & Ambrose, A. (Eds.) (2001). *The Transitional Approach to Change*. London: Karnac.

Amado, G., & Vansina, L. (Eds.) (2005). *The Transitional Approach in Action*. London: Karnac.

Ambrose, A. (2001). An introduction to transitional thinking. In: G. Amado & A. Ambrose (Eds.). *The Transitional Approach to Change* (pp. 1–28). London: Karnac.

Bridger, H. (2001). The working conference design. In: G. Amado & A. Ambrose (Eds.). *The Transitional Approach to Change* (pp. 13–160). London: Karnac.

Hjelholt, G. (1963). Training for reality. *N.T.L. Human Relations Training News*, 7: 4.

Schruijer, S. (2006). Research on collaboration in action. *International Journal of Action Research*, 2(2), 222–242.

Vansina, L. (1971). Sensitivity training binnen de organisatie. In: H. Buntinx (Ed.), *Geëngageerd Leiderschap* (pp. 99–113). Rotterdam: NIVE, Universitaire Pers Rotterdam.

Vansina, L. (2008). Psychodynamics: a field of study and an approach. In: L. Vansina & M.-J. Vansina-Cobbaert. *Psychodynamics for Consultants and Managers* (pp. 108–155). London: Wiley-Blackwell.

Winnicott, D. (1951). Transitional objects and transitional phenomena. In: *Collected Papers: Through Paediatrics to Psychoanalysis* (pp. 229–242). London: Tavistock, 1958.

CHAPTER EIGHT

Feedback or reviewing: a conceptual clarification of the differential impact on human beings and work systems

Leopold Vansina

C ompared to reviewing, feedback is an old concept. It is widely used in various fields, ranging from the training of athletes, development of motor skills, and conditioning of the autonomous nerve system to the changing of human behaviour in social or organisational settings. This chapter is restricted to the latter domain. It is an attempt to conceptually clarify the differential impact of various forms of feedback and the more recently conceptualised process of "reviewing" on (a) human beings and (b) improving the functioning of work systems.

The notion of feedback was originally borrowed from physical systems and cybernetics. A thermostat is a good example of such a feedback system, in which information about the output is returned to the heating system to trigger self-corrective action. When it was applied to individuals and groups, it became rapidly evident that the results were ambiguous in generating self-correcting behavioural change. Human beings form a complex whole. Change in one part of a person might unintentionally lead to change in other parts or areas of behaviour, especially in parts that are socially recognised as desirable and productive. For example, vehemence might be experienced as upsetting. Unfortunately, efforts to control it might turn a highly involved person into a passive co-worker. Furthermore, one discovered from experiences in "T-groups", and later in "sensitivity training", that the impact of feedback was a function of the *quality of the process* of giving and receiving feedback. In short, it was a function of the quality of the *relation* between sender and receiver. These findings, enriched by the insights from psychotherapeutic practices, led to the specification of conditions required for the process of giving and receiving feedback (e.g., Culbert, 1967; Cummings & Worley, 1993; Porter, 1979)

During past decades, the attention paid to understanding *why* a person behaves in a particular way in a given setting, and the care for *enabling insight* and *working through*, has largely been eroded by an emphasis on quick and simple feedback: *providing information* about one's impressions and observations, either directly ("I see you as . . ."), or indirectly (through questionnaires). Helping an individual learn from others and supporting him in his attempts to develop or "improve" becomes subordinated to "having told him" and making the focal person *comply*. This is most evident in structured 360° feedback. Here, human understanding and respect become socially obliterated. It often appears to be a form of collusion between managers' relief to see an alternative method that eliminates the difficulty of face-to-face individual performance appraisals on one hand and commercial interests of consultants on the other. Furthermore, such feedback procedures can easily be outsourced. External consultants take over, formulate a procedure to mobilize direct colleagues and bosses to evaluate the focal person and process their questionnaire responses to be fed back to the focal person. Beneath the surface, the 360° feedback method turns one's colleagues into a social pressure on the worker to make him/her behave as a willing instrument in the production process. In this way, "managing people" is moving one step closer to becoming the management of "instrumentalisation" and "individualisation".

The 360° method and individual feedback are based on the conception of the behaviour and performance of a human being as being the simple outcome of a person's free will. It is as if the socio-economical conditions of the organisation and management have no impact on individual performance. Or ,one takes it for granted that the current practices and systems are perfectly adjusted to the changing conditions. If they are not, it is because there are no alternatives.

The notion of "feedback" originated in the largely individualistic culture and behavioural tradition of North America (Vansina, 1970). "Reviewing", on the other hand, is a notion grounded in the psycho-analytically inspired work of the Tavistock Institute in London. It refers to a process of *reflective exchange of experiences* by the members of a work system *about their own way of functioning* and *the relevance of the work system's task and objectives* in changing conditions. Are the system's tasks and objectives still relevant, or should one be doing other things to survive in turbulent times? Eric Trist (1987) and Harold Bridger saw reviewing as an essential process in any work system to safeguard effective work under conditions of uncertainties (Amado & Ambrose, 2001). Amado and Sharpe (2001) conceived of "reviewing" as a necessary ingredient in transitional change. A few years later, the *process* of reviewing and its requisite conditions were elaborated to help managers and consultants in their practices (Vansina, 2005). Its relevance is gaining importance in modern organisations where changes require people to abandon their skills in doing "what they know how to do" for working on unfamiliar grounds, figuring out answers to "what we don't know how to do" and subsequently engaging in *new ways of doing things*. Learning to *reflect-in-action* on the progress one is making, and the courage and capability to *adjust or invent* actions to achieve goals, become requisite to success.

In the 1960s, the University of Michigan in Ann Arbor introduced Survey Feedback (Likert, 1967; Taylor & Bowers, 1967) to inform work systems, departments, and organisations as to how their employees perceived their work unit in its actual functioning, often along with how these people wished the system to be functioning. Here, too, the *system*, not an individual, became the object of feedback, albeit through the statistical elaboration of members' individual responses. The statistical distance between the actual and the desired functioning of the system was conceived as the strength of the need for change (Nadler, 1977).

The purpose of individual feedback, reviewing, or survey feedback, might be presented in terms of change, development, appreciation, or simply learning from experience. The chosen label reflects a concern to make the process acceptable to the people involved, more than it points to fundamental differences in the practice. Learning, however, might turn into *happy or unhappy learning* (Ketchum & Trist, 1992). Learning feels pleasant when it is experienced as "making progress". Happy learning is additive; it is an extension or refinement of already mastered knowledge and/or skills. Unhappy learning, on the other hand, takes place when one is confronted with experiences or information that trigger a "reorganisation of one's values, beliefs, axioms, theories and models that together make up one's personal paradigm, which has been built up slowly through one's life experiences. These form an essential part of one's identity" (Ketchum & Trist, 1992, p. 43). Unhappy learning often involves "unlearning" and a reworking of one's inner world, which is that mental space wherein personal representations of the external world, such as persons and objects, "live" and interact with each other and with one's expectations and experienced capabilities (I have added here "experienced capabilities" to the Kleinian conception of the inner world). In addition, information that normally leads to happy learning might be experienced as unpleasant when it unintentionally shakes a person's sensible roots.

In this chapter, I compare the more popular and general notion of *feedback* with the more specific process of *reviewing* in an effort to highlight their differential impacts on human beings and their learning and change.

I concentrate first on the focal unit: an individual person as opposed to a work system. Then I describe the major differences in the underlying socio-psychological processes of transforming feedback into actual change.

The unit of targeted change

Individual feedback

Whenever one speaks of giving feedback, one intends to modify the behaviour of an *individual*. The targeted change concerns the individual, either as a person (e.g., sensitivity training), or as an actor in a temporary group (e.g., a training, study, or learning group) or in a more enduring work system (e.g., a management team). The focus is on the individual, either as a person or as a person in a particular role, working on a given task.

Taking the individual as the unit of change implies a basic belief that the individual is an *all-autonomous, living entity*, as if there is a solid boundary around the individual person that separates him from the influences of the rest of the world. The person is conceived as living an isolated existence, socially and physically. This highly questionable conception of the individual person is periodically put forward in political discourses. Margaret Thatcher claimed that only individual persons, not communities, exist. More recently, the Tea Party in the USA blazes the same message. However, most striking is the absence of any scientific support for these claims.

As noted earlier, individual feedback rests on the explicit conviction that sharing information about how a person is perceived by others enables him or her to change accordingly through *conscious, personal efforts*. However, do we not know that this is only partially true?

A person does not become a human being through his biological givens only. He becomes human as he is raised in a human environment. In the process of growing up, he establishes relationships and comes to identify meaningfully with others. That process does not end with adulthood. It continues throughout life. In fact, a human being *is* his relationships with others, whether these are worked through or not. They are part of his inner world and part of his responses to the outer world. Requesting change in these responses often implies modifications or adjustments in the inner world. The latter are, psychologically speaking, more difficult to modify. They require time and space for "working through", or, in other words, for reworking parts of the inner self. The inner world, however, is to a great extent *unconscious*, although parts might become accessible through reflection. A person might strive to change how he thinks about himself, but without a reworking of his inner world—the core of his self-image—those changes remain cosmetic and temporary. They might even appear as phony and inauthentic, like a pessimist pretending to be an optimist through imitation.

Furthermore, individual feedback focuses, not always knowingly, exclusively on the *psychological* dimension of human behaviour. Thereby, it minimises, even denies, the impact of the social and physical context. The social aspect is only used as an important variable to strengthen the *forcefulness* and/or *validity* of the given feedback. In 360° assessment, the feedback informs the individual how all (or several) members of his work system (boss, peers, and subordinates) perceive him. These impressions and observations are presented as the average rating, within a given range, on the provided, standardised items. Most often, however, the measurements do not meet the statistical requirements to produce valid feedback (Toegel & Conger, 2003). Nevertheless, the procedure builds up social pressure to comply, with or without personal understanding or "insight".

The *validity* of the feedback is considered to increase with the number of people that share the same impression of the focal person. This claim is far from being a universal truth. There is a considerable amount of scientific evidence that a variety of socio-psychological processes reduce the accuracy of interpersonal perceptions and their reporting. Statistical processes neither eliminate these inaccuracies nor increase the validity of the feedback. It is sufficient to mention a few distorting processes here, such as stereotyping, myth fabrications, shared and implicit personality theories, attributions, collective projections, and other social and psychodynamic group processes (for example, Bion, 1961; Forgas, 1985; Pines, 1985; Vansina-Cobbaert & Vansina, 2008).

The behaviour of a human being is a *personal* response to an experienced *socio-physical context*, as Kurt Lewin stated more than half a century ago. Why is it, then, that so many managers and consultants become addicted to structured feedback and prefer to work exclusively on the psychological dimension of human behaviour? This runs counter to the ample evidence that human beings behave differently when put in a different work setting or a changed context. Are managers inclined to think that their organisation and its structures, technologies, procedures, management systems, and social context should not be questioned, because they are good enough? Is it that structural change is felt to be more cumbersome to realise than the psychological elements in human behaviour, or is it a cop out?

What about consultants? Are they more than eager to collude with their sponsors because it relieves them from the complex and stressful work of exploring the interactions between human beings, work, and the organisational context? Are their competences and interests limited to a feedback instrument or other impoverished forms of process consultation? Either way, one thus maintains the regrettable division where managers are responsible for the business and psychologists or consultants keep people happy and engaged, regardless of the realities in their working lives.

Based on all the requisite conditions described in the literature, three things are often neglected for an effective process of giving and receiving feedback. These are (a) a trusting relationship between the receiver and the giver(s) of the feedback, (b) a genuine willingness of the receiver to learn and to improve his or her behaviour, and (c) time and space to understand the feedback, allow it to soak in, and to engage in a "working through" process. These conditions are most frequently discarded in the popular forms of feedback provided through impersonal questionnaires, often filled out by "faceless", anonymous invitees and processed like a high-school report. The meaning of the outcome must be discovered without clarification, while a trusting relationship is absent.

In structured feedback, the *direction* of the "wished" change is almost implicit: a person scores lower or higher than the "average", whatever that statistical average might mean. It is the combination of that deviation from an "average" and the social pressure inherent in the coherence of the respondents that is supposed to motivate the person to change in a particular direction. In qualitative feedback by group members, guided or not by positive psychology, the direction of desired change is often made explicit. This might take the form of (a) wishes to engage more or less in certain activities, (b) changes in interpersonal interactions to become a more pleasant, collaborative member of the team, or (c) changes in a number of personality features, habitual patterns of responding or ways of taking action to become more effective, likeable, and/or more content with oneself. Here, the social pressure includes subtle, even unconscious appeals: for example, to be liked. How all this "feedback for change" is to be realised is left to the individual.

Reviewing

The process of reviewing is based on a *self-reflective* study of *one's experiences* of a temporary or more enduring work system in action. In a face-to-face setting, the actors reflect on and recount their *experiences* in the system, and not just impressions or factual observations. Experiences are subjective. They include implicit meanings that reveal parts of the inner world and feelings of how the work system affected the member. Yet, the *work system* is the unit under review.

Trist (1990) regularly emphasised that a work system is a social system with a mixture of more than just psychological and social factors: it is characterised by techno-structural factors that also have an impact on the task, group efforts, and choice of system objectives.

The experiences of the members embody the conscious and unconscious influences of all these factors (social, psychological, and techno-structural) and their interactions. Some factors might be felt to be central, others more peripheral, or might even be completely excluded from the conscious experience and verbalised attributions. Some members might emphasise or explain the functioning, for example, in terms of socio-psychological or techno-structural terms. An outside observer, or members who take sufficient distance, might spot elements of the culture of the work system in the offered self-reflections, or the impact of other factors that have escaped awareness. After further exploration, they might become subjects for directed improvement actions.

The aim of reviewing is twofold: (a) to learn from one's own and other members' recent experiences in the work system; (b) to improve the functioning of that system to achieve its objectives and the purpose of the organisation under changing conditions and uncertainty. Taking improvement actions is an essential part of the reviewing process. Such actions are initiated from within the work system. They are built on the internal commitment of its members.

As pointed out earlier, the unit of study is the work system. Individual members or actors in their respective roles become subject for review only to the extent that this is relevant for the functioning of the system. What is commanding attention varies with the flaws and difficulties experienced in the functioning of the system. In general, three broad, overlapping and interacting domains can be distinguished: (a) experiences related to the work done to achieve task accomplishment (called task work), such as work methods and strategies; (b) experiences of working together on the given task while coping with fields of tensions (called team work); (c) the exploration of experiences related to the actual relevance of the given task and objectives to realise the organisational purposes. The socio-psychological dimension figures only as one among the many that are explored with an explicit interest in making the system more effective.

Survey feedback

Here, too, the *unit of study* is a work system, a department, even an entire organisation. Yet, the actors report their opinions about the working of the system concerned by means of standardised questionnaires rather than a face-to-face situation. The individual data can statistically be processed in relevant categories (e.g., top, middle, and lower management and roles in staff functions *vs.* management roles), or relevant organisational units (encompassing or connecting systems), thereby providing a "sociological face" to the feedback and facilitating a better understanding of how the total system feels, thinks, and wishes to be functioning.

The most marked difference between *survey feedback* and *reviewing* is that in the latter, the boundaries between the actors and their work system are much more *fluid*. Are the members talking from their position in the system, or is the system part of the members and "talking" through them? In narrating their experiences, they willingly or unwillingly reveal their inner worlds containing the work system or parts thereof (with probable elements of idealised and incident-based experiences) that have become internalised. In other words, the information and affective colourings might well be a property of both the members and the work system. In survey feedback, the boundaries between the actors and the system studied are more neatly maintained. The emotional quality of the data, however, is largely eliminated through statistical processing. By subsequently presenting the data on a screen or a piece of paper *to look at and respond to*, it becomes further externalised. Consequently, the processes of transforming information into improvements will be somewhat different. One has to move from talking *about* the system, as if one is not a part of it, to owning one's responses in the explorations for improvement. The fact that the survey specifies and, thereby, restricts the content of change to the domains covered by the pre-established questions has the benefits of focused change, but it might not be the one most needed.

Transforming information into change

Individual feedback

A face-to-face setting has the potential benefit of sensing the quality of the relationship, checking the willingness of the receiver, and staying in touch with the responses in the process for the persons involved. The qualified sender might take time to help the receiver gain "insight" and explore with the receiver what can be done and what social support may be provided to sustain his change efforts. Space can be created to respond to questions and to attempts to understand, to clarify misunderstandings, and to deal with emotions, resistances, and anxieties. In short, there is an opportunity to engage in a genuine helping process (Schein, 2009) and to relate personal impressions and observations to specifics in the context. Regrettably, the willingness to create these appropriate conditions is often absent. Exploring the links between the psychological dimension in the feedback and the wider, multi-dimensional context becomes difficult. Too often, the recipient is left alone to "work through" the feedback and manage the required change in his work context for sustainable improvement. In this sense, individual feedback is a failing attempt to transform a person into a "change agent", in the old-fashioned meaning of that role. This is usually the case when feedback, teambuilding, outdoor exercises, or group relation seminars are organised outside the real context of the work system without devoting time and space *during* the conference to facilitate the transition from a temporary learning system to the real world of work. Some examples of how minimal conditions can be designed into conferences and management development pro-grammes to enable transitional processes to take their course are described in *The Transitional Approach in Action* (Amado & Vansina, 2005).

Individual feedback through standardised questionnaires (e.g., 360° feedback) almost always takes a less human course. The respon-dents' impressions and observations are fed back in an impoverished form of averages and ranges with a *deceptive added quality of absolute, objective accuracy*. There is no room for questions, elaborations, and "contextualisation" of the feedback, since the respondents are most often anonymous and, as such, not accountable. The focal person is deprived of any opportunity to check the *meaning that he gives* to the ratings. It is also impossible for him to *verify* his own fantasies and assumptions of why he was rated in this particular way: was it envy, leniency, an incident-based rating, or was it based on a habitual way of behaving? The respondents cannot learn from their intentions, biases, and context either. As such, standardised anonymous feedback carries with it an asocial "Weltanschauung" that infests the relations within an organisation or institution. Is it not incredible that most business schools simply pass on these values of lack of openness, respect, accountability, and enquiry to their students by requiring them to make anonymous evaluations of their teachers on standard-ised questionnaires? Does it implicitly, or even openly, entice faculty members to become popular with their students? What room is left for "unhappy learning"?

The importance attached to anonymity drives consultants to erase the "sociological faces" of bosses, peers, clients, and subordinates by averaging the scores. In 360° assessment, the potential to appreciate differences between categories of respondents, which is crucial to understanding the dynamics of the workplace as a whole, is destroyed. Furthermore, recipients are *left alone* to make sense of the given feedback, and digest and transform it into improvements. Some organisations do offer coaching sessions following the instrumented feedback; however, the results of a large empirical study regarding the effectiveness of this are complex and not very encouraging (Smither, London, Flautt, Vargas, & Kucine, 2003). Could one expect anything better? First, the company hires some consultants to admin-ister the feedback in which the employees are treated as *objects*. Subsequently, one hires the same or another consulting firm to repair the damage done through coaching!

In both face-to-face and structured feedback, the focal person is placed in a setting to learn from the experiences of *others* with him, rather than from his own experiences. Self-discovery is basically restricted to the experiences of what one has "done to" others under the codified label "feedback". *Learning from experience* does not cor-rectly describe this particular process. Too often, the emphasis is more on pleasing others in what they want you to be than on becoming more of your real self.

Reviewing

In reviewing, the whole process of transforming "feedback" into improvements of the system evolves over three overlapping phases. They follow a logical course and direct members' attention to the recollection of experiences in the *recent past*, the removal in the *here-and-now* of manifest socio-psychological obstacles in working together and understanding the underlying systems psychodynamics, and, finally, planning of changes in the techno-structural design of the work system to improve its effectiveness in *the future*. In each phase, specific mental processes are activated.

In the first phase, an observer might be struck by the similarities of the socio-psychological processes at the start of the review with those in giving individual feedback within a work group. In both, indeed, time and space are provided for sharing and comparing experiences, based on impressions, observations, and/or factual data. However, these similarities might prevent us from seeing major differences.

In reviewing, primary importance is given to *self-reflection* and sharing one's *experiences* in the group. Inviting people to collect their thoughts silently before engaging in a review enhances self-reflection. Gilmore (2006), citing Rothman (2003), underlines the importance of silence. Silence "enables people . . . to form their thinking independently rather than having it shaped by what others said". The *self-reflection* mode makes room for *self-discovery*, or insights in one's own experiences, possibly triggered by listening to those of others. This is quite different from paying full attention to what others are telling about me as the focal person. Observations and factual data, included in the narratives, are not essential. They only facilitate the understanding of one's experience by comparing them with those of others in the system. In addition, these experiences are not focused on an individual member, but on *the work system itself* (task and/or team work). Here, it is the work system, not a temporary group, that holds and contains all the exchanges and explorations. They become part of the system's history.

The process of comparing experiences, hunches, and impressions is not a search for finding sameness or similarities. On the contrary, sharing and comparing are phases in a process of exploring *differences* among the members. The finding out of differences in experiences has two important potential benefits. Exploring differences is not a search for who has, or what is, the most accurate or valuable experience, but to become aware of the wide range of perspectives, which might be complementary or contradictory, or qualify the weight given to anyone in particular, and to shed light on suitable levers for improvement actions. In short, they are highly valuable for understanding the complexity of work systems that are composed of multiple factors. The sharing of experiences enables others to recognise differences from theirs. They might learn to value and live with differences. Comparing offers opportunities for reading and exploring the behaviour of others, their emotional and intentional responses in or to the system. This kind of finding-out enables members to enrich their "mentalization capacity" (Fonagy, Gergely, Jurist, & Target, 2004). Mentalisation, here, refers to an assumed mental capacity to perceive and interpret behaviour in terms of intentional states, to imagine what others are thinking and feeling. A mental capability is of great importance in social and working life.

In addition to becoming aware of the differences in experiences, the sharing and comparing enables members to gain awareness of some discrepancies between their "organisation-in-their-minds" and the organisation (work system) operating in front of them.

> 'The organisation-in-the-mind' refers to 'what the individual perceives in his or her head of how activities and relations are organised, structured and connected internally. It is a model internal to oneself, part of one's inner world, relying on the inner experiences of the interactions, relations and activities I engage in, which give rise to images, emotions, values and responses in me, which may consequently be influencing my own management and leadership, positively or adversely . . .' (Hutton, Bazelgette, & Reed, 1997, p. 114, quoted by Armstrong, 2005)

It is the sedimentation of experiences in the inner self, built up over time about one's work system or organisation. To a great extent, these remain unconscious, but emerge in a member's behaviour and, thereby, might become accessible to outsiders. While working in the "here-and-now", members themselves might be surprised that the organisation in front of their own eyes seems to function and respond differently than expected. The healthy, human drive to stay in touch with the realities around him makes it possible to notice existing discrepancies between the *organisation-in-the-mind* and the *organisation-in-action*, as I have called it elsewhere (Vansina, 2000). This kind of self-discovery, by itself, might instigate some corrective rework. Efforts from outsiders to draw attention to possible discrepancies might not even be needed.

The work done so far has resulted in a rich plate of experiences, personal insights, and a variety of thoughts about what went well and what did not. From the whole of this data, several diagnostic views usually emerge to be dealt with in the second phase. Some could point to personal, interpersonal, or psychodynamic issues, others to more techno-structural imperfections in the design of the work system. Issues that have an obvious dominant psychological component are dealt with first. Time is taken to correct possible misunderstandings, to talk through painful experiences, to remove, or, at least, reduce, disturbing influences and tensions, and to repair the hurt done to the members in the course of hurried work. In other words, time and space is created in the "here-and-now" for "working through", for repair, and for enabling some re-working of members' inner worlds. It often happens that in this process some psychodynamics emerge or re-emerge in the here-and-now that have been disturbing good work from beneath the surface. They need to be recognised and dealt with, either directly or indirectly, by making appropriate changes in *the design of the system* itself. When these socio-psychological obstacles are cleared to a satisfactory degree, one can begin to tackle the techno-structural and design issues.

The third phase almost always calls for different skills, methods, and mental states. Consequently, the transition from phase two to three is not easy. The more reflective stance, proper for dealing with socio-psychological issues and underlying psychodynamic tensions, must make room for a much more cognitive mental state of aware-ness, known as a problem-solving mode. Some members might find it difficult to leave the highly personal involving work behind to explore the techno-structural factors and the actual relevance of task/objec-tives of the work system. Others might too quickly search for factors outside themselves to explain their functioning and that of the system, thereby avoiding or minimising their personal role in these difficul-ties. The reflective and the problem-solving mental modes alternate and are all too often complementary. If one does not deal with the socio-psychological ones first, they could continue to obstruct further serious work. However, without improving the techno-structural conditions, the socio-psychological changes and good intentions will be hard to sustain. Often, we see that appropriate socio-technical and structural modifications also reduce the field of tensions in the system and provide a good base for sustaining the earlier achieved socio-psychological improvements.

The rethinking of *the relevance of the task and objectives* of the work system to achieve purpose under changing conditions appeals to one's strategic mental capabilities, a combination of creativity and mental capacity for long-term thinking (Jaques, 1998). The request for a strategic revision then comes from the actors in the system, but the redefinition of task or objectives requires the agreement by management at a higher hierarchical level. For all changes that extend beyond the boundaries of the system, one remains dependent on these other instances in the wider organisation. However, reviewing makes it easier to gain commitment from the members of the system (they are, in fact, the agents of change) to implement the suggested techno-structural changes within their own work system.

Concluding comments

Individual feedback rests in general on the false beliefs that the individual is an *autonomous agent* and that a person can change his behaviour on request, through simple *willpower*. Social support and modifications of his context to sustain behavioural improvements are generally absent. Learning from one's personal experiences is minimal. Worse, there is no time and space in the procedures to understand what is and has been done to him in the feedback exercise and to his confidence in management. Not surprisingly, the employees largely ignore 360° feedback as a management fad.

In its conception, reviewing is a more humane and effective way to help a work system and its members improve than individual feedback, either instrumental or personal. Time and space is created for self-discovery in one's own experiences, inner worlds, *organisation-in-the-mind*, and differences in emotional and cognitive responses of members. Reviewing installs, even institutionalises, a climate of genuine learning from experiences. The group does not simply provide information, but helps to understand and support improvements along the socio-psychological dimension by introducing changes in the techno-structural design and definition of its own work system.

Survey feedback is basically a device to mobilise energy to change a department, a function, or another part of the organisation. The statistical processing of the answers of a pre-established questionnaire can be done in such a way that the various hierarchical and sub-systems acquire a *sociological face* that helps the understanding of the organisation as a complex system rather than as a monolithic big group. It compensates, in doing so, for the statistical erosion of members' engagement.

I close with a note of caution. Reviewing, along with some other forms of feedback, shares the confounding feature of retrospective interpretation. Most often, reviewing takes place, rightly so, after the members know the outcomes of the system's performance. Consequently, the causal attributions of what made the team successful or not are coloured by this knowledge. The correctness of the attributions and subsequent problem-solving efforts can only be found in the actual improvements in and of the work system.

Reviewing can genuinely be called "learning from experience". That kind of learning carries its inherent tensions and anxieties, not only for the person chairing the review session, but also for everyone involved in the learning from the process.

References

Amado, G., & Ambrose, T. (Eds.) (2001). *The Transitional Approach to Change.* London: Karnac.

Amado, G., & Sharpe, J. (2001). Review as a necessary ingredient in transitional change. In: G. Amado & T. Ambrose (Eds.), *The Transitional Approach to Change* (pp. 119–136). London: Karnac.

Amado, G., & Vansina, L. (2005). *The Transitional Approach in Action.* London: Karnac.

Armstrong, D. (2005). Organization in the mind: an introduction. In: R. French (Ed.), *Organizations in the Mind: Psychoanalysis, Group Relations, and Organizational Consultancy* (pp. 1–19). London: Karnac.

Bion, W. R. (1961). *Experiences in Groups and Other Papers.* London: Tavistock.

Culbert, S. A. (1967). The interpersonal process of self-disclosure: It takes two to see one. *Explorations in Applied Behavioral Science, 3.* New York, Renaissance Editions.

Cummings, T. G., & Worley, C. G. (1993). *Organization Development and Change.* New York: West.

Fonagy, P., Gergely, G., Jurist, E., & Target, M. (2004). *Affect Regulation, Mentalization, and Development of the Self.* New York: Other Press.

Forgas, J. P. (1985). *Interpersonal Behaviour: The Psychology of Social Interaction.* New York: Pergamon Press.

Gilmore, T. N. (2006). Briefing notes: silence in the service of development. *CFAR,* Philadelphia.

Hutton, J., Bazalgette, J., & Reed, B. (1997). Organization-in-the-mind. In: J. Neumann, K. Keller, & A. Dawson-Shepperd (Eds.), *Developing Organizational Consultancy* (pp. 478–498). London: Routledge.

Jaques, E. (1998). *Requisite Organization.* Arlington, VA: Cason & Hall.

Ketchum, L. D., & Trist, E. (1992). *All Teams Are Not Created Equal: How Employee Empowerment Really Works.* London: Sage.

Likert, R. (1967). *The Human Organization: Its Management of Value.* New York: McGraw-Hill.

Nadler, D. A. (1977). *Feedback and Organization Development: Using Data-Based Methods.* Reading, MA: Addison-Wesley.

Pines, M. (Ed.) (1985). *Bion and Group Psychotherapy.* London: Routledge & Kegan Paul.

Porter, L. (Ed.) (1979). *Reading Book for Human Relations Training.* Arlington, VA: NTL Institute.

Schein, E. H. (2009). *Helping: How to Offer, Give, and Receive Help.* San Francisco, CA: Berrett-Koehler.

Smither, J. W., London, M., Flautt, R., Vargas, Y., & Kucine, I. (2003). Can working with an executive coach improve multisource feedback ratings over time? A quasi-experimental field study. *Personnel Psychology, 56*(1): 23–44.

Taylor, J. C., & Bowers, D. G. (1967). *Survey of Organization. A Machine-Scored Standardized Questionnaire Instrument.* Ann Arbor, MI: Center for Research on the Utilization of Scientific Knowledge & Institute for Social Research, University of Michigan.

Toegel, G., & Conger, J. A. (2003). 360-degree assessment: time for reinvention. *Learning & Education, 2*(3): 297–311.

Trist, E. (1987). Keynote address. Einar Thorsrud Memorial Conference on Industrial Democracy, Oslo.

Trist, E. (1990). Culture as a psycho-social process. In: E. Trist & H. Murray, *The Social Engagement of Social Science: A Tavistock Anthology, Vol. 1: The Socio-Psychological Perspective* (pp. 539–545). Philadelphia, PA: University of Pennsylvania Press.

Vansina, L. (1970). Sensitivity training or laboratory methodology in Western Europe. In: S. Mailick (Ed.), *Newer Techniques on Training* (pp. 56–62). New York: United Nations Institute for Training and Research.

Vansina, L. (2000). The relevance and perversity of psychodynamic interventions in consulting and action research. *Concepts and Transformation, 5*(3): 321–348.

Vansina, L. (2005). The art of reviewing: a cornerstone in organisational learning. In: G. Amado & L. Vansina (Eds.), *The Transitional Approach in Action* (pp. 227–254). London: Karnac.

Vansina-Cobbaert, M.-J., & Vansina, L. (2008). Defensive processes and behaviour. In: L. Vansina & M.-J. Vansina-Cobbaert (Eds.), *Psychodynamics for Consultants and Managers: From Understanding to Leading Meaningful Change* (pp. 68–86). Chichester: Wiley-Blackwell.

CHAPTER NINE

Conversations on work

Kenneth Eisold

W ork is indisputably now our most important human activity. It is not only how we continuously build and rebuild our world, it has become our major means of knowing and valuing ourselves. Today, not only do we support ourselves financially through our careers and our jobs, but we also derive self-esteem from our competencies and construct identities from our skills. Our jobs are the primary way we have of locating ourselves in the world, the means we have of knowing ourselves, and being recognised by others.

When work is not going well, this can be a profound problem. Difficulties on the job can undermine our sense of ourselves. There are the obvious issues when one's abilities do not match the requirements of the job, but today businesses are being constantly restructured to become more competitive or to adapt to changing market conditions. As a result, a department might be outsourced or combined with other departments. On a larger scale, the company itself might be transformed as the result of a technological innovation or a dramatic shift of global supplies, or it could be taken over or merged with another company.

For these reasons and others, having little or nothing to do with competence or performance, not only can employees be let go, but

managers who have worked diligently to streamline their departments and make them more efficient will be re-engineered out of their
jobs. Executives will be reassigned as priorities change. As Jack Welch
famously observed, "Loyalty has no place in business." Constantly
seeking new ways to be more effective and profitable, businesses are
looking to reduce salaries and benefits. Or a new boss takes over a
department and replaces long-standing employees with others he has
worked with before.

Over the past few years, I have been approached by a number of
senior executives and managers to help them think through changes
in their careers, often as a result of such developments. Or they have
approached me for help when they want to make career changes for
their own reasons. Success in their jobs has propelled them to become
more ambitious. Sometimes chronic dissatisfaction has led them to
believe they would be more fulfilled in a different career.

My work with them could be seen as a form of coaching. Unlike
coaching, however, it does not target the job and the client's ability to
become more effective and efficient. It looks more generally at the
client's relationship with the world of work. It could also be seen as a
form of psychotherapy, as it often seeks to uncover hidden assumptions or motivations, but it does not presume the existence of a personal problem, or any form of psychopathology. It often resembles
advice, but actually I seldom suggest any particular course of action.

I use the term "conversation" to describe these consultations
because, in part, that is exactly what they feel like. Informal, interac-
tive, they are unpredictable and range widely from exploring personal
histories to reviewing professional issues. I feel free to draw upon
whatever I know that might be relevant to the topic at hand. Such
"conversations" aim to open up reflective space between my clients
and their jobs, to enlarge their capacity to think, and help them
develop a greater understanding of the choices that make those jobs
intrinsically worthwhile—or not.

As a psychoanalyst, I have been trained to work with the complexities of individual behaviour, to detect hidden motives and disguised
meanings. I have also been fortunate to study organisations and work
with executives on the difficulties they encounter in taking up their
roles managing complex systems. Years of participation in group
relations conferences have given me a deep appreciation of the interaction between organisational roles and the persons occupying them.

Moreover, those conferences schooled me in grasping the importance of authority in the workplace, both for those who exercise it and those struggling to accept it.

To be sure, there are others, like myself, who, by the accidents of their own careers or interests, have come to know many of these same things, both about managing organisations and understanding individual conflicts and motivation. And there are many others who have a highly developed intuitive sense of both sides. On the other hand, it can be dangerous if practitioners presume to know more than they actually understand, and introduce into their conversations with clients clichés or unfounded opinions.

There are three guidelines I have come to identify as essential to such "conversations", three principles I continually bear in mind as I am engaged with a client.

Tactfulness. It is essential to keep the conversation safe. Clients have to trust that you have their interests at heart, and that you do not aim to criticise them or make them feel inadequate. To accomplish this, you need a well-developed sense of the client's vulnerabilities.

Sensitivity. I believe you have to hear and understand what the client is saying, and sometimes that is not at all apparent. Inevitably, he or she will get into areas that arouse anxiety and confusion. Your job is to penetrate the surface that has become temporarily opaque, carefully identifying matters that need clarification, offering suggestions as to possible meanings, but not foreclosing the exploration of what you both need to understand.

Focus. While allowing the conversation to range broadly, I find it critical to maintain a clear sense of our joint objective. I do not need to keep reminding the client of it, and it will be often useful to allow or even encourage clients to let go of their pressing need for answers. It can be useful to explore tangents. However, I do believe I need to keep clearly in mind myself what the underlying issue is and how the topic at hand relates to it.

I hesitate to call these principles a method. I value the informal and interpersonal qualities of these conversations. My experience has made it abundantly clear that the process is dialectical, seemingly contradictory at times. Discredited ideas can emerge in a new form. Firm beliefs can turn out to be inadequate or wrong.

I also do not want to presume to position myself as an "expert", the one who knows. It is vital to maintain a personal, "human" contact, to allow and even encourage liveliness and spontaneity. There are sure to be moments that are humorous and those that are tearful, though it is not my aim to emphasise or uncover strong emotions. We explore important relationships for the light they shed on the client's underlying beliefs or entrenched behavioural patterns. The goal is practical understanding, insights that enhance the making of choices.

Let me give a few examples. One client, a successful mid-level executive in a firm of estate agents, faced the abolition of his job when the division he had led for several years was merged with another. Recognising his effectiveness as a manager, his company offered him several other positions, as well as a generous grace period in which to search for alternatives. At that point, he approached me to help him think through the future direction of his career.

As David reflected on his strengths as a leader as well as what he had found most engaging and rewarding in his work, he told me he had experienced particular gratification out of helping others to advance in their careers. As a manager, he made a point of keeping his door open, and was proud of being available to talk with subordinates about their problems, making sure they felt recognised for their accomplishments. When I asked him where that side of him had come from, he reflected on his role as the youngest boy in a large family. Following the divorce of his parents and a period of turmoil, in which his schoolwork had suffered, he not only developed the discipline to apply himself to his studies, but also found gratification in taking on a quasi-parental role, helping to manage conflicts between his parents. As a result of his own erratic grades, he had not gone to a top college, as had most of his colleagues in his firm, but with hard work and discipline, as well as an engaging, friendly manner, he had none the less risen through the ranks.

When we shifted to talk about areas of disappointment in work, he spoke of being hurt and upset about fellow executives who not only failed to credit him for his accomplishments, but sometimes tried to take credit themselves. He believed that as the result of such backbiting he ended up being the one edged out of his job during the firm's reorganisation. He was not so much bitter about this as rueful about his difficulty in dealing with the ambition and self-centredness of peers. But even more important, his own strong moral sense made him feel that such unethical behaviour profoundly corrupted the culture of a firm, eroding the co-operation and trust essential to long-term performance.

Not surprisingly, that was a significant factor in his evaluating the other jobs that were now available to him in the firm, but as we talked about his reluctance and fears, another thought gradually emerged, the idea of starting his own company to fill a niche that he saw emerging in the market. Minimising the idea at first as risky and challenging, it gradually became his most attractive option. Increasingly, he could see himself engaging in the necessary conversations with others and making the decisions that would be required. We talked about the concrete steps needed to implement the idea, the people he would want to hire, the risks along the way.

At first, in thinking about recruiting others to work in this prospective firm, he speculated that perhaps he would find others more qualified to be the CEO of his new firm. But as I prodded, he came to see that to get others on board, he would need to present himself, unambivalently, as the leader of the project. They would need to feel his confidence in the project and his willingness to engage it directly. Furthermore, as CEO, he could develop a team to work collaboratively with him, and that would allow him to draw upon the leadership skills of others to supplement his own. Over the course of several months, his ideas coalesced, and he went on to recruit a team of senior executives to fill the essential roles. The respect and good will he had earned over the years in the industry proved invaluable in getting others to work with him.

Had I been in the role of his therapist, we could have spent much more time on the origins of the insecurities that led him to think another might have been a better CEO. Had I been his coach, I might have helped him analyse the role of CEO or, even, helped him think through the steps of recruiting someone to fill the job. My role, however, was to help steer him through his own thought processes and arrive at a course of action that felt right for him. My clinical judgement helped me to see that, most probably, he could develop the necessary confidence as he got more experience, and that he would learn what he needed to know about the CEO role that he did not already understand. His hesitancy about taking the role of CEO himself was grounded in some residual insecurity that stemmed, I think, from his growing up the youngest boy in his family, his poor grades in school, and the fact that he had been looked down upon by colleagues who had gone to better colleges.

Another client, Yvette, came to see me as she was struggling with her role in a boutique firm in the fashion industry. She felt over-worked and stressed by her responsibility for keeping the firm afloat, and it did seem as if she was exceptionally good at managing sales and overseeing special projects. Intelligent and attractive, she readily picked up what others were thinking. Speaking with a slight French accent, in a hurried manner, as if she did not have much time to think, she proved to be highly insightful, in fact, and quick to grasp the new ideas.

I learnt that she had invested a substantial portion of her own money in the firm, at the urging of one partner in particular, and her anxiety about that contributed to the pressure she felt to make the firm successful. But it also chained her to the firm and made leaving it feel impossible. She was furious with her partner in the firm, who had so willingly taken her money and now refused to return it. But she also blamed herself for having so naïvely put herself in that position.

It soon became apparent, as we talked about her family of origin, that, growing up, she had been the glue that kept her family together. Her father, after divorcing her mother, virtually disappeared, eventu-ally leaving the country, while her self-absorbed mother went through a series of relationships with other men and struggled ineffectually to keep things together. There had been many relocations, often taken at short notice, during which Yvette functioned as a kind of head child, a mother substitute who tried to manage her siblings and plan ahead. She worried where the next meal was coming from, and how it would be prepared. She also acquired the habit of always keeping her things packed in a suitcase, ready to go.

These experiences lay behind the urgency she felt in her current role. But the chief thing that came across to me from this account of her childhood was the absence of the stability that would have allowed her to know what she actually wanted for herself. Her contin-ual focus was on being adaptable and caring for others. To be sure, she suffered from a profound sense of insecurity and craved financial stability, but she tended to drop everything to respond to the needs of others. She harboured the hope that, as she cared for others, they would care for her, but this led more than anything to a recurrent sense of betrayal, as she could not discriminate well between those who were reliable partners and those just desperate for help. When she had time for herself at weekends, she tended to hole up in her apartment, avoiding contact with others who might seek her help, as she sought to restore her depleted energy.

We did not dwell on this as Yvette easily saw the parallels between her current situation at work and her past, though she was amazed to see how thoroughly she had enacted them. She grasped how vulnerable she was and sought my help in working out how to extricate herself from the company where she worked. We quickly saw that the more important problem was for her to develop a better idea of what she herself wanted. We could have excavated the sources of her false hope in helping others, but now it felt more important to see that the roles she had tended to take up at work were often ways that neglected her own interests and needs. That was both too easy for her, based on her family identity, and too difficult, as she could not easily establish boundaries between the needs of others and her own need to be of help.

In Yvette's case, reconnecting her to work was complex. Satisfying customers was not actually the main source of the pressure and dissatisfaction she felt. The larger issue was the fact that the identity that sustained her role as the provider for the needs of others was clearly fraying. As we continued our conversations, it became clear that she had engaged in an implicit bargain with her business partner: she rescued him with her money and, in return, expected recognition and loyalty. This was the bargain that had sustained her in her family, and supported her identity. Her partner, however, felt no such obligation. It was the desperation and anguish she felt in this situation that had actually brought her to me for help.

After clarifying the "betrayal" of her partner and her need to sustain the identity as the glue that held her family together, we went beyond the problems with this job to the larger issue of work. I learnt that she had acquired a degree in philosophy at the Sorbonne before starting her career in fashion. She spoke of her degree with an odd mixture of diffidence and pride. On the one hand, she saw it as a real accomplishment. On the other, she seemed to view it as almost an accident, as if uncertain she possessed the intellectual skills it obviously had required. Exploring this further, she revealed that she was also fascinated by psychotherapy, and thought it would be exciting to study psychology and the complexities of helping people to change. No doubt the emergence of this idea was influenced by our work together, but she had thought of it several times earlier as a challenging puzzle, akin to what had engaged her in philosophy, but of greater human benefit.

The prospective identity of therapist built upon her family role as the one who helped others and held things together. At the same time, it required a degree of detachment and choice that could preserve her from being exploited. As we discussed what she might do to pursue this interest, she met and fell in love with a successful, older man who worked in a related field. Excited by the prospect of having a child—an idea she had not previously mentioned—she focused on establishing a relationship with him based on mutual care. This was not easy, but eventually she was able to establish a way of devoting herself to him and, in return, allow him of offer her the attention and love she craved.

Our work has been complex, often with an emphasis on goals that clearly were personal and therapeutic. Yvette's work history showed too great a willingness to engage with the needs of others, without adequate attention to herself. Had we neglected that, any career choice she made ran the risk of being grounded in an unreflecting repetition of the past and an inadequate self-understanding. I thought, in fact, that her interest in psychotherapy might well have been influenced by her desire to please me. As a result, I was careful in supporting that goal to be aware that it might well change, that the experiences of marriage and motherhood might well lead to other choices. Fortunately there was no rush. We continue to meet and talk, and I feel no pressure to push her into making a career choice. In other words, again, I maintain the focus on her relationship to work, not to any specific job.

Both Yvette and David were highly effective in their jobs, while feeling competent and gaining a sense of self-worth. Both were also engaged in building upon and revising their identities through their jobs. At the same time, the discontinuities of the financial and the job markets threatened their security and ability to sustain their identities. David's job had been abolished. Yvette's own money had gone into her firm to rescue it from a temporary downturn in the economy. As an investor, now, she found herself handcuffed to the other partners and felt trapped and enraged.

Conversations helped both to think through the dilemmas they faced. David's solution was to become, in effect, his own boss. That did not insulate him from the ups and downs of the economy, but it did offer him the gratification of being helpful and nurturing to others while having more control over the competitive work relationships that angered and disturbed him. Yvette's solution was a more radical rethinking of her identity, beginning a process of self-reflection on her deeper values and interests. Getting married and becoming pregnant gave her more real and appropriate relationships in which she could gratify her need to care for others while also providing a kind of moratorium to rethink and explore alternative careers.

My third example, Kevin, illustrates how such conversations can help in negotiating the stresses and uncertainties of a difficult financial environment. A highly successful executive in a public relations firm, Kevin came to see me initially as he was troubled by the anger he often felt in responding to subordinates, often losing his temper. This was usually when he was presented with inadequate work, sloppily put together and insufficiently thought through. He did not question his judgement, but felt, rightly I think, that his anger undermined the confidence of his direct subordinates without helping him get the level of performance from them he was after.

Kevin soon revealed his ambition to start his own firm based on a creative new idea, and he worried that his problem in curbing his temper would be even more of a problem under those circumstances. For some time, he had been putting aside money and keeping his eyes open for potential clients and colleagues, but just as he quit his job and launched his firm, the financial crisis of 2008 hit. Virtually every business in the country was cutting back drastically, and few were looking to expand their PR budgets. Moreover, their willingness to go with a new, untested firm was surely compromised, though he did have an impressive track record.

He forged ahead, aware of the increasing difficulties presented by the economy, yet believing he could pitch his services to potential clients as a way for them to gain competitive advantage in a declining market. He was not wrong in this, but in the beginning he could not fully appreciate how stressful this would be in this recession and how much longer than he had initially planned it would take to establish his new enterprise on a profitable footing.

At about the same time, Kevin's father died unexpectedly. A highly successful lawyer, his father represented the professional and financial achievement Kevin longed for himself. And there seemed little question that those achievements were within his grasp. His career in public relations had been stellar. Not only had he risen through the ranks, but he had also established strong relationships with colleagues and clients, impressed by his drive and accomplishments.

His life had not always looked so promising. Earlier, in school, he had been an indifferent student, more interested in pranks and sports than in his studies. That behaviour had led his father to taunt him mercilessly and call him "stupid". He felt certain his father loved him, but he was, none the less, haunted by his father's words, all the more as his older sister excelled at her studies.

Our conversations dwelt on this legacy as we explored Kevin's anger. He was disturbed by his tendency to erupt at subordinates when they turned in what struck him as inadequate or sloppy work. Gradually, it became clear that his anger largely stemmed from the pressure he had learned to apply to himself to overcome his earlier indifference to schoolwork as well as the underlying fear that perhaps, after all, he was not as bright as he needed to be. Having struggled to turn himself around, he resented subordinates who did not make the effort he had made himself, who were willing to settle for less than they were capable of achieving.

The problem with his anger became a little better, but it shifted somewhat into anxiety and self-doubt as he gradually began to fear his own ability to sustain the effort required by his new enterprise. As clients were harder to find than he had originally thought and slower to make commitments, the firm grew more slowly than he had hoped. To be sure, it was never in danger of failing. That itself was remarkable under the circumstances and a vindication of his original creative vision as well as the hard work both he and the colleagues he recruited put into it. But he felt the strain, and the strain in turn made him increasingly anxious, which, in turn, led to a renewal of his outbursts of frustration with co-workers.

Our conversations then began to uncover the importance of the fact that his father had suffered several "breakdowns" when Kevin was younger, retreating to his bed for months at a time. These were frightening, as they shook the security of the family and, on one occasion, led to his father having to sell their family home and move them into lesser, though still comfortable, quarters. Now, as Kevin recalled these events, he remembered that his father attributed these "breakdowns" to overwork and stress. In our conversations, it quickly became apparent that he feared the stress of his own work would lead to his having a comparable "breakdown".

At my urging, Kevin spoke with his mother to get a fuller picture of these events. To his surprise, he found that his father had actually suffered from manic depression, and the episodes he remembered were actually bouts of depression as his father rebounded from manic episodes in which he had not only drove himself to overwork but also overspent to the point where he had to retrench.

The effect of this revelation was dramatic. Quickly, most of Kevin's anxieties about stress lessened, as he saw that while he did have realistic worries about the business, his fears of suffering his father's fate were unrealistic. He continued to be occasionally troubled by outbursts of temper, and he had to struggle to control them as he saw the negative impact they had on the performance of his subordinates and colleagues. But now he could see them as more normal expressions of his temperament and the real pressures of managing a new business in a highly competitive environment, not to mention the additional stresses of coping with his own growing family. The solutions now, however, became the more standard ones of taking time off, working out at the gym, delegating more responsibility. And our conversations have been able to turn to the more normal issues of being the primary owner of a small but growing business.

All three clients had quite different anxieties. Kevin's were embedded in his identity as an ambitious and successful executive, but not revealed until he actually began functioning in his own firm. They presented as excessive anger that embarrassed him and interfered with his employee relations. David's anxieties were more about his ability to perform on the level he needed, not only to succeed but also to be a credible leader to other executives he needed to recruit. Both were able to modify them to be more effective. In Yvette's case, her anxiety functioned as a signal of a real danger she faced as the result of a strong identity that led her to help others too readily, ignoring information about the people she trusted. She required a more radical rethinking of her assumptions about who she was.

All three of these clients exemplify the larger points I made earlier about the dilemmas of work today. They had all struggled to prove themselves, having built confidence and self-esteem through their ability to discipline themselves and develop skills. Moreover, they had created identities, building upon earlier identity formations in their families, enabling them to establish a strong sense of what roles they could fulfil in the world, distinguishing themselves and setting them apart from others. They had come to know who they were, and they had developed a sense of purpose that enabled them to establish work relationships with others.

All, I believe, exemplify the value of conversations in creating a space to examine their particular dilemmas, linking together an understanding of weaknesses inherent in their identities, flaws exposed as they engaged the pressures and uncertainties of today's workplace. But the dialogues also enabled them to think freshly about their places in the world of work, rethinking their goals in the light of a better understanding of both themselves and the opportunities open to them.

I would like to link these three cases to a larger understanding of how work is changing now. These cases are a small sample, but they do reflect how talented and capable workers are thinking about and responding to the crisis.

Today, competence and effectiveness in those jobs is not only uncertain of rewards, as the jobs are transformed in response to rapidly changing competitive conditions, the very existence of those jobs is threatened by economic circumstances that workers have no control over—and no say in changing.

Not surprisingly all of my clients responded to their experience of this turmoil by leaving the job market. Two decided to establish their own businesses. One currently aims to be a self-employed professional. That is by no means an inevitable effect of my approach. I do not believe I am encouraging this trend of thought, but neither does it come as a complete surprise.

Kevin had made his decision early, as he rapidly rose though the ranks and gained a sense of his own potential capacity. David arrived at it as he considered the alternatives. The uncertainties of the job market made that solution more attractive than finding another job. For both of them, the promise of greater control over their own careers as well as more independence and a greater scope for success were decisive.

Yvette was motivated by similar considerations in her very different choice. The idea of being a self-employed professional was attractive not only because it gave her more control over her time, but also because it made her less dependent on others. She trusted her own ability to find clients more than she valued the seeming security of holding a job in a firm where she would be dependent on others.

To be sure, this is a small sample. However, given the speed at which companies reorganise, downsize, re-engineer, or are taken over today, the fact that the security they offer is compromised has become more and more apparent. It is easier to trust your own ability to adjust than put your fate in the hands of others to deal with the uncertainties of the market.

This might also shed light on the extraordinary growth of executive compensation and the exorbitant golden parachutes that have become standard among higher-level executives. Given the volatility of the financial system, the insecurity of job tenure goes far to explain why those who can will want to insure themselves as much as possible against losing their jobs, making sure that they will have more control over the process. Such contracts might not only serve to discourage the dismissal of the executive, but also leave him with resources adequate to pursue other kinds of work, purchasing another firm or setting up a foundation or charity to which he can devote himself and around which he can rebuild and sustain a new identity.

A number of students of organisational behaviour have argued—in the face of long-standing conventional wisdom—that organisations have to de-emphasise the role of money as the primary motivator for higher performance, particularly when work demands thought and creativity. A strong case is being made to build rewards into the workplace that are intrinsic, that give workers more control over their work, more autonomy over their schedules, more engagement with each other and determination over their output. The importance of this is more obvious with the knowledge workers, who must bring innovation and creativity to their work, but it is increasingly seen as relevant to all workers, regardless of the level of complexity of their tasks. This way of thinking is still a minority view, though its influence is growing.

> For artists, scientists, inventors, schoolchildren, and the rest of us, intrinsic motivation—the drive to do something because it is interesting, challenging, and absorbing—is essential for high levels of creativity. ... As the economy moves toward more right-brain, conceptual work ... this might be the most alarming gap between what science knows and what business does. (Pink, 2011, p. 46; see also Amabile & Kramer, 2011)

The effect of that would be to provide some insulation for the workplace from the job market, at the very least, to encourage companies to balance their commitment to their shareholders with their commitment to workers. The net effect would be to mitigate the long-standing insecurity of work, and make it far easier for workers to sustain the inclinations to loyalty and friendship that are an inevitable part of long-term work relationships. To be sure, the dynamics of capital might still make it attractive for employees to branch out on their own in order to establish their own enterprises. But businesses less prone to discarding employees in restructuring themselves are more likely to benefit from their ambition. Less driven to protect themselves, employees are more likely to put their new ideas in the service of the organisation they know, the organisation that supported them as they developed their competencies and creative new ideas.

Following the credit crisis of 2008, there is interest now in reforming capitalism, finding ways to moderate the virulence of its emphasis of profit which leads not only to exaggerated swings in stock prices and business cycles but also destructive relations to workers (Barton, 2011, Sabeti, 2011, Streeck, 2009).

But while we are waiting—and hoping—for capitalism to reform itself and become more humane, we can help individuals to widen the scope of their thinking and cope with the uncertainties of the job market.

References

Amabile, T., & Kramer, S. (2011). *The Progress Principle*. Cambridge, MA: Harvard Business Review Press.

Barton, D. (2011). Capitalism for the long-term. *Harvard Business Review*, March.

Pink, D. H. (2011). *Drive: The Surprising Truth About What Motivates Us* (Chapter 2). New York: Riverhead Books.

Sabeti, H. (2011). To reform capitalism, CEOs should champion structural reforms. http://blogs.hbr.org/cs/2011/10/to_reform_capitalism_ceos_shou.html.

Streeck, W. (2009). *Re-Forming Capitalism*. New York: Oxford University Press.

CHAPTER TEN

Enacting one's way to new thinking: using critical incidents to vitalise authentic collaboration and learning

Thomas N. Gilmore and Nora I. Grasselli

Introduction

T he work of developing one's leadership at all levels has become a major imperative as critical shifts have taken place in the wider culture away from hierarchy towards networks, from top down to widespread engagement with greater emphasis on innovation and creativity. Yet, we also need to take much more personal responsibility for our development in the flow of our work as well as in formal leadership programmes, and in both with richer links to the real work challenges. As Vansina suggests, people "need other trusted persons to open up self-confined reflections, and to enrich their perspectives to appreciate trends and practices" (this volume, p. xxiv).

E. M. Forster famously reminds us "Only connect" in his epigraph to his novel, *Howards End*, which takes up the challenges of human relationships across different identities and life perspectives. In response to the turbulence surrounding organisations, members have become more ginger, more guarded, reducing authentic collaboration and learning. Paradoxically, when we need more honest feedback and help, it has become harder to get it both in specialised development experiences and in the flow of work. This chapter describes the power of writing and working with critical incidents (Argyris & Schon, 1974) that link interpersonal dynamics with substantive stakes as a vehicle for learning about and from other and self and about the wider context. This method—in both formal development sessions and in the flow of work—can increase the ability to make sense of ambiguous situations, have richer responses, and the ability to enact them even amid the stress in ways that deepen authentic connections among the participants.

There has been a significant increase in "action learning" elements in development programmes where teams have real projects on which to apply some of the new tools and frameworks with attention to the team dynamics. However, even with projects, leadership development experiences still face the following biases.

Leadership development and business education may be overemphasising analysis at the expense of interpretative capabilities. Lester and Piore (2004) recommend that business schools

> actively stress the differences between the two approaches (analysis and interpretation) and highlight the conflicts between them, and discuss how they can be managed. [We need] to give students the skills that come through literary criticism, historical perspective, language learning, and artistic achievement—the kinds of humanistic, holistic studies that broaden and deepen interpretative capabilities. (p. 187)

More leadership writing suggests the power of linking to performance arts, the use of language, story telling.

There is too much emphasis on diagnosis and suggesting interventions as opposed to actually producing them. An analogy would be teaching tennis by having students observe a match (analogous to the case description), critique a shot selection, and suggest a better one without actually trying the recommended shot. Pfeffer and Sutton (2000) have flagged this as the "knowing–doing" gap between analytical insights about what to do and the inability to enact the recommended behaviour. A simple example is the large gap between the advice given, when doing performance appraisal discussions, to first "create a non-defensive climate" and the challenge of actually doing so. In voicing challenging interpersonal dynamics, we make aspects of our being more visible.

There is not enough attention to the development of emotional intelligence and to unconscious aspects of leadership. Empathy, listening, joining, and working with feelings (Goleman, 1997) all have become essential for both well-being and for creating sustainable value from our work. Winnicott (Phillips, 1988, pp. 12–13) writes,

> A sign of health in the mind is the ability of one individual to enter imaginatively and accurately into the thoughts and feelings and hopes and fears of another person: also to allow the other person to do the same to us.

The predominately cognitive frames in many of our interactions do not welcome exchanges in which one participant gives feedback as to the impact of the other on him or her. Yet, we know that we all have blind spots (Luft, 1969) that are not known to self, but are known to others.

There is too much external coaching of individuals as against engaging with both the key participants in challenging situations and the substantive issues. The growth in external coaching has reduced the responsibility we have to one another to "work through" difficulties, to stay in contact, to make sense of frustrating experiences, and learn.

Our unawareness of the discrepancy between "espoused theories"—what we say is our influence style or leadership practices—and what we actually do ("theory in use") (Argyris & Schon, 1974) prevents experimentation and learning to improve our effectiveness. In this chapter, we note the power of peers in a development experience or informally using critical incidents to see and experience viscerally the discrepancies and to modify their approaches accordingly.

Traditional case teaching cycles between diagnosis and proposed actions. Enactments (Grasselli & Gilmore, 2013), both in traditional case teaching and even more powerfully with participant critical incidents, can help close the "knowing–doing gap" (Pfeffer & Sutton, 2000) through playing out scenes and getting feedback on impact and effectiveness (Figure 10.1).

In this chapter, we explore how participant-written critical incidents can serve to help one "act one's way to new thinking", as well as gain insights as to their blind spots—all in the context of real stakes in the effectiveness of some aspect of their work. Enactments are

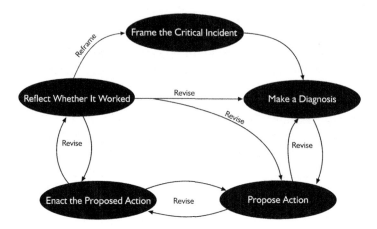

Figure 10.1.   Action–learning cycle.

powerful. Minuchin and Fishman (1981, p. 78) write, "Inner self is entwined inextricably with social context. They form a single unit. To separate one from the other is . . . to stop the music in order to hear it more clearly".

Yet, we need to acknowledge the felt risks in moving from proposing actions to their enactment. Stanley Milgram, famous for his experiments on authority, was curious about a cocktail party hunch that New Yorkers were rude. He assigned his Columbia students to ask strangers for their seats on crowded subway trains without giving a reason. A high number in the first group felt too fearful to even make the request. To explore that finding, he tried it himself.

> Dismissing his students' fears, Dr. Milgram set out to try it himself. But when he approached his first seated passenger, he found himself frozen. "The words seemed lodged in my trachea and would simply not emerge," he said in the interview. Retreating, he berated himself: "What kind of craven coward are you?" A few unsuccessful tries later, he managed to choke out a request. "Taking the man's seat, I was overwhelmed by the need to behave in a way that would justify my request," he said. "My head sank between my knees, and I could feel my face blanching. I was not role-playing. I actually felt as if I were going to perish." (Luo, 2004)

In this chapter, we overview a component of a consulting and coaching programme that worked with real critical incidents that link interpersonal dynamics with substantive stakes. This challenged both faculty members and participants to take the risk of showing, not telling, in ways that make learning more visceral and deepen relationships.

The executive participants were asked to develop, in advance, a short write-up of a *critical incident*: "an actual encounter or challenging episode, one where you doubted your effectiveness or where you felt frustrated and less successful than you felt was possible". (See Appendix A for a write-up of the request.)

As Schon (1983) has noted in the context of professionals learning on the job, we learn most from situations in which we are both surprised and do not get what we want (Table 10.1).

This framework shows how often that it is only in hindsight, after people have not got what they wanted, that they understand insights about their tacit—and often unrealistic—expectations. Too often, when disappointed, we externalise the reason for the failure to get what we want as about the other ("fundamental attribution error"). Only when we let the disappointment in do we then develop richer strategies resulting from disappointment and surprise. In the state of being puzzled, frustrated, one is ready to explore alternative

Table 10.1.   The role of surprise and learning.

	Not surprised	Surprised
Get what I want	*Low learning*, one's core skill.	*Low learning*, because one gets what one wants whether one attributes it to luck (hence no learning) or to one's skill, but rarely do we reflect when we have achieved our desired results.
Don't get what I want	*Low learning*, high externalisation of the reasons why we were unsuccessful. The constraint was immovable, the politics were all against it, etc.	*High learning*, yet an uncomfortable place to be. What went wrong? Why did it not turn out the way I expected? What might I have done differently and with what possible result?

approaches and to reflect on one's default patterns under stress—for example, to talk too much, to withdraw, etc. Zaleznik (1967, pp. 59, 61), in a classic article on leadership, notes,

> men who want power and responsibility are especially vulnerable to episodes in which reality does not conform to their wishes or intentions . . . these episodes [of disappointment] may be occasions for accelerated personal growth . . . If disappointment and the pains attendant on it are denied or otherwise hidden from view, the chances are great that the individual will founder on the unresolved conflicts at the center of his experience with disappointment.

The requested critical incidents are not at the level of major life setbacks that Zaleznik is exploring, but do involve real intentions with outcomes that disappointed them and they are still puzzled as to why. This keeps the link between an interpersonal frame and real stakes.

Following the instructions received in advance (see Appendix A), each participant has to make decisions about what episode to explore, reflecting over their frustrating experiences, having to revisit whether they really could have been more effective, or was the outcome over-determined. Thus, even the request for a critical incident where one was disappointed in a supportive climate creates a beginning for working through.

Once they have set on an episode, they have to bracket the incident: when did it begin and end? Who are the actors? What information about the context is relevant for understanding the complexity of the case? This is active practice in pulling for help from others, a concrete instance of E. M. Forster's advice to "only connect" when we too often withdraw or commiserate with colleagues rather than learn. It also builds a key skill for getting useful help: being able to frame a situation quickly with the right amount of detail. This framing of the critical incidents adds an important element to the participants' learning.

When given a request to write cases that contain experiences that were frustrating or unsuccessful, feelings of shame might be evoked. The learner's anxiety is increased: how will my incident compare with others? How will I appear in front of my fellow learners in this slice-of-life situation? If used in company development programmes, there can be political complexities of revealing issues about leaders that are known to one's classmates as well as the challenges of confidentiality. We discuss strategies to deal with this later in the chapter.

In our experience, faculty members need to anticipate two responses—a minority of participants not doing a case, or submitting a thinly masked case in which the case writer was actually effective. Yet, as we will discuss, both of these can be occasions of learning about self and others as the engagement with the critical incidents deepens.

In addition to student anxieties, faculty members also have to deal with not knowing the case as well as the case writers sitting in the room; not having a fully applicable theory, not having "the answers" to critical incidents as they most probably would for a published case study. The deeper anxiety is not knowing whether the cases will "work" as learning vehicles. Can the faculty members create a climate that is "good enough" to contain the emotions that might be stirred up? These all add an edge and a level of realism to the engagement with the mix of peer anxieties and dynamics with the faculty.

Using participant-based cases for learning

The critical incident work with enactments is composed of the following steps.

Pre-session

1. Setting the ground rules and eliciting the critical incidents (see Appendix A for the request).
2. Faculty analysis of all the critical incidents and selecting one or two for full group exploration and getting the case writers' permission to use their cases (we have never had them not agree).
3. Assigning participants the common case for the full group and 3–4 additional cases of peers to review, along with tips for reading cases—see Appendix B. We recommend participants to "pencil-read" the cases—that is, to underline words, imagery, analogies, and sentences that they found intriguing or important and write comments in the margins with their questions, hypotheses, or emotions/experiences while reading the case. Nabokov (1980, p. 3) has advised readers of novels in ways that are relevant to approaching others' cases:

[O]ne should notice and fondle details. There is nothing wrong about the moonshine of generalization when it comes after the sunny trifles of the book have been lovingly collected. If one begins with a ready made generalization, one begins at the wrong end . . . we should . . . study that new world as closely as possible, approaching it as something brand new, having no obvious connection with the worlds we already know.

Note that the frame here is to enter one another's cases with a minimum of judgement (aided by knowing that others are reading one's own case) and in a more associative and interpretative frame, jotting down "hunches" or "hypotheses". Trist (2001, p. xxiii) describes a process of *tuning in* that applies both to reading others' cases and being open to others' reading of one's own case. It

involves the ability to get in touch with new situations . . . to get a feel for their texture. . . . One has . . . to make sense of it . . . in emotional as well as cognitive terms. . . . and allow it to come in contact with what is already in oneself. . . . If one's defenses are too rigid one is not going to allow this to happen so that the novel is likely to be screened out.

In the session

1. Introduction to the overall process and full group enactment to illustrate the method with the assigned common case. We have been tempted to use a case from a previous session with a different group that has been particularly powerful, but know it makes a difference for the faculty to be at risk and for the group to feel and know this is a peer's case even if the identity of the case writer is not revealed. It begins the norm of the risk taking needed to deepen learning.
2. Mini-teams are assigned to work up a set of cases in smaller groups, so that after the full group session every case writer gets a chance to engage with their narrative, each rotating through roles of coaching the overall process, engaging with one's own case, and peer coaching and engagement with other's cases.
3. An optional component is to learn from patterns in the critical incidents, especially when they are clustered within some critical

relationship—for example, marketing and production, headquarters and divisions, or within key change challenges.

4.   A summary session in how to build this mode of quick enactments into the flow of everyday work as a form of rapid prototyping to link head and heart in understanding a complex situation and acting into it, or in a reflective, after-action review to learn.

We discuss these steps and the methods for maximising learning by illustrating the process with the following critical incident that was produced in the context of senior executives in change and coaching roles participating in a university-sponsored development programme.

An illustrative case

Situation

As a family business consultant, I am working with a business founder who is preparing for retirement as leader of his highly successful manufacturing company. At present, he leads the company, together with his son, who is second in command. His son wants to take over, but is frustrated because the company's organisation is so lean that there is almost no staff between the top management (father and son) and the workforce. The son feels the need to build a team with key skills for long-term success.

My strategy

My diagnosis is that the son has a chance to succeed as the new leader if he is supported by a team in which important roles are played by a human resources director and a financial director, thus freeing the son to be more of an operational managing director. I raised the issue during a meeting with father and son.

The results

At the next meeting, the father comes up with a solution. He has contacted two "senior consultants". These are people in their sixties who have become consultants after retirement. The father argues that these people are very experienced and very cheap. In his opinion, these two "senior consultants" can substitute for the team his son wants to build. Moreover, he thinks they can act as mentors for his son.

I am totally surprised by this initiative, and do not react.

Why it was frustrating

I still feel very frustrated by this turn of events, because I know this is neither a good solution for the family business nor for the succession process. The founder actually takes advantage of my suggestion to strengthen the management team by appointing people who are close to him and probably will not help to smooth the process of succession. Taken by surprise, I did not react adequately.

Introduction to the session

The session begins with a very brief framing and moves rapidly to engaging and enacting with the chosen case to model a key practice of "rapid prototyping" as a mode of learning and getting feedback. This draws on the traditions of "socio drama"—show *vs.* tell—and improvisation, and Weick's advice:

> In inexplicable times, people have to keep moving. Recovery lies not in thinking and then doing, but in thinking while doing and in think-ing by doing. No one has the answers. Instead, all we have going for us is the tactic of stumbling into explanations that work and talking with others to see whether what we have stumbled into is in fact part of an answer. (Weick, 1995)

Enactments of critical incidents

The voluntary case writer is brought up to the front and everyone is invited to briefly reread this critical incident and their written notes on the case. Depending on the amount of time, each participant can be invited to think about the following questions while rereading the critical incident.

- What appear to be the dilemmas or issues that are the focus of this critical incident?
- Timelining: what are the key moments (either in the encounter, leading up to it, or in the follow-up) in which you think the case writer could have acted in such a way as to take the case in a very different direction? With what possible consequences to his goals? To the relationships? Why do you think those moments are the most fateful?
- What is the influence of other stakeholders who are mentioned or implied?
- What title (perhaps playful) would you give this critical incident?

We strongly recommend against a full group discussion at this time about the critical incident and/or patterns in the critical incidents. Both the faculty members and the participants can easily collude in a mutual intellectual defence, because, as Milgram noted, enactments are anxiety provoking for all. For the faculty members, unlike situations where they are using a published case, they are in new territory themselves, confronting a slice of life someone has shared and knows more about than they do.

Before enacting one or two key moments in the case, an option is to ask small huddles of the participants to select one question to ask the case writer. We suggest limiting the number of questions, as we find getting more facts is often a defence against the anxiety of taking action. Developing better questions in a coaching frame is another area of learning, as the questions inevitably imply hypotheses about the case that reveal the enquirer's frameworks. Here, we find it useful to challenge the group: "Is this a real question, or are you making a recommendation for the case writer?" Furthermore, the questions inevitably have some aspects of projection where we put some of our own edge of awareness traits into the other's case. Faculty members, taking up the role of the director, instruct the case writer not to answer action-implying recommendations, as those are better explored via the enactments than in an analytical discussion.

Faculty members can list participants' suggestions about potential fateful moments where the case writer might have acted (not yet described) in ways that could have made a significant difference to the outcome before the key episode, during the episode, or after, as follow-up. These can be placed on a timeline to engage the case writer in choosing where in the flow he or she would like to explore different approaches.

For example in the case above, it might look like the following sketch.

- Before the meeting, ensuring that the son is attending and that there is a shared agenda.
- Coaching the son to be more effective as his own advocate for this strategy rather than the consultant doing the pitch.
- Early on in the meeting, blocking too much discussion of it if the son is absent, and not mentioning the case writer's surprise.
- Following the meeting, a session with the son or with the father to reflect on why the consultant was silent and how that might link to issues of the effectiveness of the father's approach.

We recommend giving the case writer considerable authority, commensurate with the risks, and then picking the moment he or she wants to explore.

The enactment

The case writer briefly sets the scene and identifies the participants. In this instance, the meeting was in a conference room in the consultant/ case writer's office. Right away, surprises emerged. It turns out that the case writer chose not to mention that the founder's wife was present, as was a female junior colleague of his. Participants can learn from reflecting on what they consciously and unconsciously left out of their own write-ups as these are explored with the full group case, as Sherlock Holmes does with the clue of the dog that did not bark.

We recommend that the case writer initially should take the role of the key "other" whom the writer was trying to influence—in this case, the founding entrepreneur. Invite the case writer to inhabit fully the other person's role, not to stereotype it or make it deliberately difficult for the person who is playing his role as the intervener. Useful advice comes from David Mamet (1991, p. 11), the playwright and film director. He advises against trying to show "character" but, rather, to employ the strategy of "What does the protagonist want? What does he or she do to get it?" Thus, the focus is on wants that participants can identify with and can be thinking of actions to bring it about, as opposed to trying to enact the other's style or personality. This keeps the focus on purposes and the range of ways we can achieve them in interpersonal encounters.

One of the values of this work is deepening one's feelings (empathy) and insights (perspective taking) for what might be going on with the person one is trying to influence (Shell & Moussa, 2007), in essence practising Winnicott's "ability . . . to enter imaginatively and accurately into the thoughts and feelings, hopes and fears of another person" (Phillips, 1988 pp. 114–115). Because the case writer has greater knowledge of the context, he or she can lead the improvisational dynamics of the others in the scene, including the one playing the case writer's role, which is a powerful way to imagine what purposes and motivations are in the other.

We suggest that the authority to cast fellow participants in the other roles in the enactment also be given to the case writer, rather than through asking for volunteers. When the group has been together for even a short time, these choices are unconsciously influenced by transference dynamics, whereby colleagues are seen as themselves but they are also suffused with the case writer's associations to other people: parents, colleagues, subordinates, friends, clients. Thus, the selections can amplify some of the case writer's out-of-awareness aspects of the dynamics. In this instance, the case writer selected classmates to play his role, his junior associate (a woman), and the entrepreneur's wife. One should present the participants as closely as possible to the real settings: across a table, making a phone call, behind a desk, etc. When the case writer revealed that the son was not actually present, we invited him to select a fellow participant to be the son and listen to the exchange as if a fly on the wall, but not be in the enactment. One can use this strategy for other absent stakeholders to stimulate imaginative thinking about other stakeholders' possible reactions. In many cases, we have been impressed with the way the people chosen fit with the roles they are cast in.

The faculty members then iterate that they are taking up an authoritative, theatre director role, being clear about beginnings and endings and able to interrupt at any one moment to explore what the different participants might be "thinking and feeling, but not saying"—much like the Argyris and Schon (1974) method of two-column case write-ups. At this point, the enactment begins. It can be helpful to have one of the parties actually walk into the scene to begin the meeting.

Increasing risks to increase learning

When the faculty stops the enactment at an interesting moment, several approaches can be used.

- Everyone can be invited to work quietly to think about what they are observing.
- All can be asked, if they were one of the roles in the exchange, what might they be thinking and feeling, but not saying.

This takes everyone out of the spectator role and often reveals how much more transparent we are (Luft, 1969), as people can accurately read when one of the enactors is angry, frustrated, disappointed, or pleased, even when the individual might not be aware of that feeling.

The most powerful approach is to invite each participant in the class to identify a different action that might be more effective in the exchange. But, when a participant began to share these "observer insights" with the entire group, we cut him off quickly and invited him to switch with the person playing the case writer/consultant and replay the engagement from the moment that is appropriate to the suggested approach.

For example, in the family business case, when a classmate said to the person playing the consultant/case writer, "You should involve the wife," we cut him off and had him switch chairs with the consultant to enact his strategy, not tell it. He was then required to enact behaviourally his advice to involve the founding entrepreneur's wife, and they continued the enactment. Sometimes, the new tactic enacted changes the trajectory; at other times it reverts quickly to the previous stuck dynamic. Note that, as per Schon's critical incident cycle diagram, we encourage the advice-giver to jump to *producing* the intervention, rather than just sharing his or her diagnosis or strategy. As Weick (1995) notes, we often learn more by acting into the ambiguity of the situation.

Everyone can then experience how this did or did not shift the dynamics, how it affected the founding entrepreneur, and what the wife had to say. This work resembles both improvisational theatre and socio-drama (Browne, 2007). In real life, we have to build our capacity to embrace uncertainty and co-create effective exchanges that advance our purposes, as opposed to being like lawyers in litigation, only asking questions to which we already know the answers.

While still in the large group, one can invite smaller groups (perhaps the assigned case teams) to take up a key moment in the full group case and experiment with different tactics. This gets everyone out of the spectator role, but produces a safer feeling in the smaller setting with everyone working in parallel. The class can look at the patterns of the results. For example, how many achieved the result they wanted (if it was some kind of negotiation)? The key is getting people to think beyond a single response and to develop the talents that chess players exhibit, namely to think of series of moves and countermoves, anticipating three or four moves ahead in a complex and changing game (Gilmore & Schall, 1996). Participants also deepen their appreciation for the dynamic of the exchange—one asking, the other responding—and whether and how to shift the dance or invite co-orientation to some larger shared interest.

In a recent use of this process, in the full group enactment of leaders of editorial and business, there were two major paths that were explored, one confrontational and one collaborative. When the group broke into six parallel groups to explore the same case, they came up with seven different, thoughtful strategies to explore, including several that co-orientated the pair to real strategic issues that they both faced (Mant, 1983).

Below, we touch on three specific dynamics—vicious circles, gingerness, and reparation—which can be explored via enactments.

1. *Breaking vicious circles.* What creates stalemates or "escalatory dynamics" (Hirschhorn, 2002), in which both parties feel trapped, and what might be some strategies for breaking that circle? In the enactment of this critical incident, it quickly became a dynamic of the consultant asking a question and eliciting a defensive response from the family business patriarch. What might be ways to break this circle? Even developing "recipes" for doing so (Senge, 1990) can be helpful, such as "say more" and tolerating a long silence (just as a lob in tennis gives one a chance to collect one's own thoughts and yields more information). Another tactic

invites the other to jointly explore the felt stuckness. "I feel we are stuck and wonder what is your view?" This invites both to a "balcony" perspective, where they might explore the secondary gain they or others get from the stalemate. Another tactic might be to adopt the other's point of view to see how that changes the exchange. Then the enactors and observers can step back into reflective mode to explore if and how it changed the dynamic.

2. *Care-taking or gingerness.* A major inhibitor in these exchanges is unilaterally protecting the other; what Harvey (1974) has named "the Abilene Paradox", where people do not tell each other what they really want. In enactments, people can try much more direct approaches to test what might be hearable or not and often discover that greater directness brings clarity to complex situations and deepens connections.

3. *Reparation.* Rifts in families and in organisations are costly, yet most organisations are filled with ruptured relationships that have significant organisational consequences. When one builds a connection with others that guarantees staying related despite difficult encounters—that you will be there to reflect, learn, and, if possible, repair a working alliance—greatly improves speed, connection, and creativity. In the above case, there might be a difficult reflective conversation with the son, which would raise questions about who the client is and how the consultant would handle the triangular dynamics (Gilmore, 2000). Having the courage to move closer in times of stress and building one's reparative skills are critical to preventing rifts that can persist and greatly degrade the resilience of a working group or unit. Some questions to ask could be: how did we get off track? What can we learn about our dynamic of working together? In this case, what would the next meeting with the founding entrepreneur be like if the consultant wanted to reflect on the meeting where he had felt "surprised and did not react?" This tactic is powerful in breaking vicious circles of misunderstandings. We often have insights after the encounter is over (what the French call "staircase wit"—what you think of walking down the stairs after an anxiety laden meeting), but we often do not take the next step to see how we might productively engage others with these afterthoughts. It is more likely that one will gossip and complain about the absent other to one's allies, which only widens the splits.

Parallel work in small groups to work all the assigned cases

After a full group enactment to illustrate the method, the participants meet in their assigned case groups so that each can receive help with their critical incident. It becomes more efficient as people move more quickly to a critical moment in the case and can mix discussion with brief enactments to help one another. In Appendix C, we provide an alternative method for giving every case writer some feedback and building the coaching skills of their colleagues. We recommend that each take up the coaching/facilitating/directing role in the small groups to support the group in learning how to deal with the critical incident and enactment methods. This way, the participants take away the method as a "tool", which enables them to use it in their daily work, that is, in peer coaching or supervising, in asking for help, in preparing for important encounters (future-orientated critical incidents), or reviewing self-experiences.

The faculty challenges in facilitating learning from enactments

1.   *Dealing with participants who do not submit cases.* We respect the risks each participant takes to develop a case and do not think that those who do not contribute their own cases should be in groups with other case writers. We have had positive experiences with all non case writers being in a separate group and exploring their own difficulties in writing a case. Alternatively, sometimes this brings cases to the surface and enables them to receive and give feedback. Several powerful insights have come from these conversations that go deeper than "too busy", as people bring up some of their issues about being vulnerable, or explore their resistance to the faculty's request for a critical incident, which might mask their fear of being judged by their colleagues if they submit a case.
2.   *Dealing with cases that are thinly veiled successes.* Usually, peers will challenge one another as to what grandiose outcome they had imagined when what they achieved is personally experienced as a failure, or invite the case writer to reflect on their difficulty in being vulnerable in the service of learning.
3.   *Timing of interventions in the enactments.* As noted above, enactments of situations that come from participants put both the

faculty members and the participants into new territory that is created by the enactors. The challenge for the faculty is to balance intervening too soon, too slowly, or at the wrong time. In one situation, we intervened very early after a consultant had asked his second question of the "client" (case writer), and only three to four seconds had elapsed before the consultant then continued talking. When we froze the scene and enquired about what was happening, the client felt he was not given time to think about what he felt was a good question. The consultant reported feeling anxious because of the silence, imaging it was a stupid question, and flagged that as a significant issue for him. The whole class saw the power of tolerating silence as a "pull" strategy to elicit thoughts from the other and an important tool to signal that one had finished talking and expected the other to reply. Calm silence is powerful and difficult. It is hard to know in advance what dynamics will unfold. This puts the faculty members in a co-learning mode with the participants. It does not have to be perfect, and, taking the director's prerogative, the enactors can be asked to go back to an earlier moment that, as faculty, we might have missed and now see as more interesting to explore, or, if it is flagging, suggest fast forwarding to the summation at the end of the meeting to see what are the possible next steps. In our reflective note, which we discuss later in this chapter, we mention letting an unproductive dynamic go on too long.

4. *Pulled into the expert role.* A common dynamic when doing a variety of enactments in a learning group is that participants request the faculty members to enact what they would do. This is often the result of participants' frustration, and has the unstated subtext, "if you are so smart, why don't you show us the answer?" Note that this is very much in the traditional case-teaching paradigm, where the teacher knows the ins and outs of the case deeply and has a variety of teaching points to elicit from the case. In using critical incidents, the faculty needs to stay in the role of co-learner, drawing a variety of experiences out of the group. Faculty members can suggest approaches to explore from their own experience, but they should keep the focus on what each can learn, especially because in this work nothing is more important than the fit of any approach with the personality of the enactor. People have great skills in detecting insincerity in others and it is

often forgotten how easily one can be seen as insincere when trying a "technique."

5. *Keeping tuned into the substantive stakes in the critical incidents and the related psychodynamics.* Often, the process can become too engaging at the cost of noticing key substantive issues that the case is dealing with. For example, in the above case, there are critical stakes for the business in the succession as well as for the family dynamics. Are there parallel process issues in play? Might the consultant be leading the founder towards his proposed solution (as the son's advocate), thus paralleling the founder's selling his proposed approach? Might the father be acting out rather than connecting with feelings that his son (and/or coach) does not think he has the time or capacity to develop? Faculty members have to keep in mind the level of depth that is appropriate for the setting, but always should be looking for the real substantive stakes and possible connections to the interpersonal dynamics.

6. *Faculty modelling reflects insights from their experience.* Faculty members (and working in pairs is highly recommended) often see issues, dynamics, and options after the stress of the here and now dynamics are over (staircase wit). In the above case describing the meeting between the entrepreneur and the consultant over the son's role, the faculty (the authors) had better ideas after the class had ended and they were able to share those thoughts with the class in a reflective note. This powerfully illustrates the challenges and risks for the faculty. With published cases that one teaches again and again, the lessons drawn from one presentation can be applied the next time one uses the case (Grasselli & Gilmore, 2013). With critical incidents, there will always be new facts and new dynamics that lead to new insights about oneself and the other from the dynamic. Working with participant cases puts the faculty into Bion's (1967, pp. 279–281) stated stance of "without memory or desire", connected to the uniqueness of the particular dynamics. Furthermore, given the similar stance to Heifetz and Linsky's (2002) case-in-point teaching, where everything in the class dynamics is used as material for learning, the dynamics among faculty members and with the class are fair game. Below is a portion of our reflective note back to the participants that displays our insights about our working dynamics, including possible parallel dynamics to the case itself. In writing

up the case, we noted that our reflective note in the last two imagined questions violated our espoused advice not to respond to
pull from participants to enact what we might have said as the
case writer/consultant.

Reflective note

"In the family business case, we were too slow and timid in breaking
the early dynamic of questions from the consultant and defensive responses from the entrepreneur to pose the challenge of how one could
break those cycles in real situations. Our own dynamics—as a faculty
pair comprising an older white male and a junior female—might have
paralleled the dynamics between the pair of consultants in the case.
The female might have seen the dynamic earlier, but could have been
inhibited by her junior status in ways that resembled the junior
consultant's role in the enactment. Also, gender dynamics might have
been reflected: women's voices were not heard; the wife was marginalised by not being included in the case write-up and by not having
her engage in the enactment. In the debriefing, it became clear that the
wife had been the link that brought the consultants into the engagement. The senior faculty member focused more on the dyadic encounter of consultant and entrepreneur (both men)."

Given our task of teaching the technique, we might have stopped
the case after the second question and response and invited both
observers and those in the enactment to jot down what they were
thinking and feeling, but not saying. That can be a powerful way of at
least connecting with ideas and energy that are not appearing in the
exchange. We might have introduced strategies/tactics to alter the
dynamic—they are always easier to invent cognitively than they are
to produce under stressful conditions.

A few responses we thought of for the consultant are as follows.

Consultant: "In this exchange I find myself closely identifying with
your son. It might be way off-base, but I wondered if it would be
useful for me to share some of these hunches?" Let a silence emerge,
and if the father says "All right", then some of one's hidden thoughts
and feelings can be shared.

Or: "In our conversation, it has not been easy for me to present
a counter-argument. You are very persuasive, yet I have an uneasy

feeling that I will be compliant (both in my consultancy role and in imagining your son's point of view) rather than really committed to this strategy. It is as if there has been no space for exploring a variety of paths that will respond to each of your interests. Does that resonate with you?"

Again, there might be a long silence that could break the quick question and answer exchanges. If there is some positive response, one then could say something like "I have a hunch that if you and your wife communicate your thoughts about what you want for the company, for yourselves, and for your son, say, ten years in the future, we can then more productively discuss what might be the most effective ways to get to that place."

Points to keep in mind

While critical incidents can provide a great venue for analysis and development of projected strategies, it is useful to illuminate some difficulties that are associated with the process.

- *Enactments cannot be standardised.* However, the process can be accelerated with practice. "The lesson from critical incidents is to be discovered each time rather than suggested in a teaching note or outlined in the case writer's head" (Gilmore & Schall, 1996).
- *High preparation costs.* The lack of standardisation results in a relatively time-consuming preparation and involvement from the participants as well as the faculty. Faculty members have to learn to be comfortable in situations where they do not have all the answers and do not know the case better than the participants.
- *The challenge of linking the micro-learnings to broader issues and competency developments.* Participants can become overwhelmed with the stream of opportunities in these cases and the many ways in which people can misunderstand one another. Given the increased pace in organisations, how does one select which opportunities to focus on? People can be overwhelmed if they are not helped to see the broader development of resilience and ability to be present and how valuable it can be to develop tactics that can interrupt unproductive exchanges.

Enactments in development sessions as a transitional vehicle to their use in organisational life

In the flow of one's work, one can ask a colleague to be "the other" in a forthcoming challenging encounter and, after a brief description of the context, jump into the enactment—perhaps each taking both roles to intensify the key goals of the parties. In organisations, this is most likely to happen with sales pitches, hearings, or press conferences, but can be powerfully extended to a much wider variety of challenging encounters, even internal ones, such as an appraisal, that so often create tensions rather than developmental insights.

It can be helpful to encourage colleagues to use you as an imagined other when they come to you with a difficult issue, as against just commiserating. For example, when someone complains about someone who is absent, you might interrupt quickly to ask, "What did so-and-so say when you gave them that feedback?" The usual response is, "I haven't told them", or "I can't tell them." Then you might invite him to enact some options for making it possible for the other to hear and safer for your colleague to risk saying it.

Writing up a critical incident in one's journal can be a way of getting some distance and pushing oneself beyond cognitive insights to actually imagine what one might have said, and the other's possible responses, so that one is building up a richer repertoire for situations that one finds stressful. For example, not being assertive enough across an authority boundary might be a pattern and, in the journal, one can invent possible responses for future situations. Putting in the journal imagined critical incidents that an injured or angry other might have written can be powerful. We often suggest that people write up the same critical incident that they have experienced, but from the point of view of the other in the case. What were their frustrations, tactics, projections, etc.?

Requesting critical incidents linked to key organisational issues—such as headquarters and field, shop and engineering, marketing and production—can illuminate concretely some of the difficulties and possible changes as well as build the skills to manage those boundaries more effectively. When finished with first-year paediatric interns (Center for Applied Research (CFAR), 1995), one sees patterns of their challenging collaborations: among peers over sign-out at the end of shifts, giving and getting feedback, and dealing with parents of very sick children, pushing for more feedback from attending physicians. In work with foundation programme officers, an enactment produced deep insights about the "gift giving" dynamics in the world of philanthropy (CFAR, 2003). In work with engineering and production in a microchip factory, the sets of critical incidents revealed the deep tensions in the critical work alliances between the two functions (Hirschhorn & Gilmore, 1989). In an annual executive development programme run by two European business schools, we also found patterns in organisational dynamics that reflected current business issues. The 2008 economic crisis brought up multiple cases in the following year in the context of financial reports, or a year later in changes in C-level management structures.

In a leadership development programme of a global pharmaceutical company, writing critical incidents was so anxiety provoking for the participants that the faculty decided to have them submit "typical incidents" as something between published cases and critical incidents. This way, middle management participating in the programme had the opportunity to try for themselves situations that were either typical for the setting (e.g., turnover was very high among the field force, thus one of the typical incidents was the management of a team gathering for a meeting after one or more people had left the team) or led to turmoil in the organisation that was never overtly discussed among managers (e.g., one manager went to a competitor and took all the "good people" with her). Here, critical incident work borders on organisational development and change workshops. Critical incidents are a window into the complex situations that people experience, and they often reveal new emerging challenges facing an institution, industry, or profession in transition.

Conclusions

The critical incident process offers both development contexts and their use in ongoing organisational work, links the head and the heart, offsets the excessively rational–analytical bias which focuses on thinking as opposed to acting in organisational life. We see the following advantages in using critical incidents produced by participants in both development contexts and in the flow of organisational work.

- *Reality.* Critical incidents are from real experiences. They communicate a rich sense of the context of someone's work that greatly helps peer coaching and development. When used in formal development programmes, especially early on, they convey a much richer sense of the roles each one has as well as contexts for further networking and exchange of advice.
- *No one best way.* There is no one good answer, no one best way for resolving a problem presented by a critical incident. The variety of outcomes allows for alternative strategies (Gilmore, 2000). The development of alternative strategies enhances participants' range of approaches.
- *The power of "small leadership"* (Sullivan, Gilmore, & Blum (2010). In the context of excessive grandiosity in the leadership literature, critical incidents illustrate the power of "present moments" (Stern, 2004) to alter both working alliances and the unfolding of events.
- *Developing a repertoire.* Participants develop resilience as they become more comfortable with ambiguity and learn to trust their gut in risking a variety of different approaches. They develop more "in the moment" ways of enquiring from the other, asking for time to think an issue over, inviting the parties to jointly explore their context and the pressures each are under, etc.
- *Empathy.* Participants learn to empathise and take other people's points of view. Empathy has recently been identified as a strategic issue in business that is more connected to the customers' experiences and requires a higher emotional intelligence in order to align the human resources in the organisation. It is a chance to see key roles (function, level), positions (top, middle, frontline), and professions from the inside rather than as a spectator—which often leads to stereotyping or caricature. When talking about "others", we often label them as a "resistor to change"; we rarely say that directly to their face, and neither do others describe themselves in that way, usually seeing their actions as protecting some important (to them) value.
- *Enhancing peer consultation on both substantive and process issues.* Especially in residential programmes, presenting critical incidents early in a programme provides slice-of-life views of participants that enable them to connect with each other around both change strategies and substantive issues that critical incidents bring to the surface.

- *Active practice.* Enactments are valuable because they focus on the difficulties we have in producing a strategy (the knowing–doing gap referred to earlier). Many times, people have in their minds an effective strategy, such as creating a non-defensive climate or reassuring the other that "we have shared goals". Yet, when these strategies are enacted, they do not produce the desired result. Others observing one try out the framing of an important meeting can give feedback that someone comes across very differently from what he or she might have intended. Voice is linked to presence and authority, but is too little a focus of our development. Coach to actors, Patsy Rodenburg (1992, p. 4) notes,

    > As soon as we open our mouths and speak we are judged. Instant assumptions are made about us by others. . . . Do we sound enfranchised or disenfranchised? . . . Do we sound as though we should be in charge or just subordinate? Do we sound as though we should be heard and answered?

- *Rapid prototyping for innovation.* As new products and services are developed, enactments, even with props, can deepen the sense of context and learning about the value of some new offering, taking in potential customers' point of view on the product.

Leadership and followership are more fluid, increasingly more improvisational and depends on the ability of people to move quickly from initiating to following in order to build on the work of a colleague (Weick, 1993). In today's organisations, people have to flexibly adapt to build on colleagues' strengths to accomplish the task at hand.

As with improvisation, organisations need a creative edge in relationships, but always within a superordinate valuing of the collective and co-operative task. Increasingly, the strategies and planning scenarios of organisations do not produce a definitive script for others to execute. As with improvisation, there is more real-time weaving of the two, acting and adjusting as circumstances change. Especially in a context of high uncertainty, often one must act to learn before one has a fully developed plan. Most of the significant challenges in today's organisations require collaboration with others over time to create compelling narratives about where the individuals have come from in order to animate the next stages of their journeys.

In today's context, visceral learning about risk—the interpersonal kind that Milgram described earlier—is critical to being effective in organisations. Enactments, like improvisation, create that risk for all the stakeholders taking up roles in a chosen case, as well as for the faculty.

In noting the increased ambiguity that leaders face, Weick suggests a different conception of leadership than the heroic concept of the leader who knows the way and helps or empowers followers to get there:

> The effective leader . . . searches for the better question, accepts inexperience, stays in motion, channels decisions to those with the best knowledge of the matter at hand, crafts good stories, is obsessed with updating, encourages improvisation, and is deeply aware of personal ignorance. People who act in this way help others make sense of what they are facing . . . sense making is about how to stay in touch with context. (Weick, 2001, p. 94)

Enactments in development sessions allow leaders to practise these skills in a safe, collegial learning environment. The learning that this process can produce has real-world applications and provides an outlet for reflection and analysis that would otherwise be unavailable. Context is critical. The context of the learning situation for business executives must get closer to real situations in the lives of students and executives and engage them in ways that have edge.

As we have described above, the ability to enact—to show instead of tell—can be brought into the flow of day-in and day-out work, increasing our playfulness, our creativity, and our connectedness to others in the service of meeting the challenges of a complex and rapidly changing world.

Appendix A: instructions for writing a critical incident

Following the instructions below, write up a short critical incident and e-mail it to us. These incidents will be used in class for discussion but will be held as confidential among the group. Feel free to mask your identity as well as those of others in the case.

Think of a critical incident in your work. The incident must be an actual encounter with another individual or group. It should be a challenging episode—one where you doubted your effectiveness or where you felt frustrated and less successful than you believed was possible. In considering which incident to choose for critical analysis, the following criteria should be considered.

- The episode was not a pre-determined, no-win situation, that is, one in which nothing you might have done could have significantly altered the final outcome.
- Think of episodes in which the choice of a different strategy or manner of interacting might have resulted in more favourable and satisfying outcomes.
- Avoid incidents in which you acted as the "star" or risk-taker, or where your behaviour was generally impressive or effective, given the circumstances.
- The episode is one you still find somewhat puzzling; you have not yet completely understood why it turned out the way it did.
- Begin the description with a paragraph about the purpose of your intervention, the setting, the people involved, and any other important background information.
- Write a paragraph about your strategy. What were your objectives? How did you intend to achieve them? Why did you select those goals and strategies?
- Briefly describe the results.
- Finally, write a few sentences on what you experienced as frustrating in the encounter.

In summary, your submission will have four parts.

1. Brief description of the situation.
2. Your strategy.
3. The results.
4. Why it was frustrating.

Keep your responses to one or two pages, typewritten if possible.

Confidentiality

If you wish your case to remain confidential, please mask the setting and the identities of participants, and put your name on a separate cover sheet. Selected cases will be circulated and discussed.

Appendix B: tips on reading a critical incident

Initial situation

- What appear to be the dilemmas and issues from the incident writer's point of view?
- Who is anxious among the cast of characters in the case, if any, and how is anxiety distributed?
- If you had to give the case a playful title, what might it be?

Moments

- With the benefit of hindsight, what options were available to the writer in the flow of the case? (E.g., whether to have that particular meeting, the timing, the participants, the framing, the responses, etc.)
- In the stream of events, what are some key moments where the actor could have taken the encounter in a very different direction?
- Why do you pick that moment as the most fateful?

Participants

- How clear are the relationships and identities of the actors in the case (e.g., within an organisation, across levels, functions, with important external stakeholders)?
- What is the influence of other stakeholders who are mentioned or implied?
- What are the coalitions?

Appendix C: an alternative method

Enactments might be too anxiety provoking in many settings and too time consuming. Each person who writes a critical incident should get feedback from peers at least. A powerful method for small group work with critical incidents is the following.

The case writer frames the situation in a few minutes.

- The rest of the group has a few minutes to ask clarifying questions, with an emphasis on questions being hypothesis driven rather than just accumulating more facts about the case.
- Then the case presenter pulls his or her chair back from the circle and can only listen for 15–20 minutes while the others discuss their hunches about the case and their recommendations.
- Then the case writer rejoins the group and reflects on what he or she has heard.

This is a powerful method of peer consultation. Case presenters are surprised by how much outsiders can infer that which was not directly presented by the case writer. As with the Johari window (Luft, 1969), we are often much more transparent to others. The inability of the case presenter to participate in the discussion—in a sense a balcony perspective (Heifitz & Linsky, 2002)—deepens their listening skills and increases the diversity of views, as interaction with the presenter often steers the conversation in a more focused direction and it can often take on a more defensive tone. It is a powerful lesson in the concept of being "helpfully wrong", which can stimulate the case writer to think about how the misconception was communicated and what insights might be gained from thinking about this different (but wrong) angle of vision.

References

Argyris, C., & Schon, D. A. (1974). *Theory in Practice: Increasing Professional Effectiveness.* San Francisco, CA: Jossey-Bass.

Bion, W. R. (1967). Notes on memory and desire. *Psychoanalytic Forum, 2,* 279–281.

Browne, R. (2007). Working assumptions of a socio dramatist. *British Journal of Psychodrama and Sociodrama, 22*(1): 33–46.

Center for Applied Research (CFAR) (1995). *Briefing Notes: Risk, Anxiety and Performance in Groups* (pp. 1–3). Philadelphia, PA.

Center for Applied Research (CFAR) (2003). *Briefing Notes: The Use of Enactments in Executive Learning* (pp. 1–6). Philadelphia, PA.

Gilmore, T. N. (2000). Ongoing use of "critical incidents" for self and organizational development. *CFAR* 6. Philadelphia, PA.

Gilmore, T. N., & Schall, E. (1996). Staying alive to learning: integrating enactments with case teaching to develop leaders. *Journal of Policy Analysis and Management, 15*(3): 444–456.

Goleman, D. (1997). *Emotional Intelligence.* New York: Bantam Books.

Grasselli, N., & Gilmore, T. N. (2013). Thickening case discussions through enactments. *Training and Management Development Methods, Section Three: Approaches and Techniques of Programmes Design, 27*(1).

Harvey, J. B. (1974). The Abilene paradox: the management of agreement. *Organizational Dynamics, 3*: 63–80.

Heifetz, R. A., & Linsky, M. (2002). *Leadership on The Line: Staying Alive Through The Dangers of Leading.* Boston, MA: Harvard Business School Press.

Hirschhorn, L. (2002). *Managing in The New Team Environment: Skills, Tools, and Methods* (2nd edn). San Jose: Authors Choice Press.

Hirschhorn, L., & Gilmore, T. N. (1989). The psychodynamics of a cultural change: learnings from a factory. *Human Resource Management, 28*(2): 211–233.

Lester, R. K., & Piore, J. M. (2004). *Innovation: The Missing Dimension.* Cambridge, MA: Harvard University Press

Luft, J. (1969). *Of Human Interaction.* Palo Alto, CA: National Press. *Group Processes: An Introduction to Group Dynamics.* Palo Alto, CA: National Press Books.

Luo, M. (2004). 'Excuse me. May I have your seat?' *New York Times,* section B, column 3, September 14.

Mamet, D. (1991). *On Directing Film.* New York: Viking.

Mant, A. (1983). Binary vs. ternary thinking (raiders and builders). In: *Leaders We Deserve* (pp. 9–35). Oxford: Martin Robertson.

Minuchin, S., & Fishman, H. A. (1981). *Family Therapy Techniques.* Cambridge, MA: Harvard University Press.

Nabokov, V. (1980). *Lectures on Literature.* San Diego, CA.: Harcourt.

Pfeffer, J., & Sutton, R. I. (2000). *The Knowing–Doing Gap: How Smart Companies Turn Knowledge into Action.* Cambridge, MA: Harvard Business School Press.

Phillips, A. (1988). *Winnicott.* Cambridge, MA: Harvard University Press.

Rodenburg, P. (1992). *The Right to Speak: Working with the Voice.* London: Methuen.

Schon, D. A. (1983). *The Reflective Practitioner: How Professionals Think in Action.* New York: Basic Books.

Senge, P. M. (1990). *The Fifth Discipline: The Art and Practice of the Learning Organization.* New York: Currency Doubleday.

Shell, G. R., &. Moussa, M. A. (2007). *The Art of Woo: Using Strategic Persuasion to Sell Your Ideas.* New York: Penguin Portfolio.

Stern, D. (2004). *The Present Moment in Psychotherapy and Everyday Life.* New York: Norton.

Sullivan, C., Gilmore, T. N., & Blum, R. (2010). The power of small leadership. In: *The 2010 Pfeiffer Annual: Leadership Development*. San Francisco, CA: Pfeiffer.

Trist, E. (2001). Prologue. In: G. Amado & A. Ambrose, A. (Eds.), *Transitional Approach to Change* (pp. xxi–xxvii). London: Karnac.

Weick, K. E. (1993). Organizational redesign as improvisation. In: G. P. Huber & W. H. Glick (Ed.), *Organizational Change and Redesign: Ideas and Insights for Improving Performance* (pp. 346–379). New York: Oxford University Press.

Weick, K. E. (1995). Leadership when events don't play by the rules. www.centerforpos.org, "Trying Times".

Weick, K. E. (2001). Leadership as the legitimation of doubt in the future of leadership. In: W. G. Bennis, G. M. Spreitzer, & T. G. Cummings (Eds.), *The Future of Leadership: Today's Top Leadership Thinkers Speak to Tomorrow's Leaders* (pp. 91–102). San Francisco, CA: Jossey-Bass.

Zaleznik, A. (1967). Management of disappointment. *Harvard Business Review*, 45(6): 59–61.

Epilogue

Leopold Vansina

B ecoming a leading part in creating well-being is more than a
good intention or an ambition. It is taking on a social engagement that inspires and transpires in our practices as academics,
managers, consultants, and citizens of our times. It is not an easy
engagement, since we are all exposed to the socio-cultural influence
of "virtualisation", the ideology of performance, and processes of
individualisation. All three are elements in a dominant economic
philosophy of competition and unlimited growth, from which they
derive extra forcefulness. In this book, we have focused on the socio-
psychological and psychodynamic dimensions, but it is obvious that
other disciplines also have a leading part to play—and they do.
However, listing the names of the progressive economists and engi-
neers in this field might sidetrack us from starting from where we,
managers, academics, and consultants, are.

The book focused on two starting conditions. First, we presented a
critical analysis of, or a serious reflection on, what is going on in society today that erodes humanness in the workplace, be it through
imposing "an organisational self" on the employees, or by "amputating" psychic health in organised work and eroding social relationships. Second, there is the courage and wisdom to explore the

consequences of all this for society, the future generations and the ecology of our finite planet. Facing likely consequences entails a risk. It might take us down in a spiral of helplessness in swamps of complexities and uncertainties. Yet, it can also be a source of energy for creative thinking and constructive action, and elevate the spirit to give up an easy life of "going with the flow".

"Going with the flow" is another one-liner familiar to most of us. In essence, it encourages people to go along. Originally, it meant going with the flow of movements, thereby saving energy. Later and more generally, it refers to taking the path of least resistance and going along with the emerging trends and markets in society. It saves energy; it makes us feel good to be with the latest trends, and part of society. However, *ignoring* early signs of developments and their negative consequences, or cultivating *indifference* for the complexities of the world make the trends self-fulfilling. Both attitudes create a vacuum for developments to gain strength until they reach a point of no return and will end in disaster. It reminds me of the Holocaust, which evolved in time from innocent teasing to negative stereotyping and pestering, to the atrocities that shocked the world. While we might not forget the shoah of the Nazi regime, we *must* not forget the social processes that allowed it to happen. In short, the choices we make, the decisions we take, or neglect to take, daily *create our future.* If we step out of the flow, just to reflect with *an open mind and an open heart,* we will become aware of where the flow is leading. That awareness offers choices to go along with the flow or to take action to alleviate the social undesirable consequences and to create more humane futures. However, we have to respond appropriately and in time. Human beings can do that and have done it. They have countered successfully some gloomy forecasts of overpopulation by the Club of Rome published in the last century. Can it not be achieved again?

In the book, we present thoughts and *actionable knowledge* for taking *small steps* to counter the flow. What would happen if we stopped treating or coaching individuals who bear the symptoms of mistaken organisational or work designs, or management practices, and hollow institutions, as long as management is *unwilling* to change the causal context in the workplace? What would happen if we would no longer organise training programmes aimed at resetting people's minds, reframing healthy perceptions and sentience in order to fit better the misleading slogans that the current organisational conditions are unavoidable to meet the global competition? What would happen if one would stop organising "experience-providing" programmes, popular, psychic consumption products offered under the guise of training or personal development programmes? If we stop providing crutches to shaky social systems and practices, the underlying dynamics of many current issues will be exposed. More people might come to refute the fallacy of unlimited growth, and the perverse process of the "individualisation of the social" discussed by Amado, Lhuilier, and Schruijer.

Some ideas might be transformed into small constructive changes in the way we fulfil our professional roles, from reframing research projects to include organisational contexts, to engaging in action research and teaching methods that deal with the students and future managers/consultants as whole human beings. By treating them as having both a mind and a body, we prepare them better for working in the real world, where they are not only *observers as part of the field*—as Eisenberg, the quantum physicist, noted—but also *actors in those fields*. This does require that we invent new teaching, or learning, methods, inspired or not by the "critical incident approach" described by Gilmore and Grasselli. Managers and consultants might be encouraged to invest time in "difficult talks", and in "conversations on work", as Eisold advanced. Or, find the internal strength to recognise their limits of knowing and to forego the pleasure of being seen as the expert for holding on to "not knowing". It would create space for joint exploration of alternatives and for co-creating the workplace.

Small steps that yield tangible results tend to motivate people to face bigger, more complex challenges, issues, or questions. Let me take a couple of confronting questions that stuck with me. Can organisations be healthy at the expense of the psychic health of its employees, or, the opposite, can humanity in organisations unwittingly subvert organisational health? How can we develop organisational health, and which conditions must be taken into account while working with one or more whole systems within the larger system, for example, an international company? In the context of the book, questions like these are explicitly or implicitly raised by Schein and Lhuilier.

Improving psychic health at work and organisational health might require that we take a closer look at the specifics of different parts in a modern organisation. Some parts, often comprising higher levels of global managers and staff, might become submerged in data that give rise to a virtual world, divorced from the tangible world of matter and social relationships. At the other end, but not necessarily the lowest parts in the hierarchy, people are transforming ideas, instructions, and visions in tangible structures, designs, products, and/or sensible services. Here, the virtual worlds of data and ideas (grand or small) must be turned into something real. Then, we have the various parts and interfaces, which vary widely but have no less an impact on the other parts mentioned, the psychic health of the respective employees, and the health of the overall organisation. The processes at the interfaces deserve particular attention. They largely determine the degrees of freedom for people in other parts of the system. Latitudes of freedom are incorporated in the electronic and technological means and used to send data to be transformed into products and services. In short, and more concrete, one may distinguish technologies that assist an employee in transforming from technologies that carry out the transformations and use an employee as a servant. The study of the specificities of each work setting generates sets of insights that need to be weighed and balanced with the broader requirements of organisational health. Along this line of thought, there is an abundance of action research projects.

No doubt, the world has become smaller and more complex. So are most of our international organisations (i.e., network organisations) and networks. Major decisions affecting the livelihood of whole organisational units are taken from distant headquarters based on "big data" by managers with little or no feel for the realities their people are in. We come to live with more "relatedness" and fewer "relationships". Unfortunately, only a few political and organisational leaders, and, by exception, the media, seem to be able or willing to help people understand their relatedness in a complex world. People are likely to become indifferent when they cannot grasp the complexities in which they live. Often unwittingly, they reduce the world to those parts they can directly influence or are influenced by. Others fall back on dogmatic statements or fundamentalist beliefs to govern their very simplified world.

Krantz conceives "sentience" as an indispensable element in systems psychodynamics to understand and work with relatedness in emerging "modern" organisations. "Sentience" is neither a substitution for "holistic pictures", nor a new way to set people's minds. "Sentience" is grounded in a range of conditions embedded in an "institution", expressing and evoking values, raising hopes, and offering meaning in what the organisation tries to achieve and how it actually operates. An institution requires more than "inspiring words". It transpires from tangible conditions and behaviour in *real organisations*. Still more studies are needed to see whether an institution can make "relatedness" meaningful and generate a sense of community; whether and to what extent it can evoke values, hopes, and aspirations within the ultimate purpose of organisations to better well-being for all human beings. We still lack actionable knowledge on how to withstand or counter the dominance of a mentality of competition, or "win/lose" calculation. The promising empirical findings that in *societies of more income equality* all human beings are better off, happier, healthy, and trusting still seem to lose much of their energising truth when one has to give up some of one's acquired benefits, wealth, and power.

Here, we face again a fundamental predicament. Human beings relate to, and act in, the world as a whole person: perceiving, sensing, and giving meaning. The most sophisticated ways of communication, the most inspiring statements and ergonomically designed work places, will eventually become shallow with the discovery that the ultimate purpose of the organisation does not serve humanity. It is my belief that when we, social scientists, want to be effective in enabling the development of humanity in organisations, we should be engaged in not only in studying what human beings *experience* at various times in the workplace, but also in gaining a "good enough" understanding of the different systems, structures, and processes that actually shape the "organisation-in-action", as well as with the broader socio-economic and technological streams of thought that govern society.

Is this an impossible task? I do not think so.

You and I have enjoyed meeting managers, academics, and consultants who act as leading part in fostering humanness in organisations; persons who also put sustainability before unlimited growth. They often find supporting ideas in different disciplines, for example, economy, sociology, and engineering; ideas from other disciplines that could well strengthen the endeavours of us, the social scientists. Even better, we might engage in multi-disciplinary projects, creating a kind of micro institution with a considered purpose. Thereby, we would break away from the *virtualisation* that over-specialised disciplines create. All involved will benefit from the collaborative work. Joint projects do nurture a shared understanding of the human being, with his mind and body in an *ongoing interplay* with his social, economic, and technological environments. Is it not that interplay that should be studied to enable us to *act* responsibly?

INDEX

Printed in Great Britain
by Amazon

25111742R00137